A HISTORY OF MARINE AVIATION
1911–68

The story of marine aviation is almost as long as the history of powered flight itself, and from 1911, when the young American Glenn Curtiss was experimenting with his flimsy 'hydroplanes', until the present day it has been no less fascinating.

Beginning with the early pioneering days and the First World War, this history covers the ill-fated Gallipoli campaign, where the fledgling Royal Naval Air Service had to endure the worst possible conditions; Raymond Collishaw and his aces, who earned undying fame with their famous 'Black Flight' of Sopwith Triplanes on the Western Front; and the North Sea, hunting ground of John Porte's big "Felixstowe" type patrol flying-boats.

The 'twenties and 'thirties were the record-breaking years, with aviators such as Alan Cobham and Francis Chichester, but between the wars, naval aviation in both Great Britain and the United States was haunted by penny-pinching government economies that resulted indirectly in Eugene Esmonde's last tragic Fleet Air Arm sortie with outdated biplanes against the German Fleet moving up the Channel in 1942.

All these events, and many more, culminating in the biggest and most luxurious of all sea flying craft—the Saro Princess flying-boats and Howard Hughes' gigantic Hercules of the 'fifties—make up a glorious, chequered half-century of progress, related here with the same careful documentation that made John Killen's *The Luftwaffe* such a valuable and entertaining work of reference.

Also by John Killen:

THE LUFTWAFFE: A HISTORY

John Killen

A History of Marine Aviation
1911-68

With a Foreword by

Air Chief Marshal
Sir Arthur Longmore
G.C.B., D.S.O.

FREDERICK MULLER

*First published in Great Britain 1969
by Frederick Muller Ltd., Fleet Street, London, E.C.4*

SBN:584 10124 4

*Printed and bound by
The Garden City Press Limited
Letchworth, Hertfordshire*

CONTENTS

∽∽∽∽∽∽∽∽∽∽∽∽∽∽∽∽∽∽∽∽∽∽∽∽∽∽∽∽∽∽∽∽∽∽

ILLUSTRATIONS

FOREWORD
by
AIR CHIEF MARSHAL SIR ARTHUR LONGMORE G.C.B., D.S.O.

∽∽∽∽∽∽∽∽∽∽∽∽∽∽∽∽∽∽∽∽∽∽∽∽∽∽∽∽∽∽∽∽∽∽∽∽

Various books, including one of my own, have been written about the aeroplane, airship or balloon and its uses in war or as a means of transport but I doubt if any have concentrated on the story of marine aircraft, particularly those employed in naval warfare, in such detail as this volume.

As one of the Early Birds to whom John Killen refers, I read with nostalgia of the development of the flying-boat in Britain, U.S.A. and Germany, from the day of the Curtiss boat I saw competing in the hydro-aeroplane trials at Monte Carlo in April 1912 right up to the 1950s and the late lamented Princess Saunders Roe boat on which I was a passenger at the Farnborough Air Show. The most comfortable aircraft in which I have ever flown was the Empire flying-boats on the Australia and South Africa air routes. In great contrast are more recent flights, in one or other of those crowded high-flying jets which have finally killed for me the romance of air travel as I once knew it. How has it come about that the flying-boat has faded out for air transport? Was it due to the high cost of maintaining overseas bases with the necessary boats and personnel, not to mention administrative services, or was it the result of foreign countries providing long runways for aeroplanes and airport amenities at their own government expense as a status symbol? In 1928, en route to Karachi from Plymouth in a Blackburn Iris flying-boat with three Rolls Condor engines, we had a forced landing in the Persian Gulf. I was reminded how operationally independent this aircraft could be with a skilled mechanic as one of the aircrew, who made a repair while under the lee of an island and enabled

us to continue the flight. During the evacuation of Greece in
1941 no less than sixty service personnel crowded on board a
Sunderland at Athens, and safely arrived at Alexandria.

The air battles of the 1914–18 war, in which the naval fighter
squadrons supported the R.F.C., hit the headlines, as did the
Battle of Britain in the second war, but it was largely due to the
anti-submarine operations of Sunderlands, Catalinas, Liberators
and other Coastal Command aircraft that food and war material
were able to reach Britain. John Killen covers these activities no
less well than he does the Battle of Jutland and Rutland's reconnaissance flight from the *Engadine,* while no account of the war in
the Pacific I have yet read gives such a clear picture of this
remarkable sea and air conflict as that recorded here. Primarily a
carrier war, in magnitude and the number of Allied and Japanese
ships engaged, it was unique and Mr Killen does it full justice.

As to the future, is it really true that the aircraft carrier is to be
phased out by 1971? Will it be convincing to those peoples east
of Suez who have hitherto enjoyed our military presence that we
shall still be able to reach them in emergency by air support,
using island bases or ex-colonial territory, now independent, for
air transport? Can it be guaranteed that in this era of revolutionary coups and changes in political structure these bases will, in
fact, be available? These and similar questions occur to some
whose outlook is not entirely confined to meeting the problems
which arise as a matter of political expediency, aimed at retaining
popularity with a people now so bent on individual prosperity
and social security. John Killen is wise to entitle his last chapter
'Future Indefinite'; the flying-boat is dead, but shall we not
need carriers for the foreseeable future, not for a major nuclear
war, but to meet those lesser emergencies for which we are still
expected to take some action? In years to come air congestion
over Britain in the days of Concordes and Jumbo Jets may see the
boats fly again from coastal airports; and with Russian warships
now appearing in the oceans of the world it seems unlikely that
the U.S.A. will abandon the aircraft carrier as the major weapon
in their various fleets.

But whether marine aviation assumes any real power again or
not, its past is well deserving of a special history. In these pages
it is in very capable hands.

EARLY BIRDS: 1911–14

The waters of Lake Constance, stirred by a light morning breeze, slid past only 10 ft. below the wings of the three British bombing aeroplanes as they headed for the huge Zeppelin sheds at Friedrichshafen. As the objective came into sight the leading Avro 504 biplane began to climb steadily, its 80-h.p. Gnome rotary engine throbbing sweetly in the crisp autumn air, until it was banking gently over the lake at a height of 1,000 ft. The deep coughing of the first anti-aircraft guns sounded from far below; but the Avro's bombs were already on the way. Men scattered in all directions around the airship sheds as fountains of earth and debris erupted in the military enclosure. Heavy machine-gun fire from sandbagged emplacements contributed to the racket as the second and third Avros droned overhead to drop their bombs, and a vast explosion shook one Zeppelin shed, bringing girders and roof timbers tumbling down; flame shot 100 ft. into the air from a nearby gasworks.

It was almost noon on 21st November 1914: the time and date of the first completely successful raid on Germany by aircraft of the fledgling, as yet still inexperienced, but courageous Royal Naval Air Service.

The original naval arm of the Royal Flying Corps had been formed in 1912, with its Headquarters established at Eastchurch, under the blessing of an Admiralty convinced at last that an important future lay ahead for the new heavier-than-air flying machines. Their Lordships' interest had, perhaps, been initially aroused by a number of small, yet significant, events that had taken place in the aviation world since the Wright brothers had first accomplished powered flight in 1903. Not least among these was the activities of a young, enthusiastic American named

Glenn Curtiss. A true pioneer of the aeroplane, Curtiss had come into the spotlight of fame in August 1909, when he won the Gordon Bennett Cup at the Reims Air Meeting after gaining a speed record of more than 46 m.p.h. over 20 kilometres. On 26th January 1911 Curtiss became the first man ever to fly off—and land on—water when his Curtiss-Ellyson 'hydroplane' took to the air from the surface of San Diego Bay, California. This machine was a typical, flimsy pusher biplane of the period but it featured a stubby central float (or sponson) and cylindrical tanks on the wingtips to act as floats; a crude, yet remarkably efficient, seaplane.

Within three weeks Curtiss had gained sufficient confidence and experience with his hydroplane to fly across the bay and land neatly alongside a cruiser, the U.S.S. *Pennsylvania*. As an experiment the aeroplane was hoisted aboard ship by a crane and later lowered into the water for Curtiss's return flight to his hangar on North Island. Even Curtiss could not have fully appreciated the importance of his performance at the time; but in fact the seed had been planted that would later reach fruition as the shipborne reconnaissance seaplane.

Almost exactly one year later, on 10th January 1912, Curtiss displayed for the first time in public a completely new type of aeroplane—the flying-boat. He had replaced the wide sponson float of his hydroplane with a canoe-shaped hull containing seats for the pilot and one passenger, and a 60-h.p. engine drove twin tractor airscrews by means of chains. During the summer of 1912 Curtiss hit upon a more efficient design for the flying-boat and produced his second model, which was powered by a single pusher propeller driven by an engine mounted centrally above the hull and between the mainplanes; the hull itself was 'stepped' and had a rear-mounted rudder and tailplane. The whole arrangement was remarkably advanced for the period and although considerably improved upon over the years this basic layout characterised many successors to the Curtiss boat, including the famous Supermarine Walrus amphibian.

Meanwhile a number of aviation pioneers in Europe had been attempting to adapt land aeroplanes for flying off water. In 1911 a Royal Navy officer, Commander Oliver Schwann, bought an Avro biplane, designed by the industrious young inventor Alliott

Verdon-Roe and powered by a 35-h.p. Green water-cooled engine. While working on the first British rigid airship, the *Mayfly,* at Barrow-in-Furness, Schwann utilised his spare time in fitting the Avro with floats having rather curious, turned-up 'toes' before attempting to fly his machine off the water. As Schwann had no previous flying experience he not unnaturally suffered many disappointments, but on a November morning in 1911 he at last coaxed the Avro into the air for a short flight This achievement attracted little public interest at the time but it did serve to attract more attention to the efforts of E. W. Wakefield of Blackpool, who had been an ardent exponent of marine aviation for some years. The association formed by Wakefield, named the Lakes Flying Company, had already commissioned A. V. Roe and Co. to build a seaplane, and only a week after Commander Schwann's historic flight it took off from, and later landed on, Lake Windermere.

Another Royal Navy officer, a young man named Captain Murray Sueter, had also been taking more than a passive interest in embryonic naval aviation. He had been instructed by the Admiralty to take command of a so-called naval 'Air Department' and given the task of supervising the building of an airship by Vickers Ltd. at their Barrow-in-Furness yard. The work, begun in May 1909, took two years before the dirigible neared completion, during which time it had earned itself the somewhat sad nickname of *Mayfly* from numerous critics who considered that the ability to design and build airships had been endowed only upon Germans in general and Count Ferdinand von Zeppelin in the individual. All doubts were unfortunately resolved on 24th September 1911; as the *Mayfly* emerged from her shed into the light of day a heavy gust of wind drifted her into the side of the building, resulting in a broken back for the airship and consequent total loss. Captain Sueter's enthusiasm for ligh-ter-than-air craft, encouraged by his months of supervision over the *Mayfly,* might well have been diminished by such a regrettable accident. But in common with a few other Royal Navy officers—including some, let it be admitted, of very senior rank—he had a feeling that aeroplanes and warships would soon be mixing more successfully together. How could Sueter, the junior commander of a very new Admiralty department, realise that he would, in fact, become the father of British naval aviation?

At that time there was a third Royal Navy officer whose indefatigable efforts to further the cause of sea flying would later be rewarded. During 1911 the Admiralty had given permission for four commissioned officers to receive flying instruction and out of a large number of volunteers Lieutenants C. R. Samson, R. Gregory and A. Longmore of the Royal Navy, and Captain E. L. Gerrard, Royal Marine Light Infantry, were in due course selected. These four pupils—the first 'official' naval airmen—were taught to fly at Eastchurch, in slow, cumbersome and fragile Short pusher biplanes buffeted and rocked by gusty, damp spring weather. Yet within six weeks all had gained their coveted certificates and before 1911 came to a close the exuberant Samson was pressing a surprised Admiralty to buy two training aeroplanes.

Charles Romney Samson was promoted to the rank of Commander and placed in charge of the Eastchurch naval flying school. In December 1911 he made the first successful flight from the deck of a warship in a Short biplane fitted with air bags; taking off from a special platform built over the fore-deck of the battleship H.M.S. *Africa,* Samson landed in the sea, where his aircraft gently floated. During the Naval Review of May 1912 he repeated his achievement for the benefit of King George V, lifting his Short machine from a platform erected forward on H.M.S. *Hibernia* while the battleship was under way at a speed of 15 knots.

Many of the official experiments carried out by Samson during this period with the assistance of Lieutenant Longmore were made in conjunction with two brothers, Horace and Eustace Short, already established as motor-boat builders and now exploring new fields as makers of aeroplanes: hence the increased use in naval flying of the big Short biplanes. With the establishment of the Naval Wing, Royal Flying Corps, on 13th May 1912, Short Bros. began the design and construction of that long line of Service aircraft destined to culminate in the famous Sunderland flying-boat of the Second World War. Most of the naval officers who were taught to fly at Eastchurch in the early days gained their certificates on Short aeroplanes, and one of these young pilots—Lieutenant J. W. Seddon, R.N.—in due course became instructor to many keen fledgling aviators, including the plump but energetic First Lord of the Admiralty, Mr Winston Churchill.

During 1912 the Admiralty had also ordered a few Henri Farman biplanes and one or two interesting aeroplanes built by a contemporary of Alliott Verdon-Roe, the designer and inventor T. O. M. Sopwith. During the winter months of 1912–13, Sopwith and his associate Fred Sigrist worked at Kingston-upon-Thames on the construction of a pusher-engined airframe of conventional biplane layout; meanwhile the boat-builders Saunders of Cowes were building a hydroplane 'racing hull' to Sopwith's directions. By simply bolting his biplane to the Saunders hull, Sopwith produced the first practical European flying-boat, which he gave the typically British name of Bat Boat, after the mythical flying-machine mentioned in the book by Rudyard Kipling, *With the Night Mail*.

Having some resemblance to the Curtiss boat, the Sopwith Bat Boat had a two-seater side-by-side cockpit, stepped hull and cylindrical wing-tip floats, and was powered by a 90-h.p. Austro-Daimler engine mounted centrally between the mainplanes. On 16th February 1913 it was exhibited at the Olympia Aero Show, where it interested many visitors, including Mr Winston Churchill. Some time afterwards the American sewing-machine millionaire, Mortimer Singer, put up a prize of £500 for the first amphibian type of aircraft to make at least three successive flights from land to water and vice versa; no mean achievement when it is recalled that powered flight had been accomplished for the first time within only a decade. Nevertheless, Sopwith decided to enter his Bat Boat for the prize, and fitted the machine with a primitive retractable undercarriage axled across the plywood-skinned hull.

On 8th July 1913 the Sopwith Bat Boat, piloted by the pioneer aviator Harry Hawker, and with a Lieutenant Spenser Grey aboard as official observer, won the Singer prize without any difficulty. The wheeled take-offs and landings were made at a field near Hamble, and the Solent used for the water take-offs and landings. While it must be admitted that the undercarriage failed to lower satisfactorily—the wheels had to be kicked down into position by Spenser Grey—the Bat Boat had firmly established for itself another niche in history; it was the first successful amphibian in the world.

Inspired by the success of Sopwith's Bat Boat amphibian, the *Daily Mail* now offered a prize of £5,000 for the winner of a Round Britain Race to be carried out only by marine aircraft, and at the same time interest in sea flying began to quicken all over Europe. Most of the French, German and Italian seaplanes were built on well-tried and conventional lines: biplanes mounted on a central pontoon or twin floats; machines closely resembling the Curtiss and Avro types. However, a French naval officer and engineer, Lieutenant de Conneau, had formed an association known as the Franco-British Aviation Company, which produced some excellent two-seater biplane flying-boats for the French Navy. During October 1912 an F.B.A. boat was purchased by the British Admiralty for test purposes, and was taken on to establishment at Calshot, thus becoming the first flying-boat to enter Royal Navy service. Later, the outbreak of war would bring an urgent order from the Admiralty for fifty more of the French F.B.A. boats, and many remained in service until 1918.

One of the very few foreign seaplanes of unconventional design undergoing trials at this time had been built by the Voisin brothers in France. It was of typical Voisin box-kite construction, featuring a huge central pontoon, and unusual because it was almost certainly the first attempt at a tail-first or 'canard' type of aeroplane. In Germany, where the 'lighter-than-air craze' initiated by Count Zeppelin was sweeping the country—no less than thirty airships being serviceable by 1912—sea flying continued to be sadly neglected. The first German naval officer to receive flying instruction was Naval Engineer Karl Loew, who gained his certificate in March 1911; but five months later the infant air arm of the Imperial German Navy had been allowed only another four qualified pilots. A few far-sighted designers, such as Ernst Heinkel, considered that the early Albatros and Rumpler aeroplanes favoured by the Army could be adapted for use as floatplanes; but all this lay in the future, needing the necessity and consequent impetus of war.

For these and other associated reasons, only four machines, all

British, were entered for the *Daily Mail* Round Britain Race. Of these, the big biplane to be flown by Colonel S. F. Cody, an American who had become a naturalised Englishman, crashed during trials and killed its flamboyant owner; the Radley-England Waterplane withdrew because of a faulty engine; and the Short entry failed to be ready in time. The Sopwith entry, a tractor floatplane powered by a water-cooled Green engine and flown by Harry Hawker, started the race on 16th August 1913 and reached Yarmouth, where the floats became waterlogged, rendering the aircraft unserviceable. The prize of £5,000 was therefore carried over to the following year, and T. O. M. Sopwith started work on a vastly improved Bat Boat; but in the event the race was cancelled, and Bat Boat No. 2 ended its days on training duties with the Royal Naval Air Service.

Nevertheless, 1913 seemed to be a year for competitions, perhaps encouraged by the *Daily Mail* Circuit of Britain air race of 1911 and the Aerial Derby of 1912. A French armaments manufacturer and aviation enthusiast, Jacques Schneider, presented the French Aero Club with a beautiful trophy which could be competed for by seaplanes of any nationality, the annual race to be flown over a measured course not less than 150 nautical miles in length. The first winner of this contest, in 1913, was Marcel Prevost, flying for France; he attained an average speed of 45·75 m.p.h. in a Deperdussin floatplane.

Before the 1914 Schneider Trophy Race took place, the Sopwith Company had produced a remarkable, very advanced little single seater tractor biplane, powered by an 80-h.p. Gnome engine. This tiny aircraft—later to be adopted by the R.N.A.S. and progenitor of a whole series of Sopwith scouts—was named the Tabloid. Sopwith decided to enter a machine of the type for the Schneider Trophy Race, and fitted one with floats, also changing the engine for a more powerful 100-h.p. monosoupape Gnome. In this floatplane Tabloid, Howard Fixton easily won the Trophy for Great Britain on 20th April 1914, with an average speed of 86·75 m.p.h.

About the same time, Noel Pemberton-Billing, who had founded the Supermarine firm later to become so very famous in the aviation world, was experimenting with some attractive, streamlined flying-boats with racy, cigar-shaped hulls, but despite

many brilliant ideas and long hours of hard work, he failed to lift
his P.B.I. prototype or its larger successor, the P.B.7, into the air.
Later, Pemberton-Billing would be turning his active brain over
to Service use when he joined the R.N.A.S. and planned in great
detail a bombing raid on the Zeppelin base at Friedrichshafen;
meanwhile, he remained undismayed by failure, somewhat impu-
dently exhibiting his waterbound P.B.I. at the Olympia Air Show
in 1914.

So the flimsy biplanes and fragile monoplanes that had never
carried guns into the air continued to putter around the sky at
meetings all over Europe, intriguing many and amusing not a
few; but the war clouds were gathering, and flying for the sheer
pleasure and daring of it would shortly be ended. War and naval
aviation were only too soon to walk hand in hand; in the autumn
of 1913 the first armed Whitehead torpedo to be launched from
an aeroplane had been dropped by Lieutenant-Commander A.
Longmore, flying a Short floatplane. Also, Commander Samson
and an assistant, Lieutenant E. E. Clark-Hall, undertook various
experiments in bomb-dropping from seaplanes during that year;
and Lieutenant Reginald Gregory lifted a Short machine into the
air carrying a 300 lb. bomb, a very heavy missile for the time.

On 26th October 1913 Mr Winston Churchill formulated the
types of aeroplane he considered to be most suitable for work
with the Royal Navy, recommending "an overseas fighting seaplane to operate from a ship as base, a scouting seaplane to work
with the fleet at sea, and a home service fighting aeroplane to
repel enemy aircraft. . . ." From the beginning, the First Lord of
the Admiralty had shown great interest in the possibilities of
naval aviation; and undoubtedly his special mixture of boyish
charm, twinkling persuasion and downright stubbornness
influenced the decision to form the Royal Naval Air Service from
the Naval Wing, Royal Flying Corps, on 1st July 1914. Three
weeks later, the new R.N.A.S.—seventeen Short and Farman seaplanes and two flights of miscellaneous aeroplanes—flew in formation over the ships of the Home Fleet, lined up at Spithead for
review by H.M. King George V.

The gilded Royal yacht *Victoria and Albert,* symbol of a happy
comfortable era almost at an end, stood at anchor off Cowes
beyond the lines of grey battleships that tragic golden summer of

1914; but when the Review was over the R.N.A.S. remained fully mobilised, while the Home Fleet steamed quietly up to war stations at Scapa Flow. Much later it became apparent that the astute First Lord had, in fact, deliberately kept the Fleet in a state of mobilisation to watch over the sea lanes so vital to Great Britain, with the full agreement of the First Sea Lord, Prince Louis of Battenberg. The value of Mr Churchill's foresight was to be emphasised by the terrifying series of events that led up to 4th August 1914. On that fateful day, 11 p.m. brought the deep, booming voice of Big Ben, echoing across a silent London to hammer out the last few seconds of peace between Great Britain and the German Fatherland.

The previous evening, Sir Edward Grey, the British Foreign Secretary, had stood at his window in Whitehall, watching darkness settle over a gaslit London. "The lamps are going out all over Europe," he commented sadly to his companion. "We shall not see them lit again in our lifetime."

On the outbreak of war, the Royal Naval Air Service could muster 52 seaplanes and 39 aeroplanes, flown or maintained by a hundred officers and some seven hundred non-commissioned officers and men. These aircraft and personnel initially operated from six air stations—including the three large bases at Yarmouth, Felixstowe and Calshot—and for some weeks did little except carry out coastal patrols from the Humber down to the mouth of the Thames. Meanwhile, the seven airships belonging to the R.N.A.S. patrolled the Channel between Dover and Dunkirk, keeping a watchful eye open for the Zeppelins expected at any time to attempt an attack on London.

On 27th August 1914 Commander Samson took the Eastchurch squadron to Ostend, where the Admiralty hoped to establish the first British naval base on the continent; but it was impossible to carry out any useful work with so few aircraft, and three days later Samson found himself back in England. Nevertheless, the Admiralty fully realised the necessity of naval air bases in France and Belgium, and by October the energetic Samson had established a seaplane station at Dunkirk and commanded nine aircraft, a formidable force of men and a number of touring cars. Using these vehicles, armoured with boiler plate and armed with Maxim guns, Samson led repeated daring reconnaissance sorties into enemy territory, on one occasion engaging a German staff car near Cassel and later clashing with Uhlan cavalry with some success. When the Germans captured Douai, Samson retook it with his primitive armoured cars and held the town until compelled to fall back by the overwhelming weight of enemy forces.

Unfortunately, Commander Samson remained desperately short of aircraft; and indeed the R.N.A.S. as a whole needed more rapid expansion to cope with the many tasks being crowded upon it. The Admiralty had given permission for the conversion into floatplane carriers of three cross-Channel steamers, the *Riviera,* the *Empress* and the *Engadine,* and there was already talk of flying off seaplanes from these ships to bomb targets in Germany. The first attack on the German homeland had already been made on 22nd September 1914, when four naval aeroplanes took off from Antwerp to bomb the airship sheds at Düsseldorf and Cologne; but regrettably only one aircraft reached its target, all the bombs except one—which inflicted no damage—failing to explode.

On 6th October a more successful raid on Germany was carried out by two little Sopwith Tabloid single-seater scout biplanes of the R.N.A.S., one flying to Düsseldorf and the other to Cologne. Squadron Commander Spenser Grey arrived over Cologne in thick fog and dropped his small 20 lb. Cooper bombs in the area of the main railway station; Flight Lieutenant R. L. Marix, on the other hand, found wintry sunshine brightening the sky over Düsseldorf and dived towards the airship sheds, releasing his bombs from a height of 600 ft. A moment later, the Tabloid was shaken by the blast of a great explosion within the Zeppelin shed, and Marix saw a fountain of red flame leap into the air. He zoomed away, pursued by heavy rifle and machine-gun fire, and with great skill nursed his tiny biplane slowly along on the weary journey back to base. Riddled with holes, the Tabloid finally gave up and Marix was forced to make a landing only 20 miles from Antwerp. Later, it was learned that his bombs had destroyed the new Zeppelin Z IX and caused other extensive damage.

And so to the historic raid on Friedrichshafen by Avro aircraft on 21st November 1914. This long-range attack had been planned with great attention to detail by Lieutenant Noel Pemberton-Billing, who had actually crossed Lake Constance from the Swiss side in disguise to study the Friedrichshafen Zeppelin sheds and factories at first hand. For an advanced base, the French frontier town of Belfort—the nearest point to Friedrichshafen—was selected, the four Avro 504s from Southampton being moved secretly at night to the aerodrome there. Eleven mechanics arrived quietly at Belfort to service the aeroplanes, and four pilots were chosen to fly them. Those selected were Squadron Commander E. F. Briggs, Flight Commander J. T. Babington, Flight Lieutenant S. V. Sippe and Sub-Lieutenant R. P. Cannon; all outstanding airmen, with justifiable confidence in their first-class machines.

The remarkable Avro 504, developed by Alliott Verdon-Roe in 1912 from his Series 500 racing aeroplane, was destined to have only a brief moment of glory as a bomber before settling down to become probably the most famous training aircraft of all time. Simple in the extreme to fly, and very stable, with none of the unexpected vices that characterised some other early aeroplanes, the 504 gained a special place in the affections of all those pilots who had their first experience of flying seated in the deep cockpit of a Mono Avro. More than any other aircraft, it symbolised the era when flying really was flying, conjuring up a hundred sights and sounds that are now gone for ever: instructor and pupil tramping out to the waiting Avro, armed against the early-morning chill in leather helmets and sidcots, fug boots and gauntlets; taxiing with a finger on the blip-switch, the engine firing in short bursts, drowsy mechanics steadying the wing tips; then gazing out over the high, drum-tight fabric decking, the bitter tang of the castor oil used as an engine lubricant twitching the nostrils, the face whipped by the icy slipstream lashing back over the little windscreen; and finally drifting in to land, the unforgettable, throaty blip-blip of the Gnome rotary; the altimeter needle falling away round the dial, the gentle rocking of the wings as the wheels swished through the damp grass. Over 8,300 machines of that immortal Avro 504 type were manufactured between 1914 and 1918, of which 5,446 were used as trainers, including the colourful aircraft operated by the famous

Smith-Barry school of flying training at Gosport. After the war
the 504K (and later the 504N) remained the standard initial training aircraft of the R.A.F. until 1932, being superseded by another
Avro design, the Type 621 Tutor.

At 9.30 a.m. on the morning of 21st November, then, Squadron Commander Briggs led his flight of bombing 504s out
across the grass field at Belfort. Unfortunately, Sub-Lieutenant
Cannon's aircraft broke its tail skid and taxied forlornly to a
standstill; but the other three Avros were soon in the air and
steadily gaining height. Following a rather crooked course to
avoid infringing Swiss neutrality, Briggs led his flight of biplanes
to Mulhausen and then over the Black Forest. They reached
dreamy Schaffhausen, turned, and dived down over Lake Constance. "Arrived extreme end of lake and came down to within
10 ft. of water; continued at this height over lake, passing Constance at very low altitude . . ." Stated Flight Lieutenant Sippe in
his log, the bare, direct facts giving little indication of the dan-
gers involved. Directly ahead was the target: Friedrichshafen.

Despite the heavy anti-aircraft fire, a number of direct hits
were made in the Zeppelin works and hangar area, with the
devastating results already described. Squadron Commander
Briggs' machine was hit repeatedly by accurate machine-gun
bursts; but he managed to make a forced landing not far from
Friedrichshafen, soon becoming surrounded by a menacing
crowd of civilians from the town. Fortunately, a squad of German soldiers appeared in time to save the ugly situation, treating
Briggs with great respect and taking him to hospital for treat-
ment.

Their mission completed, the two remaining Avros throbbed
back across Lake Constance at zero height—and their maximum
speed of 80 m.p.h.—to land safely at Belfort in the early afternoon. Within four hours they had travelled 125 miles to successfully bomb an important target in enemy territory, and returned
to base; an astonishing achievement at the time, so alarming to
the Germans that they poured troops and guns and searchlights
into Friedrichshafen in quick time to defend the Zeppelin sheds.
But they succeeded only in locking the stable door after the horse
had been stolen; British bombers were destined never to attack
Friedrichshafen again in the First World War.

On Christmas Eve the fourth and last raid of the year 1914 to be carried out by naval airmen had been set in motion. That night the seaplane carriers *Riviera, Empress* and *Engadine,* each with three Short aircraft below decks, and escorted by the light cruisers *Arethusa* and *Undaunted* and eight destroyers, were steaming across the North Sea; before dawn the small but powerful force lay some twelve miles north of Heligoland on a calm sea, awaiting the opening of another bitterly cold day. Then one by one the nine floatplanes were hoisted out and went skimming away. Seven of the Short biplanes rose without any difficulty into the air, but the remaining two machines refused to become airborne with their heavy weight of bombs and had to be swung back aboard their parent carriers. The seven pilots committed to action—Flight Commanders Douglas Oliver, F. E. Hewlett, R. Peel-Ross and Cecil Kilner; Flight Lieutenants Arnold Miley and C. H. Edmonds; and Flight Sub-Lieutenant Vivian Caskell-Blackburn—huddled deeper into their draughty cockpits in the clear, icy air and set course for Cuxhaven.

Over the German coast, the floatplanes encountered a swirling mist which soon resolved into dense fog, and the pilots consequently failed to locate their primary objective, the Zeppelin sheds at Cuxhaven. A number of bombs were therefore dropped in the dockyard area, causing only slight damage; but a reconnaissance of the German harbours and roadsteads was more successfully carried out. By great good fortune, Flight Commander Kilner and his observer, Lieutenant Erskine Childers, surprised a large part of the German fleet in the Schillig Roads, startling the German crews by buzzing angrily around their decks at minimum height. Indeed, the ships got under way in such great haste that the battle cruiser *Von der Tann* collided with another warship in the confusion and was badly damaged.

By 10 a.m. on Christmas Day three of the raiding floatplanes had returned to their parent ships and were being swung aboard. Of the other four machines, three had landed on the water near the British submarine E11, which barely had time to pick up the aeroplane crews before crash diving to avoid bombs dropped by a watchful Zeppelin. It later transpired that the remaining seaplane had alighted alongside a Dutch trawler, the crew being interned for some time in Holland.

During its three hours sojourn off the German coast, the British naval squadron had also come in for a fair share of the action. Two attacks by Zeppelins had been easily turned away by a rapid bombardment from high-angled 6-in. shrapnel; but a third, more determined, attack by a number of enemy seaplanes failed only because the barrage of machine-gun and rifle fire put up by the warships made accurate bombing impossible.

The Christmas Day raid could, perhaps, be considered only a very small success. Nevertheless, the young Royal Naval Air Service, with little more than a handful of flimsy aeroplanes, had struck mightily at the enemy on his own homeland during the first few months of war—and within three years of the first four Royal Navy officers receiving flying instruction at Government expense. A hard year lay ahead for the R.N.A.S. with the onset of 1915; but there would be an increased number of aircraft, more trained crews, and—by no means least in importance—a new seaplane carrier, named *Ark Royal*. What nation had achieved more? Not France, with only one *escadrille* of floatplanes and a few F.B.A. boats to her name. And certainly not Germany, with her steadfast faith in the huge airships of Count Zeppelin and consequent neglect of naval aeroplanes. As for the United States, Glenn Curtiss had inspired considerable interest in flying-boats; but America was still at peace, and aviation remained a hobby for wealthy young sportsmen; the drums of war were beating too far away.

2

DARDANELLES TRAGEDY: 1915

∽∽∽∽∽∽∽∽∽∽∽∽∽∽∽∽∽∽∽∽∽∽∽∽∽∽∽∽∽∽

The 7,450-ton seaplane carrier H.M.S. *Ark Royal* was designed as a merchant ship, being converted at Blyth late in 1914 to carry ten floatplanes. She was just over 350 ft. in length, with a flight deck (or launching platform) of some 130 ft. and had a speed of about eight knots in favourable weather conditions. The spacious single hangar of the *Ark Royal* was in the hold, and the ship was well fitted out with cranes, workshops and small machine tools. Initially, she carried Short, Wight and Sopwith aircraft, with six or seven machines operational at any one time; but of these, only the stable Short seaplanes could be flown off in really bad weather. However, despite the shortcomings of her equipment, the *Ark Royal* was destined to prove an excellent carrier, and early in 1915 would play an important part in the ill-fated Dardanelles campaign.

Great Britain had been at war with Turkey since the end of August 1914, when the series of events that had been set in motion by the German cruisers *Goeben* and *Breslau* taking refuge in the Dardanelles ended with the bombardment of Russian ports in the Black Sea by Turkish warships. In the November, Britain, taking action as the ally of Russia—and also demonstrating the might of the world's greatest sea power—despatched her Mediterranean fleet to bombard the Turkish forts in the Dardanelles; but Winston Churchill, the First Lord of the Admiralty, had long been of the opinion that a full-scale campaign should be mounted there. "I wanted Gallipoli attacked on the declaration of war . . ." he wrote on one occasion to H. H. Asquith, the Prime Minister.

With his remarkable love of side-shows and unquenchable thirst for new adventures, the dynamic Churchill visualised forcing

the entrance to the Dardanelles, and then striking across the
Sea of Marmara to the Turkish capital of Constantinople; a
sword in the Near East to relieve hard-pressed Russia and surprise Germany, at a time when world opinion assumed that Britain was wholly committed on the Western Front. But it would
be no easy task to force a passage. After the Royal Navy's bombardment of the Dardanelles, the Turks had strengthened the
defences, and large numbers of howitzers and other heavy guns
commanded the entrance from the Gallipoli peninsula. Nevertheless, the persuasion of Churchill and his supporters, together
with urgent Russian requests for a 'second front' to ease the
Turkish pressure, finally to some extent succeeded; the Admiralty was allowed to commence naval operations against Turkey
"to bombard and take the Gallipoli Peninsula, with Constantinople as the object." The Secretary of State for War, Lord Kitchener, could not be moved to promise any military support,
despite an increasing weight of opinion at the War Office that
troops should be made available.

During the winter of 1914–15, the aircraft of the *Ark Royal*
had meanwhile been getting modified for active service in the
Dardanelles. A young air mechanic, Chief Petty Officer Teasdale—now Squadron Leader J. J. Teasdale, R.A.F. (Retd.)—was
one of those ordered to Blyth to join the carrier. "The first task
was to co-ordinate aircraft and armament," he has recalled. "I
had already experienced the problems brought about by bombs
rolling around loose in the cockpit, and considered that their
proper place should be somewhere outside the aeroplane. I therefore constructed a bomb rack. This was made by suspending a
length of light angle iron under the fuselage; the angle iron
having six slots to take eyed set screws which it was intended to
fit to the bombs. The bombs could be dropped by using split
pins attached to the end of a length of cable, the other end of the
cable being passed through to the cockpit and fitted with a handle, a tug on the handle thus pulling out the split pin and releasing the bomb." Teasdale then had to face the problem of fixing
the eyed set screws to the bombs. "I had no knowledge of explo-
sives and nor had anyone else on the ship," he said. "However, I
knew that a detonator had to be inserted before the bomb was
ready for use. I therefore hoped there would be no danger in my

drilling a hole in the bomb casing so that it could be threaded to take the set screw; but I took the precaution of clearing everyone out of the workshop. Then I placed the bomb under the drilling machine." The casing of the bomb proved to be much thinner than Teasdale had anticipated, and when the drill had penetrated about ⅛ in. white powder (the T.N.T. filling) came up the flutes of the drill—a somewhat alarming experience. "Of course, the unarmed bombs could be drilled quite safely, provided the drill was not allowed to get warm; so the problem of properly arming the *Ark Royal* aircraft with bombs had been solved."

It is interesting to note here that the Lewis machine-guns on these naval aeroplanes had their cooling jackets removed, and then were mounted to fire forward through the propeller arc; thus anticipating by six months the introduction of an interrupter gear. "Only one drum of ammunition could actually be fired," recalls Teasdale, "because obviously a number of bullets were bound to pierce the propeller. As some precaution against splintering, adhesive tape was wrapped around the airscrew where the bullets would pass through; but the propellers were usually rendered unserviceable after one drum of ammunition had been fired."

Vice-Admiral S. H. Carden, in command of the combined British and French naval expedition to the Dardanelles, opened his attack on the outer Turkish defences on 19th February 1915, renewed the bombardment on the 25th, and put ashore small 'commando' parties of Marines over the following ten days. These actions resulted in the destruction of most of the Turkish heavy guns forming the entrance defences, but regrettably with very little assistance from the *Ark Royal*, which failed to get any aircraft off in a week of appalling weather. On 5th March an indirect bombardment of the inner forts was commenced by the huge battleship *Queen Elizabeth*, firing across the Gallipoli peninsula at 14,000 yd. range, with a Sopwith floatplane ready to spot the fall of shot from a height of 3,000 ft. Unfortunately, ill luck continued to dog *Ark Royal* and her airmen; before observing could be commenced, the propeller fell off the aeroplane and it dropped like a stone into the sea. With some difficulty, the crew were rescued, and a second Sopwith two-seater then took off from the carrier and also climbed to 3,000 ft. At once, it was hit by rifle fire which wounded the pilot. He struggled back to base, and during the afternoon the floatplane took off again with a new crew; but visibility was fading and operations had to be suspended until the following morning.

During the next few days, the *Queen Elizabeth* continued to drop her enormous 15-in. shells on the Turkish inner defences while floatplanes from the *Ark Royal* carried out reconnaissance flights far up the Dardanelles. However, the Turks were moving up mobile guns under cover of darkness, the thickly sown mine-fields could not be located and cleared, and a deadly stalemate was developing which had to be broken. On 18th March, Admiral Carden's successor, Vice-Admiral J. M. de Robeck, therefore ordered an attack by the Allied fleet to silence the forts in the Narrows, using no less than eighteen battleships—including the *Queen Elizabeth*, *Agamemnon*, *Lord Nelson* and *Inflexible*—and large numbers of cruisers and destroyers: the kind of awe-inspiring, grey, majestic armada that Churchill loved. At 11.30 a.m. this great array of ships opened fire.

The bombardment continued for most of the day in fine, cloudless weather, and a floatplane from the *Ark Royal* was sent aloft every hour to observe results; but most of the messages sent back to base carried only bad news, and some told of tragedy and disaster. A number of the Turkish guns had been knocked out and others half-buried under rubble with their crews during the morning, although by the early afternoon most of the attacking warships had been slightly damaged by the intense enemy counter-fire. The French battleship *Bouvet* was hit as she turned at speed in a wide arc, wavered beneath the blast of a great explosion, then capsized and sank. Within the space of a moment six hundred men had been lost. In the ensuing withdrawal, *Inflexible* shuddered as she struck a mine, and began to list badly. Three minutes later, the *Irresistible* was also mined; and *Ocean*, a third British battleship, was hit so badly she began turning in wide circles, out of control. The disabled *Inflexible* eventually laboured back to Tenedos, but *Irresistible* sank and *Ocean* foundered after drifting helplessly for hours. The remainder of the Allied fleet withdrew, having shaken the Turkish defences and caused the enemy gunners to expend all their available ammunition—but at the terrible price of three battleships sunk, a number of other warships damaged, and seven hundred men killed.

It now began to seem clear that if the campaign was to be successful a joint naval and military operation was essential. Indeed, General Sir Ian Hamilton had already been ordered by Lord Kitchener to the Dardanelles with a large body of troops but no agreed plan of campaign, although Kitchener had told him, "I hope you will not have to land at all; if you do have to land, why then, the powerful Fleet at your back will be the prime factor in your choice of time and place." After the failure of the Allied naval force to penetrate the Straits on 18th March, it became obvious that a military landing would have to be effected, but day after wasted day of uncertainty and indecision slid past, while the grateful Turks first repaired and then strengthened their inner defences. On 26th March the German General Liman von Sanders arrived at Gallipoli to take command of the Turkish Fifth Army, and immediately called for heavier artillery, a squadron of aircraft and more infantrymen. "The British," he wrote later, "allowed us four good weeks of respite . . . before their great disembarkation."

The respite so welcome to Liman von Sanders existed because of the sadly unprepared state of the Allied expeditionary force; stores and equipment badly loaded in England; a drastic shortage of ammunition; no raw materials; and many essential items lost in a sea of confusion. Into this chaos arrived Commander C. R. Samson, his boundless energy undiminished by a winter of armoured-car sorties from Dunkirk, together with No. 3 Squadron, Royal Naval Air Service—a curious collection of eighteen aircraft of various types. By dint of much hard work over the next two or three weeks, Samson established the first naval aerodrome in the Near East, at Tenedos. On 28th March a reconnaissance flight over the Straits was undertaken for the first time by a No. 3 Squadron aeroplane; and during the following month Samson had machines up almost every day, plotting enemy gun positions, observing fall of shot from the bombarding Allied warships, and reporting in great detail on the increasing enemy defences. Meanwhile, the floatplanes from *Ark Royal* ranged far

and wide on similar duties until 17th April, when they were
returned to Mudros to prepare for the infantry landing, planned
to take place one week later.

Slowly the problems of supply and demand were sorted out,
despite the limitations of the base at Mudros. The main Allied
landings were to be made on three small beaches, code-marked
V, W and X; all, as it turned out, heavily defended. Other forces
were to be put ashore at various points along the peninsula,
including about two thousand men on the sandy strip named Y
Beach and a large number of Australian and New Zealand troops
at the later famous Anzac Cove. A certain Commander Edwin
Unwin, R.N., had suggested that a merchantman could be used
as a landing ship to run ashore at the important V Beach, and by
20th April the old collier *River Clyde* lay anchored at Mudros
ready for action, her upper structure reinforced with sandbags
and narrow gangways—along which it was hoped two thousand
men would speedily effect a landing—fastened to her rusty sides.
Eleven machine-guns mounted in the armoured bows of the
River Clyde were placed under the command of Lieutenant-
Commander J. C. Wedgwood, of No. 3 Squadron's armoured car
section—yet another striking example of the many tasks being
undertaken by R.N.A.S. units at that time. Around the landing
vessel at her base were clustered a great number of warships,
liners, steamers and transports of various types, all packed with
troops about to "take a good run at the peninsula and jump
plump on—both feet together," in the words of General Hamilton.

At 6.20 a.m. on 25th April 1915, after a heavy supporting
naval bombardment, the converted collier *River Clyde* ran gently
aground on V Beach, under the lee of Sedd-el-Bahr castle, together with a number of ship's boats carrying men of the Royal
Dublin Fusiliers. But as the flying gangways were run out from
the *River Clyde* and lighters placed in position, the rapid, murderous clamour of machine-gun fire broke the silence and at once
the landing dissolved into screaming confusion. The beach suddenly became littered with dead and wounded; boats drifted
away in a sinking condition, riddled with bullets; the gangways
of the *River Clyde* ejected a tangled mass of shouting men, dying
under the continuous, raking fire; and from the fore-deck of the

old ship Wedgwood's Maxim guns flayed the Turkish emplacements and trenches in reply. Throughout the long, tragic day the
slaughter went on, the doomed infantry still trying to struggle
ashore while the sea literally ran red around them, the battleship
Queen Elizabeth hurling great shells into the defences almost
without respite.

When darkness fell on the scenes of carnage around the peninsula, the machine-guns of No. 3 Squadron had wrought fearful
havoc around the natural amphitheatre of V Beach; and Wedgwood would continue to produce those deadly Maxims whenever
and wherever they were needed until the end of May, by which
time the crews were completely exhausted. The expeditionary
force, then, had succeeded in landing before nightfall. Troops
were ashore, if somewhat precariously, on all the beaches, at the
cost of heavy casualties; and the Turks were still fighting with
undiminished fierceness on Y, X and W Beaches and at Anzac
Cove. On V Beach, the attacking force had been tragically decimated, but the defenders had also been virtually wiped out, and
the silence of the moonlit night was disturbed only by a crackle
of spasmodic rifle fire and the pitiful cries of the many wounded.
The Gallipoli campaign—the 'side show' so dear to Churchill
and Kitchener—had begun to take its fearful toll of human life,
every day increasing the suffering, achieving nothing.

During the next month bitter fighting raged on the Gallipoli
peninsula in the long battle for the commanding heights of the
hill Achi Baba. The floatplanes from *Ark Royal* and the aeroplanes of No. 3 Squadron were again constantly in the air to spot
targets for the bombarding warships or to chase away the occa-
sional high-flying German reconnaissance machine. Early in
May, Commander Samson established a rough forward landing-
ground at Helles, in close contact with even the most advanced
Allied troops, and despatched his aircraft far and wide to shoot
up and bomb Turkish positions. In the beginning, darts were
sometimes carried for use against personnel, but without any
success. "They were contained in boxes of 500, the boxes being
fitted with shutter lids," recalls Squadron Leader Teasdale. "The
darts were about the size of a pencil, and were intended for
dropping on formations of troops or cavalry; indeed, it was

claimed that they were capable of passing clean through a man and horse. The containers were secured to the side of the fuselage clear of the lower wing, so that when the lid was withdrawn the darts scattered away point downwards on to the target. In fact, they were found to be quite useless, as they tended to wobble during their descent, depending on the weather conditions; and when they wobbled they would not penetrate anything."

Bombs were of infinitely greater value, and the Turkish infantry soon began to dread the sound of aeroplane engines. On 17th May, Flight Commander R. I. G. Marix, flying in a Breguet two-seater with Commander Samson acting as his observer, dived low over the port of Ak Bashi Liman, where Turkish reinforcements frequently landed, and dropped a number of bombs, causing some damage and widespread confusion. In the same area, Samson spotted large numbers of Turkish troops moving up to face the Anzac positions; and his subsequent report to Headquarters ensured that the Allied forces were ready when the enemy attack came on the night of 18th–19th May. Again, on 4th June, Samson dropped a 100-lb. bomb on a German submarine, unfortunately without success; an incorrect fuse setting caused the projectile to explode before striking the water. Before the end of June, the bombing of Turkish columns and entrenched infantry by R.N.A.S. machines had become a regular occurrence, despite the many difficulties that arose when operating aircraft of the period in such intense heat and primitive conditions.

Meanwhile, another seaplane carrier, the 2,650-ton H.M.S. *Ben-my-Chree,* had arrived at Imbros to join *Ark Royal,* soon to become a depot ship for all the naval aircraft in Mediterranean waters. A converted Isle of Man packet built in 1908, the *Ben-my-Chree* was commanded by Squadron Commander C. J. L'Estrange Malone, one of the pioneers of British naval aviation. She was a small, but fast carrier with stowage for four two-seater torpedo floatplanes, and there seems little doubt that she was sent to the Dardanelles because there was some hope in Admiralty circles that her aircraft might sink the German cruisers *Goeben* and *Breslau,* then at Constantinople. However, that little pipe dream was destined never to become reality, either by good luck

· ·

Above, Blimp-type naval airship S.S.24; *below*, the Felixstowe F.4
Fury triplane of 1919 arrived too late for operational service

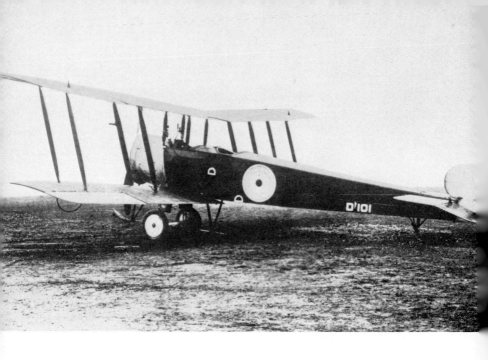

Above, the R.N.A.S. Avro 504 was the first successful bomber on land or sea; *below,* No. 1 Naval Squadron: Sopwith Triplanes which saw considerable action in support of the R.F.C. in 1916

or judgement; such wishful thinking took little consideration of the shortcomings of carrier-borne seaplanes in 1915.

The torpedo aircraft carried by the *Ben-my-Chree* were of the then very modern Short 184 type, so new that the first two prototypes (numbered 184 and 185) were included, about to be plunged into active service in the Dardanelles. Specifically designed by Horace Short as a torpedo-carrying biplane, the 184 was a large, somewhat sprawling two-seater machine initially powered by a 225-h.p. Sunbeam Mohawk engine, and carried a standard 14-in. Whitehead torpedo between the floats. Early models were unarmed, but later versions were fitted with a Lewis gun on a ring mounting around the rear cockpit. Pilots found it by no means perfect as a torpedo-carrying seaplane; indeed *The War in the Air*[1] comments, "The torpedo-loaded Short seaplane could only be made to get off the water and fly under ideal conditions. A calm sea with a slight breeze was essential and the engine had to be running perfectly . . ." Uninspiring and slow— the maximum speed was only 75 m.p.h.—the 184 nevertheless continued to give such good reliable service in various capacities from the spring of 1915 until the Armistice that by the end of 1918 about a thousand aircraft of the type had been produced, including later versions powered by Sunbeam Gurkha or Maori engines.

Some indication of the unspectacular but inherent good qualities of the Short 184 may be gathered from the activities of the Short floatplanes of that type operating from the *Ben-my-Chree* in the Mediterranean theatre of war during 1915. On 12th August Flight Commander C. H. K. Edmonds, flying from the Gulf of Xeros, sighted a large Turkish merchant ship off Injeh Burnu and dived to a height of some 15 ft. above the water, launching his torpedo at a range of 300 yd. The vessel was hit amidships, and Edmonds thus became the first man in history to torpedo an enemy ship from the air; although it later transpired that the steamer had been put out of action by the British submarine E.14 four days earlier. However, on 17th August Edmonds repeated his achievement by torpedoing one of three large supply ships he

[1] Vol. II, by Sir Walter Raleigh and H. A. Jones (Oxford University Press, 1922–37).

spotted heading for the port of Ak Bashi Liman, and the other Short 184/185 prototype, piloted by Flight Lieutenant G. B. Dacre, also scored a success within the hour by torpedoing a Turkish steam tug in False Bay.

The fearful Dardanelles summer of heat, sweat and flies dragged on, and Sir Ian Hamilton still could not break the stalemate of the Gallipoli campaign. He had asked for more reinforcements in preparation for a fresh onslaught, and by the end of July had no less than thirteen divisions in the field; but Hamilton also needed at least one energetic young subordinate General to command the attacking force. Instead, he received the elderly Sir Frederick Stopford, who knew nothing of modern war, and so the hopeful Allied offensive was doomed before ever a shot was fired. The attack was launched on the night of 6th–7th August, the Australians striking in the Anzac Cove area and some two thousand men being landed without opposition at Suvla Bay. But, having achieved a landing, Stopford congratulated his troops and did nothing more, despite urgent pleas from Hamilton to advance, and the surprised observers in the British aeroplanes droning over the beach were soon looking down on hundreds of troops making breakfast, relaxing, even bathing in the clear water. There were no Turks to fight, so "why bother to advance?" seemed to be the general opinion that day, but it was a selfish, unfortunate reasoning; three miles south of Suvla, at Anzac Bay, the Australian infantry were fighting bitterly to retain their meagre foothold on enemy soil.

Stopfold finally decided to move his troops inland on 8th August, after the Turks had employed two useful days moving heavy reinforcements into the area, and the Allied attack ended in the inevitable, dismal failure. It was stalemate once again by the September, and Hamilton was looking gloomily forward to the prospect of a blustery autumn and hard winter in the Dardanelles; but the Suvla Bay fiasco turned out to be the blunder that would bring about the end of the whole campaign. Stopford was recalled to England, and the flow of reinforcements dwindled to a mere trickle, although No. 2 Wing of the Royal Flying Corps—some two hundred men and twenty-two aircraft—arrived in the September. On the other hand, the R.N.A.S. armoured car squadrons were disbanded in the same month for absorbing into the

Army, many of the cars being stripped of their armour for use as staff vehicles and ambulances.

In Whitehall, it was at last realised that the Dardanelles campaign no longer had any hope of success. When Lord Kitchener was asked if he still believed there was a chance of driving on to Constantinople, he said, "By God, no! I have been let into this thing, but never again. Out I come, the first moment I can!" Nevertheless, the arguments and discussions drifted on into October, when General Sir Ian Hamilton was recalled to London. An outstanding commander from the Western Front named Sir Charles Monro next arrived in Gallipoli, with orders to report on the situation. He recommended immediate withdrawal as the only feasible solution to the problem, thus stoking up fresh disputes in the British Cabinet. Despite the later comments about Monro from such ardent supporters of the campaign as Winston Churchill—"He came, he saw, he capitulated"—there could have been no more realistic assessment of the facts; the Allied troops were desperately short of supplies, including food and water, and dysentery was rife over the whole peninsula. Meanwhile the Turkish forces were daily growing stronger in numbers and material, assisted by the constant flow of munitions and equipment from Germany trundling along the Berlin–Constantinople railway, re-opened after the entry of Bulgaria into the war.

Still the British Government could not find agreement on the subject of evacuation. Finally, Lord Kitchener himself visited Gallipoli, and returned prepared to admit what was already known beyond any doubt; the costly 'side-show' in the Near East had got to be abandoned. Detailed plans were soon being drawn up for evacuation, but in the meantime the overworked aeroplanes of the R.N.A.S. went on attacking the Turkish communications, with a fine disregard for the hard living conditions and the onset of winter. On 8th November, Commander Samson, flying a Maurice Farman biplane and leading two Short floatplanes from the *Ben-my-Chree,* made a round trip of 180 miles to bomb a vital railway bridge on the Berlin–Constantinople railway—soon to be attacked six more times by British naval aircraft. Two weeks later, Squadron Commander R. Bell Davies,

flying a single-seater Nieuport biplane, led Lieutenant G. F. Smylie, in a Henri Farman, on a raid against the railway station at
Ferejik; but after the two airmen had dropped their bombs,
heavy enemy rifle fire brought Smylie's machine down. As the
pilot climbed out and set fire to the wreckage, with Turkish
infantry running towards him, Bell Davies landed his Nieuport
neatly alongside. Smylie ran across and supported himself against
the struts of the little aeroplane, Bell Davies took off under fire,
and in due course both men arrived safely back at their base. For
this remarkable achievement, Bell Davies was awarded the Victoria Cross; and subsequent attacks on Ferejik completely destroyed the vital railway station.

On 19th–20th December 1915 Anzac and Suvla Bays were
quietly evacuated in the dead of night, long columns of weak-
ened, tired men filing on to motor barges which took them,
four hundred at a time, out to the waiting ships in a silence
broken only by spasmodic rifle fire. The R.N.A.S. stayed on,
flying continuous patrols over the beaches and Turkish trenches;
and still remained in action three weeks later, when the final
withdrawal from Cape Helles was also carried out without loss.
There followed a few days when the British naval airmen suffered
a number of casualties before they relinquished Imbros, then the
last weary Allied forces departed from the Dardanelles, leaving
behind them vast quantities of supplies, and much, much more:
all the dreams of forcing the Straits with a mighty battle fleet,
opening a line of communications to Russia, knocking Turkey
out of the war, marching in triumph through Constantinople.

It remained only to count the cost of failure. The British
casualties for the whole Gallipoli campaign totalled 213,980 sick,
killed and wounded, and the French had lost another 47,000
men; against about 251,000 enemy losses, according to official
Turkish figures As might have been expected, Churchill became
the scapegoat, and left the Government, receiving the nominal
position of Chancellor of the Duchy of Lancaster; a year later, he
would be commanding a battalion of infantry in France. In
Whitehall, thoughts were already turning to other side-shows,
with an eagerness to forget those many disasters of Gallipoli
enriched only by the unswerving courage of the men who had
fought and died on that forbidding peninsula. Not least of the

bravery there had been shown by the Royal Naval Air Service; in the worst possible conditions of intense heat that warped wood-work and bitter cold that shook exhausted bodies, aircraft and crews had carried on flying to the end. When that end came, the British naval airmen had reluctantly withdrawn; but they remained cheerful in spite of everything and, in truth, unde-feated.

3

BLIMPS AND ZEPPELINS: 1915

∽∽∽∽∽∽∽∽∽∽∽∽∽∽∽∽∽∽∽∽∽∽∽∽∽∽∽∽∽∽∽∽∽∽

On the morning of 7th June 1915 Flight Sub-Lieutenant R. A. J. Warneford, a young naval airman based at Dunkirk, was flying in a single-seater Morane Parasol monoplane over Belgium, when he sighted a large German airship moving like a vast silver pencil through the cloudless sky near Ostend. Warneford was on his way to make a solitary attack on the Zeppelin sheds at Berchem St Agathe, but quickly changed his mind and decided to have a crack at the unsuspecting airship sliding past before him; a courageous decision by a man whose machine was no fighter at any time and slower than ever when weighed down by six 20-lb. bombs. He turned towards the Zeppelin—actually the LZ 37, commanded by Oberleutnant von der Haegen—and gradually overhauled it, soon coming under a raking fire from machine-guns mounted in the airship's gondolas.

Warneford drew back on the stick, and the Morane climbed sluggishly to a height of 10,000 ft. Then he glanced over the side at the Zeppelin flying steadily along beneath him; far below it, the city of Bruges was a cluster of miniature buildings on the vast chequerboard of the Belgian countryside. The stick went forward in Warneford's gloved hand and the Morane dived, rapidly increasing speed, until he was pressed back against his seat, the gleaming silver back of the airship filling his windscreen. When he was about 150 ft. above the Zeppelin, Warneford levelled out with a great roaring of engine, his free hand jerking at the bomb release levers. The bombs fell away in rapid succession with perfect timing, seeming to hit all along the broad upper surface of the airship—or so Warneford must have hoped at that critical moment.

The result was decisive, and much more spectacular than Warneford could have thought possible. A great gout of flame erupted from within the depths of the LZ 37, to the accompaniment of a tremendous explosion that shook the little Morane like a toy and threw it upside down. Stunned by the blast, Warneford reeled in his seat, fighting the darkness that threatened to cloud his brain, while the monoplane plunged headlong earthwards, with great pieces of the burning Zeppelin falling all around it. At last, he struggled back to consciousness and eased back on the stick; the Morane trembled, then came out of the dive screaming and regained level flight. Still feeling dazed and ill, Warneford centralised his controls and looked down.

He saw a strange and fearful sight. The German military airship LZ 37 had been utterly destroyed, and the smoke and flame of its passing besmirched the pleasant Belgian countryside. Wreckage was scattered over a wide area, but much of the heavier machinery had fallen on a convent, killing two nuns. Of the Zeppelin's crew, there was only one survivor, a helmsman named Muller, who had hurtled like a human projectile through the tiled roof of the convent and crashed on to a bed below. Though very badly injured, Muller made such a good recovery that eventually he returned to duty with the Zeppelin service.

Circling far above the plume of greasy black smoke that marked the end of LZ 37, Warneford suddenly heard the Le Rhone engine of his Morane sputter and then stop, the propeller windmilling slowly around before his startled gaze. He could do little except keep the machine steady as it gradually lost height; silently, the monoplane glided over a wood and dropped to a bumpy landing in the field beyond. Only too well aware that he was far behind the German lines, Warneford jumped out and made hurried preparations to set his Morane on fire—then hesitated. All around him the countryside was still; nothing moved to show that his landing had been observed. What if he could repair the engine and get away?

Examining the Morane's rotary motor, Warneford soon located the fractured oil pipe that had caused all the trouble; and then spent anxious moments striving to effect a temporary repair. At last the job was done. Warneford now had to start the engine again without assistance, perhaps the most difficult task of all on an aircraft of that type. He swung the propeller, the warm motor thundered into life, and immediately the light Morane began to move; Warneford leapt for the cockpit, dropped into his seat as the speed increased—then the Morane was up and away. Within the hour it had safely crossed the Belgian lines. For his great courage and tenacity during the action, Warneford was awarded the Victoria Cross; but ten days later he tragically crashed outside Paris, and was killed.

The first German airship to be destroyed in the air had thus fallen to bombing attack by a British naval airman; and indeed the activities of the R.N.A.S. were to be largely concerned with fighting the Zeppelin menace during the remainder of 1915. Most of the Royal Flying Corps squadrons were engaged in France, and the Admiralty had become almost entirely responsible for the defence of the United Kingdom, including the formation of a special branch of the R.N.A.S. to man the handful of anti-aircraft guns and searchlights scattered around London. The North Sea air stations—especially Great Yarmouth and Felixstowe—were flying reconnaissance machines out on many hundreds of monotonous, but very necessary, patrols in the hope of sighting Zeppelins or submarines. There was a very real fear of an airship offensive by the enemy at this time, and many false alarms—later to become known as 'Zeppelin scares'—were received, sending aeroplanes aloft on fruitless missions that brought only frustration. Nevertheless, this arduous work was carried out without complaint, frequently at night, without the use of any blind-flying instruments. Also, it may not be appreciated that lack of experience in proper organisation led to anomalies that seem quite remarkable in retrospect; it was not unusual for Avro 504 and B.E.2c landplanes to undertake patrols far out over the North Sea, or Short and Sopwith floatplanes to be sent up in search of airships that information indicated had already crossed the English coast.

All the R.N.A.S. aircraft in service at that time suffered from the same deficiencies—lack of speed and inadequate armament. The last-named defect was partially remedied by the introduction of synchronised machine-guns later in 1915; and the Ranken incendiary darts, followed by the electrically fired le Preur rockets and finally the devastating mixture of Brock explosive and Pomeroy tracer ammunition, proved effective enough to combat the German airship campaign a year later. Some experiments had been carried out in the early days of British naval aviation with a Sopwith floatplane fitted with a 1½-pounder Vickers naval quick-firing cannon, and during the summer of 1915 the Davis gun, a 6-pounder recoilless cannon, was installed for testing purposes in a Short 184 flown by Flight Lieutenant W. G. Moore. But the Davis cannon was too unwieldy for service use, and was soon abandoned; only rapid-firing light automatic weapons such as the Vickers and Lewis guns were turning out to be of lasting value in air warfare. The first movable gun mounting available to the R.N.A.S. was the Scarff socket-and-pillar mounting, later replaced by the Scarff ring; Lewis guns were fitted to these for use by observers in two-seater machines and the big reconnaissance flying-boats.

The development of the flying-boat type of seaplane in Great Britain had made only slow progress since the outbreak of war, despite the encouragement of Glenn Curtiss, and also T. O. M. Sopwith, with his Bat Boats. Much of the credit for the work that was done on the craft during 1914 must inevitably go to a certain Lieutenant John Cyril Porte, who had been invalided out of the Royal Navy with pulmonary tuberculosis in 1911. During his career, Porte had become intensely interested in aviation, and after taking his flying certificate he helped to form the British Deperdussin Company, making French designs under licence. Unfortunately, the firm collapsed in 1913, by which time Porte had earned himself wide fame as a brilliant display pilot at Hendon. He next joined White and Thompsons, a Bognor boatbuilding works branching out into the aviation world, undertaking test flying and similar duties. At about the same time, a Captain Ernest Bass who had also been a member of the Deperdussin Company purchased a Curtiss flying-boat; and in due course this craft arrived at Brighton. It thus came about that John Porte was introduced to Glenn Curtiss outside Volk's Seaplane Base—actually a canvas hangar just capable of holding one flying-boat—on Brighton beach one morning, and at once became another enthusiastic exponent of that type of seaplane.

Early in 1914 the American millionaire Rodman Wanamaker, who had originated the idea of department stores in the United States, commissioned Glenn Curtiss to build a large twin-engined

flying-boat capable of crossing the Atlantic, and John Porte was
delighted to be offered the job of pilot. He left for America at
once, joining Curtiss at Hammondsport on Lake Keuka, in the
State of New York, and the large biplane flying-boat later to be
named *America* quickly began to take shape. However, initial
taxiing trials soon proved that the two 90-h.p. Curtiss OX-5
engines mounted between the wings of the *America* had insufficient
power to lift it off the water; and before modifications could be
carried out, Great Britain was on the brink of war. On 4th
August 1914 John Porte returned to England.

Despite his serious disability, Porte was accepted into the
R.N.A.S. and placed in command of the Hendon flying training
station. While there, he discussed the Curtiss *America* flying-boat
at length with Captain Murray Sueter, the Director of the Admiralty Air Department, and a number of R.N.A.S. inspecting
officers were sent to the United States to report on the craft and
another Curtiss design, the J.N. two-seater training biplane.
Large numbers of the J.N. type—or 'Jenny' as it soon came to be
called—were eventually purchased for use by the British air arms,
and the Admiralty did indeed buy the original *America* boat; but
Their Lordships were only prepared to take the risk of ordering
one sister-ship—surely an indication of the little value placed on
flying-boats at the time.

The two Curtiss H.4 boats, as they were officially designated,
duly arrived at Felixstowe for testing in December 1914, and a
further small batch of the type was cautiously ordered. However,
even when powered by twin 100-h.p. Anzani radial engines, the
H.4 or Small America, boats were far from perfect for operational use; and John Porte therefore arrived at Felixstowe air
station to work on the development of a more reliable craft.
Largely on his advice, Glenn Curtiss designed a similar flying-
boat to the H.4, but much larger, and with a longer range. This
machine was the H.8, inevitably named the Large America type,
from which evolved the H.12, powered by two 250-h.p. Rolls-
Royce Eagle engines. Basically a good design, the H.12 could
remain in the air for over six hours, carry 400 lb. of bombs, and
had a maximum speed of 85 m.p.h.; but it had the serious defects
of a weak hull and inadequate defensive armament. Nevertheless,
about seventy H.12 boats saw active service with R.N.A.S. squad-

rons between July 1916 and the Armistice, and performed very well.

The shortcomings of the H.12 boats encouraged Porte to enlarge the scope of his experiments at Felixstowe, and in due course he developed the famous 'F' (for Felixstowe) series—the F.2 prototype, F.2A production version, F.3, and finally the F.5. During 1915, Porte also designed a big three-engined flying-boat intended for long-range patrol work. This craft, named the Porte-Felixstowe Baby, turned out to be somewhat slow and cumbersome at first, but Porte improved the performance by fitting very powerful 360-h.p. Rolls-Royce engines; and by 1918 his Babies were operating with great success from Killingholme and Felixstowe air stations.

Some mention must be made here of the development of British lighter-than-air craft since the outbreak of war. Early in 1914, the Admiralty had become responsible for all airships in use or under construction—despite the failure of the *Mayfly* and consequent lack of faith by the Royal Navy in the rigid type—and by August these included a number of small but very useful ships. Since the turn of the century, the influence of Germany with her growing fleet of Parsevals and Zeppelins had lain heavily upon British air thought, experiments with balloons leading in 1907 to an airship named the *Nulli Secundus,* which was driven by a 50-h.p. Antoinette engine, and three years later to the *Gamma,* a very similar craft. During 1913, a Parseval semi-rigid airship, powered by two 170-h.p. Maybach engines, had been purchased from Germany, an Astra-Torres non-rigid airship had been bought from France; and another smaller non-rigid airship designed by a Mr T. E. Willows had also been obtained. To this assortment of lighter-than-air craft were soon added three Army types, the *Delta, Eta* and *Beta,* all designed and produced by the Royal Aircraft Factory at Farnborough.

In anticipation of North Sea patrols and the hunting of enemy submarines by its airships, the Admiralty decided that the crossing of the British Expeditionary Force to France in August 1914 should be covered by the Astra-Torres and Parseval craft, flying between their base at Kingsnorth, near Chatham, and Dunkirk. The redoubtable Lord Fisher, at that time First Sea Lord of the

Admiralty, had already advocated the production of a number of small but fast airships of the Willow type, and Wing Commander E. A. D. Masterman, together with Commander N. F. Usborne, who had worked on the *Mayfly* project, were given the task of organising a building programme in the shortest possible time.

Due to the efforts of Masterman and Usborne, the first of the S.S. (or Submarine Scout) airships appeared early in 1915. The type was simple in the extreme; nothing more than a Willows gas-bag with the fuselage of a two-seater B.E.2c aeroplane, complete with engine, slung underneath to contain the crew. About thirty of these early naval airships were built, soon to be undertaking long patrols over the Straits of Dover and the approaches to the Irish Sea, often in the worst possible weather conditions, the crews exposed to the bitter cold of winter in open cockpits. Later, proper crew nacelles were turned out by a firm of furniture manufacturers, and larger gas-bags of various sizes were produced; the earlier S.S. ships had a gas capacity of 20,500 cu. ft. but those which appeared later in the war had a capacity increased to as much as 70,000 cu. ft. Endurance was in the region of eight hours, with a maximum speed of over 40 m.p.h. The curious name 'blimp' commonly applied to these first Royal Navy airships has been credited to the seaplane designer Horace Short, who is said to have exclaimed, "Look at that blimp!" upon seeing one for the first time; and when asked, "But why blimp?" he replied, "Well, what else could you call it?" Before the Armistice, the name 'Colonel Blimp' had become synonymous with any stout, hidebound staff officer with outdated ideas, the term being derived from the portly shape of the naval airships' gas-bags. Some 150 ships of the S.S. type continued to serve with the R.N.A.S. during the war years, including the final S.S. 'Twin' series, powered by twin Rolls-Royce engines.

Also in 1915, some new and still larger airships came into service; these were the 'C' (or Coastal) class machines, originally intended to replace the S.S. craft, although in the event both types were found to be of equal value. Designed with a three-bag trefoil structure in mind—the Astra-Torres principle developed with such success in France before the war—the 'C' class ships had a gas capacity of 170,000 cu. ft., were powered by two engines and carried a defensive armament which included a machine-gun mounted on top of the gas-bag. Endurance on patrols was lengthened with the big 'C' machines to over eleven hours; the maximum speed was about 45 m.p.h. Before the end of 1916, twenty-seven 'C' craft had been produced, and were proving so useful that a development with still greater range and increased speed, the 'C Star' class ship, was envisaged for service in 1917.

The demand for an increasing number of airships for naval patrol work had in turn brought an urgent need for airship bases with suitable large hangars to accommodate the corpulent craft. Following upon the original Kingsnorth base, only three British stations, at Folkestone, Polegate and Anglesey, had been established in 1915, with a fourth sited at Marquise, near Calais; but during 1916 other stations sprang up at Pembroke, Howden, Mullion and Peterhead. However, in due course many more bases would be erected—indeed, it was becoming increasingly obvious that the home-based R.N.A.S. squadrons of non-rigid airships and flying-boats were to play an important part in the constant struggle against the German U-boat and Zeppelin menace.

Having so vigorously set in motion the high-speed building programme for naval airships ordered by Lord Fisher, Masterman and Usborne persisted with their research in developing and extending the uses of the craft; the latter officer reaching out without hesitation into an entirely new field of flight, and persevering with the experiments until they brought about his tragic end. Together with Lieutenant-Commander de Courcy W. P. Ireland, at that time in command of Great Yarmouth seaplane station, Usborne sought to increase the range and ceiling of an aeroplane by slinging it under the gas-bag of an airship, the pilot releasing his machine when he wished to start the engine and fly away. It was hoped that a solution to the problem of getting an aircraft up to the great heights at which Zeppelins frequently operated over England might thus be achieved; but during 1915 many difficulties were experienced with the release catches fitted to the wings and tail of the machine Nevertheless, by early 1916 the defects appeared to have been remedied, and on 21st February Commander Usborne and Lieutenant-Commander Ireland took off from Kingsnorth airship station in a complete

B.E.2c biplane suspended from the gas-bag of an S.S.-type airship. The so-called 'airship-plane' climbed to a height of some 4,000 ft. then the B.E.2c abruptly dropped away from beneath the gas-bag at a steep angle, throwing the unfortunate Ireland out; his body was later recovered from the river Medway. Usborne was in the front seat, and could do nothing to regain control—in the B.E.2c type the pilot occupied the rear cockpit. The machine went into a spin, and Usborne was killed when it crashed outside Strood railway station.

For some time the accident seemed to have ended any 'airship-plane' experiments, but Usborne and Ireland, two very courageous officers and a credit to their Service, had not died in vain. During 1918, research with a view to carrying a fighter aircraft under a rigid airship (and so provide an aerial escort for the lighter-than-air craft) was ordered by the Admiralty, and before the Armistice single-seater Sopwith Camels had been successfully slipped from beneath the airship R.33; while some years after the Great War it became possible to re-attach a De Havilland D.H.53 aeroplane to the same airship when both machines were in flight.

4

OVER LAND AND SEA: 1916–17

At the outbreak of the 1914–18 War, the Imperial German Naval Air Service had only about twenty aeroplanes and a few seaplanes, including an early Sopwith floatplane and a Sopwith Bat Boat purchased in March 1914 by von Pustau, the aircraft buyer for the German Navy at the time. The latter machine was later photographed for propaganda purposes as "a captured British flying-boat"; but in truth almost two years were to pass before the German naval aeroplane arm became anything more than a poor relation of the greatly admired airship service. The first seaplane stations were formed at Kiel, Heligoland and Wilhelmshaven, and others were commissioned in due course at Borkum, Sylt, Norderney and Zeebrugge. The principal duties of all these small and often primitive bases were laid down by the Naval High Command, and followed much the same lines: reconnaissance, protection of friendly shipping, and defence against enemy aircraft. These apparently simple instructions actually covered a vast amount of arduous work, including patrols along the coasts of England, France and Holland, the sighting and bombing of submarines, and provision of air cover when strong German naval forces put out to sea—a multitude of impossible tasks for an air arm unable to keep more than a handful of slow, inferior machines aloft at any one time.

During 1915, the number of reconnaissance floatplanes taken into service by the main German seaplane bases slowly but surely increased, and *staffels* (or squadrons) were formed, including a remarkable unit of Marines-cum-airmen based on the Channel coast, under the command of an officer commonly known as 'Ludwig the Prickly'—Admiral von Schroeder. Some of the earlier Albatros and Rumpler biplanes had already been adapted as

floatplanes to satisfy the urgent need for more aircraft, and a few
Ago and Friedrichshafen two-seater machines followed in 1915;
but the German naval pilots required faster, more reliable and
better-armed aircraft for their long-range patrol duties—seaplanes actually designed to operate over the sea. Without such
machines, many hundreds of patrols were being flown to little
purpose, for the enemy was only too seldom encountered. As a
typical example, over eight hundred patrols were undertaken
from Borkum seaplane base during 1915, for the loss of seven
aircraft, with two officers missing and two captured.

Meanwhile, the German airship offensive against Britain had
been launched, with bombs even falling unexpectedly on an
indignant, if somewhat fearful, London; and the High Command
in Berlin beat the big drum over the success of its courageous
Zeppelin crews and forgot that an equally brave, if badly
equipped, naval aeroplane arm was striving to gain air superiority over the North Sea and the Channel—without which the
airship attacks might soon be ended. It was true that the British
coastal air defences were sadly lacking in co-ordination, and the
home defence aeroplane bases remained desperately short of
machines—neither the Admiralty or the War Office wanted the
responsibility of tackling the airship attacks—but the worried
German naval airmen knew nothing of the controversies raging
at a high level in Whitehall. They might have troubled less over
their own problems had they learned of the latest attempt by the
hard-pressed R.N.A.S. to increase the range of its 'Zeppelin-
seeking' scout patrols at night: two paddle-steamers, each carrying two or three little Sopwith Schneider (or Baby) single-seater
floatplanes, chugging out from Great Yarmouth and Killingholme respectively, to stop engines some 60 miles east of the coast
and send their aircraft aloft. Muddling through at any price and
sheer neglect of its most vital services were indeed not exclusive
privileges of the German High Command.

The autumn of 1915 dragged on into winter, and the naval
airmen of both sides continued to wait impatiently for more—
and better—aircraft. In the November, Flight Lieutenant H. F.
Towler, flying a Bristol C Scout biplane, took off from the small
deck platform of a new seaplane carrier, the *Vindex,* and thus
became the first man to fly his machine from the deck of a ship

specifically designed and constructed as what we now call an aircraft carrier. From early 1916, German experiments were being undertaken in the Baltic to release torpedoes from aircraft against ships in harbour or at sea, with such success that a special Wing of torpedo-carrying seaplanes was later formed at Flensburg. The designer, Ernst Heinkel, produced the first German operational torpedo-carrying machine, the large, twin-engined Hansa-Brandenburg GW type, in time to be superseded by an even larger (GWD-type) biplane, which could carry a torpedo weighing 4,000 lb. A number of these aircraft were sent to Zeebrugge to commence operations over the North Sea, together with some twin-engined Gothas modified for the same purpose. The first British ship to be sunk by an enemy aerial torpedo thus went down off the mouth of the Thames on 9th November 1916; but the German High Command abandoned the use of torpedo-carrying aeroplanes only a year later, on the grounds that the losses in men and machines had not been justified.

From such small beginnings were sown the seeds of naval air action in future wars, though the events seemed of little significance at the time. However, 1916 proved to become a decisive year for the R.N.A.S. in Flanders, still operating from the air station established at Dunkirk in the October of 1914 by Commander C. B. Samson. The unceasing demands from units both at home and on active service for new aircraft finally brought, in the early summer of 1916, two outstanding Sopwith designs; the two-seater 1½-Strutter and the single-seater Pup. The conventional 1½-Strutter tractor biplane (so called because it had only one pair of outer struts between the wings and short centre section struts between wings and fuselage) arrived on the Western Front for trials with No. 5 Wing of the R.N.A.S. and soon achieved great success as a reconnaissance aircraft. Powered by a 130-h.p. Clerget rotary engine which gave it a maximum speed of 102 m.p.h. at 6,500 ft. the 1½-Strutter was the first British machine to be fitted with a fixed Vickers machine-gun synchronised to fire through the propeller arc by means of an interrupter gear; and it was also the first two-seater aeroplane to have a Scarff ring mounting for the observer's Lewis gun around the rear cockpit. Within a month, the first Sopwith Pup had also entered service by joining 'A' Squadron—then equipped with

Nieuport Scouts for the air defence of Dunkirk—and at once endeared itself to the naval pilots at that base. A delightfully nimble little aircraft without any vices, the Pup was a direct descendant of the very advanced Tabloid scout of 1913 which had proved so adaptable in the early months of the war—yet another product of the fertile brains of T. O. M. Sopwith and his assistants at Kingston-on-Thames. Either an 80-h.p. Le Rhone or a 100-h.p. Gnome monosoupape engine was used to power the Pup, which had a maximum speed of about 100 m.p.h., and the usual armament consisted of a single fixed Vickers machine-gun synchronised to fire through the airscrew; although some of the later R.N.A.S. machines were fitted with a Lewis gun and external racks for light Cooper bombs.

On 10th June 1916 'A' Squadron of No. 1 Wing, R.N.A.S., was moved from Dunkirk to the French aerodrome at Furnes, and soon afterwards a third new type of aeroplane for the Service joined that unit—another Sopwith design, the remarkable single-seater Triplane. In fact, the R.N.A.S. should never have received this machine, for it had originally been ordered for the Royal Flying Corps; a new French scout, the S.P.A.D. S.7 having attracted more attention for Navy use. However, when deliveries of both types commenced, the R.F.C. took a liking to the Spad biplanes, and by a series of agreements they were exchanged with the Sopwith aircraft. Like all such triplanes, the Sopwith 'three-decker' was very manoeuvrable and had an astonishingly high rate of climb; indeed, it could fly rings around almost everything the Germans could put into the air for some time. Possessing many of the Pup's excellent qualities, the Triplane became successful enough to replace not only that little scout in due course but also the 1½-Strutter, being without doubt the finest British scout in Naval service until the appearance a year later of the Sopwith Camel. Powered by a 130-h.p. Clerget rotary engine, the Triplane was armed with a single cowling-mounted Vickers gun, synchronised to fire forward through the propeller.

These three types of aircraft—the 1½-Strutter, Pup and Triplane—thus arrived almost at the same time on the Western Front to form the equipment of the R.N.A.S. squadrons destined so soon to find glory at the side of the R.F.C. units meeting the shock of savage air fighting during 1917. The introduction by

Germany into the air war over France of the single-seater Fokker monoplane scout, with its revolutionary interrupter gear enabling machine-guns to be fired through the propeller arc had already brought one black period for the Allies; the time when British airmen became known as 'Fokker fodder' and their fragile observation machines were only too frequently to be seen trailing banners of flame and smoke down the heedless sky. That fearful situation had been remedied to some extent by the appearance of the De Havilland 2 and F.E.2b pusher types, and the Fokker monoplane was finally beaten when the Nieuport 17 scout entered service. But the Germans worked energetically for the next few months to recapture the ascendancy; and by the summer of 1916 the pendulum was swinging back in their favour once more.

The tragic, ill-fated Somme offensive was opened by the Allied High Command on 1st July 1916, and from that date the R.F.C. aircraft were in action from dawn to dusk almost every day. On the cratered, shell-torn battlefield as well as in the smoking, bullet-streaked air it was a long, weary struggle that seemed to drag on like an endless nightmare, showing nothing for so much bravery and endurance except mountainous lists of casualties. By September the German Air Service was reaching eagerly for the advantage, with the entry into active service units of the Albatros 'D' and Halberstadt single-seater scout biplanes; armed with twin forward-firing Spandau guns, they had a better performance than any R.F.C. machine in action at the time. The British Commander-in-Chief, Field-Marshal Sir Douglas Haig, had already asked that the number of R.F.C. squadrons in France should reach fifty-six by the spring of 1917, and now, hard·pressed by that father of so much in military aviation, General 'Boom' Trenchard, he again demanded reinforcements—and at once.

Haig wrote that "we shall undoubtedly lose our superiority in the air if I am not provided at an early date with improved means of retaining it . . ." and the War Office immediately responded to his letter by forming No. 8 Squadron, R.N.A.S., from personnel and aeroplanes based on Dunkirk. The later famous 'Naval Eight' under Commander G. R. Bromet, an outstanding seaplane pilot, was originally equipped with one flight of Nieuports, one of Sopwith 1½-Strutters, and one of Pups; but within a few weeks the squadron became equipped entirely with Pups, to the joy of the naval pilots and the detriment of many a German airman. A beginning had thus been made, and other R.N.A.S. squadrons soon joined the R.F.C. in the embattled skies over France: Nos. 1, 3, 4, 9 and 10—particularly No. 10 with its flights of swift devastating Sopwith 'Tripehounds'—all fought well, mourned their dead, and brought forth their aces.

Typical of those young naval airmen was Raymond Collishaw, from British Columbia, twenty-three years of age when he joined No. 3 Wing, R.N.A.S. on 2nd August 1916. The following October he scored his first victory, shooting down an enemy scout near Oberndorf, destroyed two more German single-seaters soon afterwards, and was himself shot down in the December. Shaken but miraculously unhurt, Collishaw was soon back in action, and his Vickers gun took toll of an Albatros D.III on 4th March 1917. A month later he was posted to No. 10 (Naval) Squadron to take over command of the famous 'B' Flight, five black-painted Sopwith Triplanes, each flown by a Canadian pilot. In only four hectic months of 1917, this magnificent 'Black Flight'—the *Black Maria* of Collishaw; the *Black Death* of J. E. Sharman; the *Black Prince* of W. M. Alexander; the *Black Roger* of E. V. Reid; and the *Black Sheep* of G. E. Nash— accounted for no less than eighty-seven enemy aircraft. During just one of those months—June—Collishaw shot down sixteen enemy machines in twenty-seven days; and before the year ended he had been shot down for a second time (again without injury) and gained forty victories.

Robert Alexander Little was another naval scout pilot from the Dominions; an Australian, born in Melbourne, he was posted to No. 8 Squadron, R.N.A.S. on 26th October 1916. Flying the new Sopwith Pups with great skill and daring, Little had shot down nine enemy aircraft by March 1917, and when the squadron re-equipped with the Sopwith Triplane he became an outstanding exponent of that type, on at least one occasion whirling into single-handed combat with a number of Albatros scouts of the celebrated Richthofen *Geschwader*. By July 1917 Little had shot down more than thirty enemy machines.

A third brilliant Triplane pilot was Roderic Stanley Dallas, commissioned into the R.N.A.S. in June 1915. He joined No. 1

Wing (later renamed No. 1 (Naval) Squadron) early in the December, and between then and June 1917, when he took over command of the squadron, he shot down some thirty enemy aircraft. Some of his most hard-won victories were achieved during the bitter days of 'Bloody April' when losses were so heavy that afterwards pilots had to be transferred to No. 1 from the decimated—and consequently withdrawn from service—No. 9 Squadron. Like Collishaw and Little, the tall, relaxed Dallas had also come from beyond the seas to fight for the mother country; a native of Queensland, he was destined to gain ten more victories before falling to his death over Lievin in June 1918, heavily engaged by a number of Fokker Triplanes.

The combats these young men fought were frequently close and deadly; battles of attrition, with death the penalty for a single error of judgement. "I saw three tracers actually go into the pilot's head," wrote Flight Sub-Lieutenant J. S. T. Fall, of No. 3 (Naval) Squadron, after shooting down an Albatros scout. While heading west for home, the victor in this lonely duel, Fall was again engaged, this time by a Halberstadt in the hands of a determined and skilful opponent. For some moments, Fall could do little except use every quality of his Sopwith Pup to take evasive action; then, suddenly, he saw his chance. "When he was about a hundred and fifty yards behind me I looped straight over him, and coming out of the loop I dived at him and fired a good long burst," summed up the British naval airman. "I saw nearly all the tracers go into the pilot's back just on the edge of the cockpit. He immediately dived straight into the ground . . . My machine was badly shot about."

Who could blame the R.N.A.S. aviators flying and fighting over the Western Front if occasionally they envied their fellows based on the North Sea air stations or experimenting with deck-flying and gun-spotting from the comparative security of the seaplane carriers?

But air power at sea was also no bed of roses. Attacks had to be made on the German airship bases as a partial deterrent to the Zeppelin offensive; even the latest floatplanes were so fragile that they could only be taken-off or landed under perfect weather conditions; and the Royal Navy still possessed only one large aircraft-carrier, the 20,000-ton *Campania,* and that was a converted Cunard liner. Much hard work was being done at this time in developing the new art of directing naval gunnery from the air, and on 7th April 1915 the battleship *Revenge* successfully hit her target at a range of 11,000 yd. entirely as a result of radioed fire direction from a floatplane out of sight in the clouds overhead. On 16th August research in sea-flying was taken a step further when Flight Lieutenant W. L. Welsh, in a Sopwith Schneider single-seater floatplane, took off smoothly and neatly from the 120-ft-long flight deck of the carrier *Campania* while the ship was steaming at 17 knots into wind.

On the last day of May 1916 an event took place that the Commander-in-Chief of the British Grand Fleet, Admiral Sir John Jellicoe, had been expecting for some time; the German High Seas Fleet, under Admiral Reinhard von Scheer, put to sea from Wilhelmshaven. The German commander knew that he dared not risk a full-scale naval battle—his ships were strong in numbers but heavily outgunned—yet he was a dynamic leader, unwilling to let his fleet rust away in harbour. In March, and then again in April, his battle cruisers had sallied forth to make lightning bombardments of the English east coast, rapid, unexpected hammer blows that did little damage but caused great public consternation. Where is the invincible Grand Fleet? was the outcry, uttered by a British public weary of increasing hardships at home and the endless slaughter on the Western Front. Reassured by the success of his daring sorties, von Scheer next planned a bombardment of the coastline between Sunderland and the Firth of Forth; but thanks to the constant tapping of German radio signals by a series of secret direction-finding stations, Jellicoe was ready and waiting to engage the enemy fleet in battle.

Half an hour before midnight on 30th May 1916 the British Grand Fleet, under Sir John Jellicoe, and the Battle Cruiser Fleet, commanded by Admiral Sir David Beatty, weighed anchor at Scapa Flow and the Firth of Forth respectively to steam in a mighty array of powerful ships eastwards through the night. Unfortunately, Jellicoe's seaplane-carrier, *Campania,* with her fourteen up-to-date aircraft, was left behind in port; by an inexplicable oversight she had received the signal to raise full steam but not the final orders to put to sea. Sir David Beatty therefore had with his battle-cruiser squadron the only carrier available to the whole Fleet for the battle, the little 1,700-ton former Channel packet *Engadine,* equipped with four seaplanes. It was perhaps as well that in the event mist and fog restricted air reconnaissance by both sides, and von Scheer's Zeppelins—the 'eyes' of his great fleet—would throb uselessly back and forth over unseen British warships, unable to report their movements until it was too late.

On the afternoon of 31st May the British light cruiser *Galatea* made the signal "Enemy in sight" and soon afterwards transmitted, "Have sighted large amount of smoke as though from a fleet . . ." On the bridge of Beatty's flagship, the 30,000-ton battle-cruiser *Lion,* the jaunty, square-jawed Admiral prepared for action. "At 2.45 p.m. I ordered *Engadine* to send up a seaplane and scout to N.N.E.," he wrote after the battle; this aircraft was a Westland-built Short 184 floatplane, flown by Flight-Lieutenant F. J. Rutland, with Assistant-Paymaster G. S. Trewin as his observer. Approaching the enemy fleet at a height of only 900 ft. because of the low clouds, the seaplane came under heavy anti-aircraft fire from every ship that could bring guns to bear, but at least three German cruisers and an escort of ten destroyers were identified; and when these unexpectedly changed course their manoeuvre was signalled back to the parent carrier. Using a searchlight, *Engadine* endeavoured to pass the message on to the *Lion* but her urgent flashing remained unobserved. However, the watchful *Galatea* had also seen the enemy's alteration of course and duly signalled the flagship. At their full 25 knots the British battle-cruisers turned to meet the German ships—actually the Imperial Battle Cruiser Fleet under Admiral von Hipper. When the two squadrons were about 12 miles apart von Hipper in his flagship *Lutzow* gave the order to open fire. At once the *Lion*'s main armament thundered in reply; the Battle of Jutland had begun.

Meanwhile Flight-Lieutenant Rutland—soon to become famous as 'Rutland of Jutland'—was in difficulties with a faulty engine, a defect which made him only a few moments later almost certainly the first pilot in aviation history to make a forced landing in the sea during a naval battle. A man endowed with a cool head and a calm acceptance of events, Rutland swung out of his cockpit on to the seaplane's float and quietly went to work repairing the broken petrol pipe that had so abruptly terminated his flight. Then *Engadine* came alongside and the Short machine was hoisted aboard. Later the sea became too rough for aircraft to take off; so the only worthwhile reconnaissance flight of the battle had been made by Rutland and his observer. "Flight-Lieutenant Rutland and Assistant-Paymaster Trewin are to be congratulated on their achievement, which indicates that seaplanes in such circumstances are of distinct value," wrote Sir David Beatty in his report included in Jellicoe's despatch on Jutland.

However, there was still more work at hand for the little *Engadine* and yet another courageous act in store for Rutland. On the evening of 31st May, with the battle still raging as the German High Seas Fleet waited for darkness and a chance to crash through the British Grand Fleet and escape for home, a squadron of British cruisers strayed in the mist across the line of enemy ships. At point-blank range von Hipper's battle-cruisers opened a devastating fire, completely destroying the 14,000-ton *Defence* and badly damaging a sister ship, the *Warrior*. A moment later the battleship *Warspite* was also heavily hit and swung in a large circle, by chance shielding *Warrior* from the murderous enemy guns. With her superstructure ablaze the British cruiser slowly reeled away and set course for Scotland, struggling gamely along through a night lit up for many miles around with the glare of searchlights and the flash of gunfire.

Just before daybreak the limping *Warrior* was met by the carrier *Engadine* and taken in tow. But it soon became obvious that *Warrior* would never make port; her stern was sinking so low that her main deck was awash in an increasingly turbulent sea. It was therefore decided to transfer the cruiser's officers and men to *Engadine* and this appallingly difficult task was duly carried out, the many casualties being passed across on stretchers while the two ships rubbed and ground together with a fearful rending of wood and metal. Suddenly a wounded man slid out of his stretcher and dropped into the sea between the two ships; but Flight-Lieutenant Rutland at once slipped down a rope into the water, ran a line around the sailor and had him hoisted back aboard—all despite the great risk of both being crushed when the ships came together. For his exploit Rutland was awarded the Albert Medal, First Class, a decoration granted only to those who "have, in saving or endeavouring to save the lives of others from shipwreck or other peril of the sea, endangered their own lives."

The ebb and flow of the Battle of Jutland, its outcome and aftermath, have no further place in this story of naval aviation, but it is worth recording briefly that the action was indeed brought to a conclusion with the German High Seas Fleet in full retreat; but did the terrible British casualties really justify the London Press hailing Jutland as a great victory? The superb German gunnery had wrought awful havoc with Jellicoe's and Beatty's squadrons: the battle-cruisers *Queen Mary, Invincible* and *Indefatigable* blown up, with the loss of over three thousand men; eleven other ships of the Grand Fleet sunk, including the cruisers *Black Prince, Defence* and *Warrior* and the sadly familiar lists in the newspapers soon showed a further three thousand casualties. Against this toll of disaster the Germans had lost von Hipper's flagship, the battle-cruiser *Lutzow*; an old battleship, the *Pommern*, four cruisers and five destroyers; and about three thousand men. Nevertheless, Admiral von Scheer had been taught a bloody lesson, which had given him a new respect for British sea power. "It may be possible for us to inflict appreciable damage on the enemy," he reported to the Kaiser, "but there can be no doubt that even the most favourable issue of a battle on the high seas will not compel England to make peace in this war . . ."

After Jutland, the Admiralty came to realise more fully the pressing need for new aeroplane-carriers comparable with the *Campania* in size; better ships than the old, coal-burning, converted Isle-of-Man packet *Manxman,* carrying only four Sopwith Baby floatplanes, commissioned at Chatham in December 1916. Flight-Lieutenant Rutland, in his capacity as Senior Flying Officer on the *Engadine,* was in the meantime urging a more general use of aircraft with a wheeled (land-type) undercarriage, thus making proper use also of the carrier's flying-off decks, and eventually won officialdom over to his side. Early in 1917, Sopwith Pup single-seater scouts were supplied to *Campania* and *Manxman,* and later that year Rutland advanced his research a step further by taking off in a Sopwith Pup from a 20 ft.-long platform fitted over the forward gun turret of the cruiser

Yarmouth while the ship was steaming head to wind in the outer waters of the Firth of Forth.

The value of Rutland's experiments were to be proved much sooner than he or the Admiralty had anticipated. On 21st August 1917 the British First Cruiser Squadron, including the *Yarmouth,* was on patrol off the coast of Denmark when the German Zeppelin L.23 was sighted. A Sopwith Pup, flown by Flight Sub-Lieutenant B. A. Smart, immediately took off from the *Yarmouth*'s platform, and intercepted the airship at a height of 9,000 ft. Using the Lewis gun fixed to fire upwards at an angle through the centre section—an armament peculiar to the shipborne Pups—Smart opened fire, closing to 20 yd; and the L.23 fell burning into the sea, with the loss of all her crew. This success prompted the Admiralty to have one light cruiser in each squadron fitted with a flying-off platform, while Rutland was encouraged to broaden the scope of his experiments after a suggestion had been made that aircraft should also be flown off the gun turrets of capital ships. On 1st October, he successfully took off in a Pup from the fore turret of the 32,700-ton battle cruiser *Repulse.*

Also in 1917 the first British Fleet aircraft carrier to match the *Campania* made an appearance. This was H.M.S. *Furious,* originally laid down as one of three fast, unarmoured battle-cruisers ordered for the Royal Navy by Lord Fisher when he was First Sea Lord. The *Furious,* however, had been converted to a carrier on the recommendation of the Grand Fleet Aircraft Committee, appointed in February 1917 to knit together more closely the threads of our air power at sea. With a displacement of 22,000 tons, the *Furious* was a very large and impressive ship for the time; her flight deck was 228 ft. long (later extended to 284 ft.) and 50 ft. wide; she had a top speed of 31 knots; and could carry eight aircraft. Her Senior Flying Officer was Squadron-Commander E. H. Dunning, a very experienced pilot who had taken part in the Dardanelles campaign, and the scout pilots under him were, according to Rutland, "certainly second to none in the R.N.A.S. They had exercised for three months at Fort Grain in both seaplanes and Sopwith Pups, and when *Furious* commissioned in June 1917 with these superb pilots, the effect was exhilarating . . ." These were the men about to attempt a solution to the constant problem of recovering land aeroplanes of the Pup type from the sea, by landing on their parent carrier's flight deck—if that could be achieved.

On 2nd August 1917 Squadron-Commander Dunning, flying a Sopwith Pup, took off from the flight deck of *Furious,* then came around to attempt a landing, drifting gently and skilfully in over the deck to place his machine almost into the hands of a crew of waiting officers who held it down as he cut the engine; the very first occasion such a deck landing had been accomplished by an operational aircraft. A second landing was also successful, but in a third attempt a few days later Dunning's little aircraft came in with more speed, bounced into the air, then stalled and cartwheeled over the starboard side of the carrier. Knocked unconscious by the impact, the unfortunate Dunning drowned before his machine could be recovered; and experiments in deck-landing therefore came to an end until the development of arrester wires, which owed much of their success to the efforts of the tireless, enthusiastic Rutland.

The first arrester gear was produced for *Furious* after the carrier had been fitted with a so-called landing-deck aft of the bridge during a refit at Newcastle-on-Tyne. This modification was a compromise between the Admiralty and Rutland, who had succeeded Dunning as Senior Flying Officer, and after trying one or two deck landings, considered that the *Furious* needed a flush deck almost the length of the ship—the first clear conception of the true aircraft carrier. The arrester gear developed by the R.N.A.S. Marine Aircraft Experimental Depot at the Isle of Grain consisted of parallel wires running fore and aft of the ship and raised slightly off the deck by wooden blocks commonly known as 'fiddle-bridges' in the Service. The aeroplanes—usually Pups or $1\frac{1}{2}$-Strutters—were fitted with hooks on the undercarriage axles which engaged the wires immediately after landing; the wires sprang back, the aircraft slowed down, and with luck was brought quickly to rest.

However, the basic principle of such an arrester gear was not very satisfactory in operation, and it was not even a new idea. An American naval airman named Eugene Ely had managed to alight on a platform erected on the after deck of the cruiser U.S.S. *Pennsylvania* in 1912, landing his machine by means of wires stretched across the platform and attached at the ends to sand-bags; the aircraft hooking up the wires in rapid succession as it ran along, until the weight of the bags brought it to a stand-still. On the *Furious*, it was soon found that wheeled undercarriages were frequently damaged or badly strained when landings were made by use of arrester wires, and a ski-type undercarriage was therefore designed and fitted to a few Pup aircraft. Rutland alighted a number of times on the landing-deck of the *Furious*, using both skids and wheels, and on at least one occasion plunged over the side into the sea, before he finally developed the best technique for hooking on to the wires. But, as Rutland had foreseen in the first place, the turbulence which swirled aft from around the bridge and funnels when the carrier was steaming at any speed made deck landings possible only by the most skilful of pilots; a flush deck and an island super-structure (including funnels) set to one side out of the way was the only real solution.

Fortunately for the Admiralty, it was not too late to remedy the situation. The *Conte Rosso*, an Italian liner requisitioned when first laid down, was being built on the Clyde, as the 15,750-ton H.M.S. *Argus*, another Fleet carrier; and a battleship under construction by Armstrong-Whitworth on the Tyne would soon be turned into the *Eagle*, a third large carrier. It was decided that both these new ships should have completely flush decks and offset island superstructures, and that similar refinements would be included in the next reconstruction of the *Furious*. Due to much hard work, endless research and not a little courage, Great Britain was thus to possess by 1920 three of the world's leading aircraft-carriers, destined to form the backbone of her Fleet Air Arm for over a decade.

5

VICTORY WITH WINGS: 1917–18

∽∽∽∽∽∽∽∽∽∽∽∽∽∽∽∽∽∽∽∽∽∽∽∽∽∽∽∽∽∽∽∽∽∽∽

During 1917 the R.N.A.S. air stations at Great Yarmouth and Felixstowe greatly extended their flying-boat activities over the North Sea, despite increasing enemy opposition, particularly from the *staffel* of two-seater floatplane fighters based on Zeebrugge under the command of that brilliant sailor-airman Friedrich Christiansen. In only eight weeks of 1916 the young German designer Ernst Heinkel had projected the very fast and heavily armed Hansa-Brandenburg W 12 biplane; and soon afterwards followed this success—by way of the larger W 19—with the W 29, a greatly improved monoplane version of the same machine. Due to the ingeniousness of Heinkel and the resolution of Christiansen, who led his mixed formations of W 12s and 29s out against British aircraft and shipping regardless of weather conditions, the big R.N.A.S. 'F' boats were soon having to fight hard to retain their air superiority, so vital at a time when U-boat warfare was at a height. Also, the German airship offensive against England, though unsuccessful, had not yet been entirely defeated.

On 14th May 1917 an H.12 flying-boat, *N8866*, with Flight Lieutenant C. J. Galpin as commander, Flight Sub-Lieutenant R. Leckie as pilot, Chief Petty Officer V. F. Whatling as observer, and Air Mechanic O. R. Laycock as engineer, was about two hours out from Yarmouth, on patrol north-west of Texel Island, when a Zeppelin was sighted at a height of some 3,000 ft. "The Zeppelin turned north and then north-east exposing her broadside, and I conclude she was coming south-west when we first saw her, and had now reached the limit of her patrol . . ." wrote Galpin afterwards in his report. "I opened fire with both (Lewis) guns at 50 yards range and observed incendiary bullets entering the envelope on the starboard quarter slightly below the middle. After a few rounds the port gun jammed, but the starboard gun fired nearly a complete tray before jamming also. We were then 100 feet from her and turned hard-a-starboard while I tried to clear the starboard gun . . ."

As the flying-boat banked, Galpin glimpsed a tiny flame spring to life underneath the airship, and by the time the H.12 had come around he could see that the whole belly of the Zeppelin was well alight. Within a few seconds, the long, cigar-shaped ship was burning from end to end, plunging vertically by the tail towards the sea. "C.P.O. Whatling, observing from the other hatch, saw the number L.22 painted under the nose before it was consumed," reported Galpin. "We also saw two of the crew jump out, one from the after-gun position on the top of the tail fin and one from the after gondola. They had no parachutes . . ."

Thus the Zeppelin L.22, commanded by Kapitänleutnant Dietrich Bielefeld came to an untimely end, a ship first commissioned on 3rd March 1916. In just over a year she had undertaken forty-one war flights, including eight over Britain. Now, as the flying-boat circled, nothing remained except a column of brown smoke snaking over 1,000 ft. up into the air; there were no survivors. The L.22 was, of course, the first airship to be destroyed by a flying-boat, but on 14th June—exactly one month later—the achievement was repeated when the L.43 was shot down in flames off Vlieland by an H.12 boat from Felixstowe air station, piloted by Flight Sub-Lieutenant B. D. Hobbs, with Flight Sub-Lieutenant R. F. L. Dickey as his gunner. A year later, the third and final Zeppelin to be destroyed by a flying-boat fell burning into the sea off Heligoland; this was the L.62, set ablaze by Lewis gun fire from an F.2A based at Killingholme and piloted by Captains T. C. Pattison and A. H. Munday.

The big 'F' type flying-boats developed by John Porte proved to be invaluable for patrolling large areas of water in the relentless search for enemy submarines. From the spring of 1917, the famous 'Spider Web' system of patrols with 'F' boats began to operate from Felixstowe, covering some 4,000 square miles of sea; a vast circle—or 'web'—sixty miles in diameter, with the hub of that circle the North Hinder Light Vessel, from which eight imaginary arms, each 30 miles in length, were projected. The octagonal figure thus created provided eight sectors for patrol purposes, which could be checked or double-checked as desired, so that every square mile was, in one combination or another, covered. The patrols from Felixstowe were arranged to overlap with many of those from Great Yarmouth, and all reports on the sighting of enemy submarines were carefully plotted on charts at the parent bases until the prey was finally pinned down. On 20th May 1917 an H.12 flying-boat commanded by Flight Sub-Lieutenant C. R. Morrish bombed a U-boat, the UC.36, on the surface of the North Sea and destroyed it; the first submarine to be sunk from the air. Two more German submarines were similarly bombed and sunk in the July, the opening of a determined campaign by the R.N.A.S. against the U-boat menace, sixty-seven enemy submarines having been sighted and forty-four attacked before the end of the year.

The air combats became more frequent as time passed, short, savage dogfights hammered out over the empty sea many miles from shore. On 19th June 1917 a Short 184 floatplane was on patrol out from Dunkirk, escorted by two Sopwith Baby single-seater scout seaplanes, when the flight was attacked by three German machines and a typical battle took place; when it was over, all but one of the six floatplanes had been destroyed or forced down on the water. The survivor, Flight Lieutenant R. Graham, flying a Sopwith Baby, obtained assistance from a French destroyer for the wounded of both sides. Such flights were commonplace before the end of the year, and undoubtedly for some time Friedrich Christiansen and his crews reigned supreme along the Flanders coast. Also, the German naval airmen were no less aggressive than their British opposite numbers when it came to hunting submarines; as an example, on 6th July 1918 Christiansen, leading a flight of W 29 monoplanes—his 'Fighters of Zeebrugge'—attacked the Royal Navy submarine *C.25* off Harwich, killed the commander and five ratings, and damaged the craft so badly that she had to be towed back to port, awash, by another submarine.

Perhaps the most memorable battle between the R.N.A.S. flying-boats and the German fighting seaplanes took place on 4th June 1918, when Captain Robert Leckie led a force of four F.2As and one H.12 out on patrol in the direction of the Haaks Light

Vessel. After about two and a half hours, one of the F.2A boats, piloted by Captain R. F. L. Dickey, was forced to drop out of the formation due to a broken petrol feed pipe, and finally alighted on the water ten miles north of Terschelling Island. Captain Leckie signalled Dickey by Aldis lamp, giving him permission to taxi into Dutch territorial waters for internment; but twenty minutes later a number of German floatplanes turned up from Borkum to attack the crippled flying-boat. Leckie immediately swung his flight around to engage the enemy machines, which broke off the action after a sharp exchange of fire. They retreated eastwards, followed by the H.12 boat, and the three remaining F.2As circled slowly over Dickey's machine as it continued to trundle along towards the Dutch coast, rocking gently on the water.

Then more black-crossed seaplanes abruptly arrived on the scene—a whole *staffel* of fifteen or sixteen aircraft—and a roaring, free-for-all dogfight took place. Leckie, leading his big boats in a neat V formation, attacked the enemy scouts head-on, raking them with Lewis gun fire at close range, then switched his formation to 'line ahead' and again swept the German seaplanes with tracer, first from the bow and then the port guns of the flying-boats. Riddled with bullets, three enemy aircraft staggered away, losing height; while the redoubtable Leckie brought his flight around to administer another withering broadside.

"Everybody seemed to be firing away like blazes, and the air was thick with the smoke from tracer bullets ..." reported one of the F.2A pilots afterwards. A burst struck the cockpit beside Leckie, smashing some of his instruments; another hit the interplane struts beside his head. A German floatplane, its pilot shot dead, went into a spin and plunged into the sea, to be followed almost immediately by a second, and the H.12 flying-boat was seen to land heavily on the water in a shower of spray. At last, after forty hectic minutes, the enemy had had enough; the surviving floatplanes quietly broke away and made for home at top speed. One of the battle-scarred F.2A boats, flown by Captain A. T. Barker—his co-pilot had been killed—was forced to land on the Zuider Zee with a broken petrol pipe, but the engineer managed to effect a temporary repair and the machine struggled back to Felixstowe. Captain J. Hodson, flying another F2A, also had

Above, left, Wing Cdr. C. R. Samson, who formed the first British attack squadron in the Dardanelles campaign; *right,* Lt. R. A. J. Warneford, first to destroy a Zeppelin in the air, received the V.C. for courage during the action and was killed ten days later in an air accident; *below,* Major R. Collishaw, outstanding as a Sopwith Triplane flyer, destroyed sixty enemy aircraft

Top, the Short S.184 two-seater floatplane, in action throughout most of 1914–18; *middle,* one of the successful Felixstowe series of flying-boats, the F.3, operational over the North Sea from 1915–18; *below,* Sqdn.-Cdr. E. H. Dunning making the first deck landing by an operational aircraft. Shortly after he lost his life when the Sopwith Pup shown here ran over the side

engine difficulties but continued on course with only one work-
able motor, repairs to the other actually being carried out during
the return flight to Great Yarmouth. Only two of the flying-
boats had thus been lost (the H.12 having been so crippled that it
had to taxi to the Dutch coast for internment) in a battle against
superior odds and very much faster enemy aircraft; at least two
of which had been shot down and a number of others damaged;
a lasting tribute to John Porte, his remarkable Felixstowe boats,
and the men who went out in them on the long North Sea
patrols.

Following upon the heavy losses in Allied aircraft over the
battlefields of Arras during the spring of 1917—that 'Bloody
April' of ill repute—and the blatant appearance over London in
broad daylight of enemy long-range Gotha bombers, it became
increasingly obvious that a complete re-organisation was needed
of British air power; there had already been far too much muddling through in Whitehall, too many arguments between the
Admiralty and the War Office. Now the Cabinet would have to
act as mediator; indeed, public indignation demanded that decisive measures be taken without delay. On 17th August 1917 the
great South African, Lieutenant-General Jan Christian Smuts,
was thus able to place before the War Cabinet a report which
recommended the creation of an Air Ministry and Air Staff, to
direct and control a unified Air Force. The principle of this
report, later to be described by the official historian as "the most
important paper in the history of the creation of the Royal Air
Force", was accepted by the Government within a week; and on
29th November 1917 the Air Force (Constitution) Bill, 1917,
received the Royal Assent.

On 1st April 1918 the Royal Air Force came into being, amal-
gamating the Royal Flying Corps and the Royal Naval Air Service. By this time the R.N.A.S. had grown out of all proportion
to the expectations of 1914, with 126 air stations at home and
abroad, and a force of 67,000 officers and men, manning or servicing some 3,000 aeroplanes and airships. Aircraft of the R.N.A.S.
were fighting and flying everywhere; at sea, from air bases and
carriers and the fore turrets of warships; in the Middle East,
the Western Desert, Palestine and Arabia; Mesopotamia and East

3—AHOMA * *

Africa; and always on the embattled Western Front. Truly, the inestimable value of naval aviation had been displayed by Britain to the whole world.

Perhaps because both Services had achieved such stature in almost four years of war, the change brought many regrets and minor domestic upheavals; traditions died hard in both the military and naval units, and there was a strong reluctance to accept new ideas in the heat of battle. And there were many, many new ways of life to be adopted: all the old R.N.A.S. squadrons were renumbered as R.A.F. squadrons; all R.N.A.S. officers lost their naval ranks on transfer to the R.A.F. and received military titles; and the blue R.N.A.S. reefer jacket and trousers were all too soon to be replaced by the unfamiliar, light blue R.A.F. uniform. Nevertheless, in time the naval airmen became accustomed to their strange new guise, and of course all flying operations remained unaffected.

In France, the ex-R.N.A.S. pilots put up their new military badges of rank amid grumbles, arguments and rude comments; and the bitter war high above the trenches continued as before. On 21st April—only three weeks after the amalgamation—Captain A. R. Brown, flying a Bentley-powered Sopwith Camel of 209 Squadron (formerly No. 9 (Naval) Squadron), shot down the German ace of aces, Manfred von Richthofen. About the same time, Raymond Collishaw, the leading naval ace pilot in France, was proving himself to be a as much of an expert with the tricky Sopwith Camel as he had been an exponent of the same manufacturer's Triplane; his score of forty victories by January 1918 would reach a total of sixty before the Armistice. A month after Richthofen fell to his death, Robert Alexander Little, one of the few men to cross swords, single-handed, with the colourful Richthofen circus and survive, was also killed. After shooting down forty-seven enemy aircraft, he had returned to England, and on 27th May 1918 was on the tail of a raiding Gotha bomber when searchlights blinded him and he crashed, the victim of a tragic misfortune. The death in action of Roderic Stanley Dallas, after gaining forty victories, has already been mentioned; he was shot down on 19th June 1918.

With the S.E.5a, the single-seater Sopwith F.1 Camel is generally considered to be the other outstanding British fighting scout of 1918. An amazing total of 1,294 enemy aircraft was destroyed by the type; and 386 of those were shot down by Camels in R.N.A.S. use. From 4th July 1917, when a flight of five new naval Camels from Dunkirk air station attacked a formation of Gothas crossing the coast after a raid on England, until November 1918, the nimble little Sopwith biplanes formed the main equipment of the naval fighting squadrons, replacing the Pup to a great extent and entirely supplanting the Triplane. Armed with twin, fixed synchronised Vickers machine-guns built into the cowling, the Camel had a maximum speed of 115 m.p.h. at 6,500 ft. The original naval Camels had 130-h.p. Clerget engines, but Bentley Camels—fitted with the 150-h.p. Bentley engine—soon took their place in the Service.

The shipboard version of the Sopwith Camel was designated 2F.1, and originally intended for operation from carriers or warships as a successor to the Pup and 1½-Strutter. The prototype 2F.1 flew for the first time in March 1917, and although the German airship offensive against England had virtually been broken by the time the type entered service, routine Zeppelin patrols over the North Sea continued well into 1918. Envisaged as a high-flying scout to intercept such troublesome enemy reconnaissance airships, the 2F.1 soon proved itself to be a very successful light bomber; for in June 1918 a specially trained force of naval Camels embarked in the carrier *Furious* to undertake the first carrier-launched strike against a land target in the history of aviation—a fore-runner of the great attack by Fleet Air Arm Swordfish against Taranto in 1940.

Shortly after dawn on 19th July the *Furious,* escorted by the First Cruiser Squadron, was off the Schleswig coast. In the early morning, seven 2F.1 Camels, each machine carrying two 50-lb. bombs, took off and set course for the German airship sheds at Tondern, a distance of some 80 miles. Led by Captain W. D. Jackson, the first flight approached the town at a height of about 3,000 ft. and dived towards the huge Zeppelin sheds, dropping their bombs from 100 ft. directly over the hangars. "Captain Jackson dived right on to the northernmost shed and dropped two bombs, one a direct hit in the middle and the other slightly to the side of the shed," reported Captain W. F. Dickson, another of the attacking pilots, afterwards. "I then dropped my one remaining bomb and Williams two more. Hits were observed. The shed then burst into flames and an enormous conflagration took place rising to at least 1,000 feet and the whole of the shed being completely engulfed. After dropping, Jackson went straight on, Williams to the left and I to the right . . ."

The second flight, led by Captain B. A. Smart, came in very low over the sheds ten minutes later, and bombed with equal success, hitting another shed, which burst into flames, and also setting fire to a captive observation balloon. It was later discovered that the new Zeppelins L.54 and L.60, in the sheds at the time of the attack, had been completely destroyed. Unfortunately, bad weather forced four of the 2F.1 scouts to land in Denmark and a fifth was lost at sea, the remaining two machines, piloted by Captain Dickson and Smart, successfully returning to their parent carrier. Due to the many imperfections still inherent in deck-landing techniques, the Camels had to ditch alongside *Furious,* but both the pilots were rescued.

During the spring of 1918 experiments had also been taking place with 2F.1 Camels flown off lighters towed by destroyers of the Harwich Light Cruiser Force, and on one occasion Charles Romney Samson, the ebullient hero of the armoured car units in Flanders and subsequently active during the Dardanelles campaign, almost lost his life. When racing forward to take off, the Camel he was flying failed to rise from the lighter, plunged into the sea over the bows, and was then run down by the craft. However, on 31st July 1918 a successful take-off from a similar lighter was achieved by Lieutenant S. D. Culley of Great Yarmouth air station; and the following week, when the Harwich Force, under the command of Rear-Admiral Sir Reginald Tyrwhitt, put to sea bound for Heligoland Bight, a 2F.1 Camel—with Culley as pilot—was carried on a lighter towed by the destroyer *Redoubt*. Six flying-boats also accompanied the flotilla. The main task of this very powerful spearhead into enemy waters was to put to sea light motor torpedo boats, which would then make a 'commando' sortie into the bight, attacking any German ships they sighted.

On 11th August the force was hove to off Terschelling when a Zeppelin was sighted to the north-east, flying at a great height.

Lieutenant Culley successfully took off from the heaving deck of the lighter and slowly but surely coaxed his 2F.1 scout up to over 18,000 ft.—higher than the official ceiling of the type. At last, he was only 300 ft. below the airship—the L.53 commanded by Kapitänleutnant Prolas, based at Nordholz—and opened fire with his twin Lewis guns. Within seconds the Zeppelin was in flames and plunging towards the sea, shedding debris of all kinds: bombs, engines, gondolas, even one or two pitiful, whirling human beings, without parachutes. Culley lost sight of his flotilla for some time, and had just decided to attempt a landing near a Dutch fishing boat he had spotted, when he saw the squadron steaming at full speed almost underneath him; ditching his machine in the sea, he was picked up, and the force returned to Harwich.

Meanwhile on the night of 5th–6th August, the last German airship raid on Britain had taken place; and been utterly defeated by naval aeroplanes from Great Yarmouth. During this attack the latest Zeppelin to be built at Friedrichshafen, the slim and beautiful high-flying L.70, under the command of Fregattenkapitän Peter Strasser, the dedicated and courageous Chief of the German Airship Division, was attacked by a De Havilland 4 two-seater manned by Major Egbert Cadbury and Captain Robert Leckie. Set ablaze by bursts of mixed Brock and Pomeroy ammunition, the L.70 fell in flames into the sea some forty miles off Yarmouth; and with the death of Strasser and his crew the airship offensive against Britain ended. "After the loss of L.70 . . . there were no more airship raids on England, primarily because the driving force behind them [Strasser] was gone," writes one historian of the German airship service, but in fact the long-range Gotha and Staaken Giant heavy bombers had virtually replaced the Zeppelins during 1917 and proved much more effective as air weapons, particularly against large cities such as London.

Since the April of 1917, when the United States had declared war on Germany, American naval aviation had increased to astonishing proportions—over 1,850 machines, with a strength in personnel of some 37,000 officers and men. However, very few American-built aircraft saw any action during those last twenty

months of war, for a decision had been made to concentrate on
the production of training aeroplanes and flying-boats—the tried
and trusted Curtiss Jennies and 'H' patrol boats—while relying
upon the Allies for a supply of fighting and bomber types. The
United States air units which began to arrive in France from
September 1917 were therefore equipped with French and a few
British machines, mostly Spads, Nieuports, Breguets and Camels;
but a number of Curtiss H.16 flying-boats were operated by U.S.
crews out of Killingholme air station. These craft were improved
versions of the H.12 type, larger and with modified hulls—not
unlike the Felixstowe boats developed by John Porte, but
powered by American 330-h.p. Liberty engines.

Meanwhile, the U.S. Navy Department, encouraged by the
success of Glenn Curtiss with his big 'H' boats, had requested
the design of an even larger flying-boat for anti-submarine patrol
work, capable of flying the Atlantic and landing in the roughest
of seas. In due course Curtiss displayed to the Department Chief
of Construction his initial plans for two types of machine, the
first a three-engined craft, the second to have four engines. Both
designs were unusual in featuring short hulls, with the tailplanes
carried on outrigger booms and struts in much the same way as
the Sopwith Bat Boat or the British pusher aeroplanes of 1916
such as the De Havilland 2 and the F.E.2b. The biplane wings of
the Curtiss boats had a span of 140 ft. (later somewhat reduced)
and the length of the hull was 44 ft.; like John Porte, Curtiss was
a man whose big ideas could produce really big aircraft. It had
been anticipated that very powerful engines would be needed,
and special 12-cylinder versions of the remarkable new Liberty
motor were therefore constructed, each capable of developing
400 h.p.

In the spring of 1918 the Secretary of the U.S. Navy placed an
order for four of the three-engined Curtiss boats, designated
NC-1, 2, 3 and 4, but even with the new Liberties the huge craft
were so under-powered that many difficulties were experienced
when take-offs were attempted with a full load. Indeed, on one
occasion NC-3 failed to rise until over 300 lb. in weight—
including a flight engineer!—had been put ashore. Because of
these problems, and similar teething troubles, the NC boats had

still not entered service by the Armistice, but development continued into 1919, eventually to be crowned with success, as will be seen.

In this closing year of the Great War, there seemed to be something of a mania for bigger and better flying-boats, a specification having also been issued by the Admiralty in London for a very large, four-engined craft to be used for co-operation duties with the Royal Navy. Three prototypes were authorised, two designed by the Fairey Company and a third by the Gosport Aviation Company; but all were to be built on much the same lines, with wing spans of nearly 140 ft. and hulls 66 ft. in length. The engines were 650-h.p. Rolls-Royce Condors, arranged in twin tandem units between the biplane wings, and driving huge, four-bladed propellers. Named *Atalanta I, Atalanta II* and *Titania,* the N.4 Class boats—as they were officially designated—were unfortunately to be dogged by somewhat curious subcontracting agreements that involved the building of hulls at Southampton and Gosport, and the construction of superstructures at Lytham, near Blackpool, and Bradford. The transport by road of the huge, unwieldy hulls to the north for assembly with the wings and engines took so much time and organisation that months passed without any appreciable results; then when everything was found to fit properly together, the boats had to be dismantled again for despatching to the Isle of Grain to undertake flight tests. It was a ridiculous, completely unsatisfactory state of affairs, and not surprisingly the maiden flight of the first N.4 boat did not take place until 1923. By that time, economy measures were ensuring that British air power would soon amount to little more than a handful of aircraft; so the colossal N.4 boats were dismantled for the last time, and by 1927 all three had ended up in the scrapyard.

The main German designer of big flying-boats between 1914 and 1918 was Claudius Dornier, who conceived some really gigantic craft powered by Maybach engines for the Zeppelin combine, making extensive use of a new alloy at the time—duralumin. Some flights were made from Lake Constance to Norderney and other air stations, and one Dornier type—the Rs III—is said to have been used operationally over the North Sea on at least one occasion; but the Armistice put a stop to further development, and the huge boats had all been destroyed by 1921 on the orders of the Allied Commission. Claudius Dornier, of course, had benefited enormously from his four years of experience with the Zeppelin concern, and later would use his famous sponson principle in a long line of successful German flying-boats destined to emerge between the two World Wars.

Glancing around the air forces of the belligerents in 1918, it is strange to find that during four years of war only a very few really startling naval aeroplanes had been produced by any nation other than Great Britain. Apart from the Hansa-Brandenburg floatplanes, Germany possessed the excellent, but very uninteresting, Friedrichshafen series of two-seater seaplanes in fairly large numbers, and while it is true that at least one of those became famous—the FF. 33E, nicknamed *Wölfchen* because it was carried by the German merchant raider S.M.S. *Wolf* during her exploits in the Indian Ocean—they were still simple, sturdy, conventional biplanes. Incidentally, the success of *Wölfchen* as a shipborne reconnaissance aircraft encouraged Ernst Heinkel to design a very small biplane flying-boat powered by an 80-h.p. Oberursel engine, capable of operating from large ocean-going submarines; but there were too many assembly, dismantling and stowage problems involved, and the type had still not entered service when the war came to an end.

In Austria and Italy there had been a tendency since 1915 to use quite small flying-boats typified by a succession of Lohner biplane boats constructed for the Austrian Navy, and a series of very similar Macchi craft in service with their Italian enemies for over three years. Poor, tragic Russia, at war since 1914 and torn by internal revolution from October 1917, had also depended to a great extent on flying-boats for the air arm of her Imperial Navy; many effective operations being undertaken over the Black Sea and Baltic areas by the single-engined 'M'-type craft conceived by the young designer D. P. Grigorovich. All these machines—Austro-Hungarian, Italian and Russian—had many common design features: biplane configuration; pusher-type engines; small but surprisingly comfortable cockpits—the basic Curtiss layout of 1912, with a few modifications.

On the continent, therefore, development in naval aviation had progressed only slowly despite the spur and necessity of war (with the obvious exception of Germany, of course) and indeed for some years only Macchi of Italy would come near to rivalling Short Brothers and Supermarine in Britain or Curtiss in America in the unceasing search for bigger, better—and always faster— seaplanes. Meanwhile, the new floatplanes and flying-boats continued to leave the factories all over the world; but not for long once the summer of 1918 was over. With Ludendorff's last great offensive in the west defeated and the German Fleet in a state of mutiny at Kiel, peace was in sight after four years of guns and death, mud and rats in the trenches. On 9th November, at his headquarters at Spa, Kaiser Wilhelm II was told by his generals that they could no longer hold out any hopes of victory; and the following day he arrived in Holland, soon to sign his formal abdication as Emperor and become an exile who would never enter Germany again.

Two days later, the fighting stopped and the guns fired for the last time. "On the morning of the Armistice at the eleventh hour I stood at the window waiting for Big Ben to tell that the war was over," wrote Winston Churchill of that great moment. "The bells of London began to clash. From all sides streams of people poured out, hundreds, thousands, screaming with joy. The tumult grew like a gale. After fifty-two months of gaunt distortion, suddenly, everywhere the burdens were cast down . . ."[1] Later, through great cheering, dancing crowds, Churchill and his wife drove along Whitehall to offer their congratulations to the Prime Minister; and the wild rejoicing continued far into the night and throughout the following day. In strange contrast, the victory was celebrated only quietly in France, crushed by four years of terrible casualties, her countryside turned into a charnel-house.

But the burdens had only for a brief span of time been dropped from weary shoulders. In truth, ten months later, on 28th June 1919, the First World War officially ended in the long Hall of Mirrors at Versailles, and eighteen months later the Royal Air Force was axed down to a mere twenty squadrons to fulfil a host of duties; but it all amounted to nothing more than wishful

[1] From *The World Crisis, 1911-1918,* by Winston S. Churchill (Macmillan version, 1943).

thinking; the tired eyes blinded by the bright dawn that preceded a tempestuous day and fearful night. Within twenty years, British air power—that "extravagant luxury which might easily be dispensed with"—would be called upon to fight in another major war; all the old burdens, and many new ones, would have to be taken up again.

6

SCHNEIDER TROPHY: 1919–31

For the Schneider Trophy Contest of 1919—the first race of its kind for over five years—Great Britain entered three aircraft; two floatplanes by Fairey and Sopwith respectively, both powered by 450-h.p. engines; and the third a Supermarine flying-boat, named *Sea Lion I*. This latter machine bore some resemblance to the small, single-seater N.1B Baby produced by the same company the previous year, and was the brain-child of a comparative newcomer to marine aviation, the brilliant young man later to achieve fame as the designer of the Spitfire—R. J. Mitchell. There were also three French entries, two Nieuports and a Spad-Herbemont, and one machine from Italy, a Savoia S.13 flying-boat. Bournemouth was chosen by the Royal Aero Club as the most suitable venue, with ten laps of a triangular course to be flown, making a total distance of 200 nautical miles.

Unfortunately, the day selected for the 1919 Contest—10th September—turned out to be dull and foggy, and only the three British machines and the Savoia managed to get off the water, in the late afternoon. All the British entries had to retire after only a few laps, but the Italian pilot, Janelli, succeeded in completing the entire course, although on one lap he missed the turning point at Swanage. Despite Janelli's skill and courage, it was felt that the race had been spoiled by the bad weather, and it was therefore declared null and void. The Italian achievement was complimented by a suggestion that the next contest should be held at Venice.

There followed two dead Trophy years from the British point of view, for the simple truth was that we had nothing good enough to enter the race before 1922. The fourth Contest, flown at Venice in September 1920, was won without any difficulty by

Italy, represented by a Savoia S.19 flying-boat. The pilot, Bologna, had only to complete the necessary ten laps at a fair speed, for his French opponents had failed to pass the preliminary seaworthiness tests. The 1921 Contest, again held at Venice, brought forth one French entry—a Nieuport—and three Italian defenders, all Macchi flying-boats. Again, a most unsatisfactory situation arose. The Nieuport crashed before the race, and two of the Italian machines had to retire with engine trouble; but the third, piloted by Briganti, completed the course, attaining an average speed of 117·8 m.p.h. Two successive races had thus been won by Italy without opposition; and under the rules a third win by the same country meant outright victory for that nation, with a consequent end to the Contest and retention of the Trophy for all time.

It was agreed that the 1922 Contest, to be held on 10th–12th August, should be flown at Naples, to the relief of the people of Venice, who had twice endured the ear-shattering noise of powerful aero engines over their placid canals and lagoons. Two French machines were entered—in the event they failed to be ready in time—and there were two Italian defenders, a high-performance Macchi M.VII flying-boat and a Savoia S.19 flying-boat. For Great Britain, Supermarine entered the *Sea Lion II* flying-boat, developed from the *Sea Lion I* of 1919, and powered by a 450-h.p. Napier Lion engine; a noteworthy joint achievement by Mr Hubert Scott-Paine and Mr H. T. Vane of the Supermarine and Napier companies respectively, both men having shown great enterprise in undertaking such a private venture.

The two Italian machines, piloted by Passaleva and Zenetti, thundered round the course only seconds behind Captain H. C. Biard, flying the *Sea Lion,* until the final lap; then the British aircraft seemed to hurtle forward as Biard gave it full throttle and it crossed the finishing line well ahead of the opposition, with a recorded average speed of 145·7 m.p.h. Lacking any financial assistance from the Government, Great Britain had yet managed to recover the Trophy at least for another year; but it had been no easy task to get the *Sea Lion* ready in time, and the next race would prove beyond any doubt that the exciting, if worrying days of private endeavour were almost ended.

The 1923 Contest was arranged by the Royal Aero Club for

27th–28th September over a course at Cowes, Isle of Wight, with turning points at Selsey Bill and Southsea. The British entries were the Blackburn Pellet biplane flying-boat, piloted by R. W. Kenworthy, and an improved version of the Supermarine Sea Lion—*Sea Lion III*—piloted by Captain Biard. Both machines were powered by the tried and trusted 450-h.p. Napier Lion engine, and seemed to have an excellent chance of success. However, in comparison with previous Schneider Trophy races, the challengers were many and varied, including an Italian team and French C.A.M.S. and Latham flying-boats; but it was the American entries, all Curtiss floatplanes, that aroused the most interest when they arrived at Cowes. Small, neat, and obviously built for speed, the Curtiss Navy Racers for the 1923 Trophy had in fact been sponsored by the United States Government, and formed a trio amounting to nothing less than a special High Speed Flight, although the fact was not generally realised at the time. The pilots selected to fly these very fast seaplanes were Lieutenants Irvine, Rittenhouse and Wead, all of the U.S. Navy.

The usual seaworthiness tests, more exacting than in previous Contests, quickly narrowed down the field, for the Italians dropped out with mechanical trouble and the Blackburn Pellet suddenly porpoised and sank at speed, fortunately without serious injury to the pilot. For the actual race, two out of the three French entries were non-starters and one of the Curtiss floatplanes also failed to rise; so the Contest became a hammer-and-tongs battle between the remaining two Curtiss Racers and the Supermarine boat. The French C.A.M.S. biplane retired on the third lap, and soon afterwards the trim little Curtiss machines forged ahead, Lieutenant Rittenhouse winning the coveted Trophy for the United States with an average speed of 177·3 m.p.h.

The remarkably advanced design and superb quality of the American seaplanes came as a rude shock to British aviation prestige; and the reverberations continued to echo around Schneider Trophy circles for the next two years. When the 1924 Contest came along, Great Britain could produce nothing likely to have any chance of beating the Curtiss Racers, and France and Italy also failed to provide any entries, which gave America the opportunity to claim the Trophy again. Nevertheless, the United

States showed great sportsmanship by officially postponing the
race for a year; and during those twelve months young R. J.
Mitchell of Supermarine designed the first aircraft of the series of
floatplanes destined to win the Trophy outright for Britain
within a decade.

The eighth of the Schneider Trophy Contests took place on
26th October 1925, and was flown over a triangular course at
Chesapeake Bay, Baltimore. The British entries were both twin-
float seaplanes: the Supermarine S.4, piloted by Captain H. C.
Biard, and the Gloster-Napier III, piloted by Captain Hubert
Broad. Another Gloster-Napier III was held in readiness as a
reserve machine, with the famous Bert Hinkler as pilot. There
were three American defenders, all Curtiss R3C-2 biplane floatplanes, piloted by Lieutenants Cuddihy and Ofstie of the U.S.
Navy and Lieutenant Doolittle of the U.S. Army; and Italy
entered two Macchi flying-boats, both conventional enough in
appearance but driven by powerful 500-h.p. Curtiss engines.

It should have been a lively and exciting Contest, but the
British machines were dogged by misfortune and the risks
involved when introducing so many novel experimental features.
Undoubtedly, the S.4 designed by R. J. Mitchell was such an
aircraft: a mid-wing, unbraced monoplane constructed almost
entirely of wood, a surprisingly complete departure from the
previous Supermarine biplane flying-boats; and by no means
least in importance for a Schneider Trophy entrant, it was so slim
and streamlined that even the little Curtiss Racers were put to
shame. And the S.4. had speed—so much speed that just before
being sent to America it had established a World Speed Record
of 226·752 m.p.h. As for the Gloster-Napier floatplanes, they too
were very fast; indeed, all three of the British entries were
powered by the W-type 700-h.p. Napier Lion engine specially
produced in time for the Contest.

In view of the possibilities for the British team, the actual race
came as something of an anticlimax. On 23rd October the S.4
suffered wing flutter at speed and crashed with tremendous force,
though without injury to Captain Biard; and one of the Gloster-
Napiers was badly damaged by rough seas three days later. The
other Gloster-Napier aircraft, with Captain Broad as the pilot,
flew extremely well and completed the course at an average speed

of just over 109 m.p.h., but the U.S. Army pilot, Lieutenant Doolittle, was easily the fastest with an average speed of 232·5 m.p.h. The Trophy was thus retained by America for another year, with every chance that it would be won outright by the same nation at the next Contest.

Before moving on to examine the remaining Schneider Trophy races, it is as well to pause here in 1925 and see what had been achieved by American naval aviation since 1918—the stepping-stones that helped the United States to become proud owners of the fastest single-seater floatplanes in the world in less than ten years. The genius of Glenn Curtiss, had, as always, been sparkling everywhere, and most of the problems troubling the big NC boats designed by him were ironed out soon after the Armistice. On 16th May 1919 three of the huge biplanes took off in an attempt to fly non-stop for over 1,400 miles—from Trepassey Bay, Newfoundland, to the Azores. As the route lay entirely over water, a fleet of destroyers was dispersed at 50-mile intervals for the whole distance, but despite the elaborate precautions one NC boat force-landed and broke up in tremendous seas—her crew being rescued by a passing steamer—and the second NC boat was also seriously damaged when landing in thick fog after managing to remain in the air for fifteen hours. However the third boat—NC-4—encountered no difficulties and eventually skimmed to a perfect landing on the waters of Horta harbour in the Azores, fifteen hours and eighteen minutes after leaving Trepassey Bay.

Five years later, the United States Army Air Service undertook a similar project using two-seater Douglas biplanes for a record round-the-world flight that is of some interest in the story of marine aviation since floats were exchanged for the more usual wheeled undercarriages when large stretches of water had to be covered. The Douglas World Cruisers were very large for single-engined aircraft, with a top speed of only 100 m.p.h., and carried no radios or indeed any other special equipment; but despite all the disadvantages two machines successfully completed the long, arduous flight from Seattle, around the world and back to Boston—a distance of 23,377 miles. A year later, two PN-3 biplane flying-boats of the U.S. Navy attempted a non-stop flight from California to Hawaii; but both aircraft were unfortunately forced to land on the water short of their goal, owing to lack of fuel.

In the field of smaller and faster seaplanes in America, many unwanted machines from the Great War days had been altered for commercial and joy-riding use, but there remained a need for a more comfortable aircraft, designed for civilian use. In the early twenties, young Grover Loening introduced his Air Yacht, a single-engined flying-boat having comfortable accommodation for the pilot and three passengers with light luggage; a very advanced design for the time that bore a surprising resemblance to the Republic Seabee produced more than twenty years later. The Air Yachts operated between Newport and New York about twice a week, with great success; while Loening next came up with a remarkable new biplane amphibian, the COA-1. Powered by the inevitable Liberty engine—over 18,000 had been built during the war years and many still remained in perfect condition—the COA-1 was chosen by the National Geographic Society to undertake photographic work in the wilderness of the Arctic Circle, a trio of the Loening machines covering vast areas during 1925 and 1926. Other COA-1 amphibians, taken into service with the U.S. Army and Navy, were sent on goodwill flights around South America.

Meanwhile, Glenn Curtiss was busy making a name for himself as the man who produced racing aircraft that really won races. The little Curtiss CR-3 biplane flown to victory by David Rittenhouse in the 1923 Schneider Trophy Contest had already won the 1921 and 1922 Pulitzer Trophy races when equipped with a land undercarriage; and the 1924 Pulitzer race had been won by the same Curtiss R3C-2 that roared around the course at Chesapeake Bay the following year to retain the Schneider Trophy for America. This was at a time when the growing popularity of National Air Races all over the United States meant that the American people were becoming increasingly air-minded—an interest enlivened by the activities of that great champion of air power, Brigadier-General W. Mitchell. Against much high-ranking opposition Mitchell had proved that capital ships could be sunk by bombs or aerial torpedoes. In June 1921 he assembled a small force of bombers for demonstration purposes and sank three surrendered German warships, the battleship *Ostfriesland,* the cruiser *Frankfurt,* and a destroyer; then hammered his point firmly home by conducting further tests that brought about the sinking from the air of three old and unwanted U.S. battleships, the *Alabama* later in 1921 and the *Virginia* and *New Jersey* in 1923.

The simple fact that after 1923 the American entries for the Schneider Trophy Contest were backed by the weight of the U.S. Government brought the swift realisation that aircraft design and general performance were being improved through the experience gained each year with racing machines; but Italy also came to understand that she too needed a High Speed Flight, and for the 1926 race entered a team of very streamlined Macchi M.39 monoplane floatplanes. The American defenders were again Curtiss R3C-type seaplanes, the pilots being Lieutenants Cuddihy, Schilt and Tomlinson. Great Britain and France failed to produce any entries, which was, perhaps, as well—nothing that year could have possibly matched those amazing Italian seaplanes.

On 13th November 1926, over a triangular course at Hampton Roads, U.S.A., Major Mario de Bernardi, flying a Macchi M.39 floatplane, averaged 246·442 m.p.h. and reached a maximum speed of over 248 m.p.h. on at least two laps, to win the Schneider Trophy for Italy; thus succeeding in holding the lead over his nearest rival—Lieutenant Schilt, who averaged 231·363 m.p.h.—for the whole Contest. This striking accomplishment came as surprise enough to the aviation world, but the victorious Macchi went on to raise the World Speed Record to just over 258 m.p.h. Indeed, Italy had become a startlingly revived challenger in the constant race for more speed, thanks to Government backing, the willingness to benefit by American experience, and an extremely good 800-h.p. V-type Fiat engine.

Great Britain could no longer ignore the vital necessity for special Government-sponsored racing seaplanes, flown by pilots trained to a high degree of efficiency, and by 1927 the first Royal Air Force High Speed Flight had been formed, with its headquarters established at Felixstowe. When the Air Ministry set about organising the British entries for the next Schneider Trophy Contest, there was no lack of new designs, which included a Short Crusader, powered by a big 800-h.p. Mercury radial engine; two Supermarine S.5s, powered by 900-h.p.

Napier Lion engines; and three Gloster IV biplanes, also using the Napier Lion engines. The R.A.F. racing team, under the command of Air Vice Marshal F. R. Scarlett, was composed of Squadron Leader L. H. Slatter and Flight Lieutenants S. M. Kinkead, S. N. Webster and O. E. Worsley, all experienced pilots who had undergone intensive training in flying and banking at high speeds before leaving with their machines for Italy in the aircraft carrier *Eagle*.

The 1927 Contest had been arranged to take place on the Lido, near Venice, with a determined team of four Italian serving officers of Mussolini's air force—the Regia Aeronautica—ready and waiting to enter the fray. These young men—Colonel Mario di Bernardi and Captains Ferrarin, Guasconi and Guazzetti—were each to pilot a Macchi-Fiat M.52 low-wing monoplane powered by a 1,000-h.p. Fiat engine. There should have been at least one American entrant to thrust his sword into what promised to be an Anglo-Italian duel, but the machine failed to be ready in time; a most unfortunate loss in the light of later events, for it might well have been the ancestor of the high-speed fighter America was to need so badly at the time of Pearl Harbour.

Before 26th September, the actual date of the race, there were teething troubles in plenty for both the British and Italian teams, aside from a certain amount of inclement weather. The Short Crusader crashed on a preliminary flight, due to crossed aileron controls, seriously injuring the pilot, Flying Officer Schofield. Then two of the Glosters proved not too satisfactory in general performance; and all the Fiat engines presented their worried mechanics with a host of problems. In the event, only half a dozen aircraft were able to take part in the Contest—one of the Gloster IVs, both the Supermarine S.5s, and three of the Macchi M.52 floatplanes. At five-minute intervals, commencing from 2.30 p.m., all six entrants streaked across the water and lifted smoothly into the air, gaining height as they headed for the starting line.

So the race began, quietly enough at first but soon bringing many surprises. The beautiful, scarlet-painted Macchis hurtled noisily around the course for the first few laps, showing great promise for Italy, but then the engine troubles began to crop up again. Ferrarin was compelled to drop out, and soon afterwards di Bernardi vanished from the view of the crowd, gliding down to land on the water well outside the course. All the British machines continued to perform sweetly for some time in a way that must have warmed the hearts of their designers; but at last the Gloster-Napier was seen to lose speed before it eventually retired. The two Supermarines were thus left to battle it out with Guazzetti, who was piloting the remaining Macchi with great skill.

The sixth lap brought about a decisive turn of events, just as Worsley and Guazzetti were flying neck and neck for the Lido hairpin; the Macchi banked violently around, leaping higher into the air than the pilot intended, and Worsley turned neatly beneath the Italian machine, thus gaining the lead. At once, Guazzetti made a desperate attempt to recapture the advantage, but the overtaxed engine of the Macchi had lost heart and faded out a few moments later. With Italy's last hope gone, Worsley was able to relax his efforts, and Flight Lieutenant Webster in the other Supermarine S.5, finally won the Contest for Great Britain, with an average speed of 281·65 m.p.h.

For many reasons, including the realisation that it was no longer possible to impose a time limit of only a few months for the designing and building of complicated high-speed racing sea-planes such as Macchi and Supermarine were able to put into the field, it was agreed that after 1927 the Schneider Trophy Contest should be held only at intervals of two years. The eleventh Contest was therefore arranged by the Royal Aero Club to take place on 6th–7th September 1929 at Spithead, off the Isle of Wight; and the R.A.F. High Speed Flight—disbanded after returning from Venice in 1927—was hurriedly re-formed at Felixstowe. Now that Great Britain had a good chance of winning another, successive, victory, her Government was willing to open the Treasury coffers once again, and the Supermarine and Gloster companies were soon preparing their latest machines for the race. Two Supermarine S.6 floatplanes were produced, developed from the successful S.5 type but slightly larger, and powered by special V-type Rolls-Royce engines of 1,900 h.p.; while Glosters brought out improved versions of their 1927 biplane, again using Napier Lion engines, but with the thrust increased to 1,400 h.p.

The only challengers for the 1929 Contest came from Italy—
three Macchis, a Fiat and a Savoia, all floatplanes. However, it
was decided that the two competing teams should be each limited
to three machines, so in the event only the Macchis—two new
M.67s and a re-designed M.52—took part in the race. The R.A.F.
entrants chose to rely entirely on Supermarine types; the two
S.6s, to be flown by Flying Officers R. L. Atcherley and H. R. D.
Waghorn, and an S.5, with Flight Lieutenant D'Arcy A. Greig as
the pilot. Extensive training took place for some months before
the Contest, the S.5s used for practice by the British team becoming as familiar a sight at Calshot as the Italian Macchis at Lake
Garda, where tragedy struck when Captain Motta lost control at
over 300 m.p.h. and was killed when the seaplane he was flying
plunged into the water. On the Supermarines and Macchis alike,
the wings were small, the fuselages so streamlined they resem-
bled arrows, and the speeds had become so great that one tiny
error, a momentary lack of concentration on the part of the pilot,
could bring instant disaster.

At one minute after two o'clock on 7th September, the starting-gun at Calshot boomed out the opening of the 1929 Contest,
and immediately the Supermarine S.6 flown by Waghorn roared
past the great crowds along the Solent, a streaking blue and-
silver monoplane rocketing down the course and around the
pylons. The first Italian pilot, Dal Molin, thundered away in
pursuit, then the S.5, then one of the Macchi M.67s, and finally
the other S.6 and the second M.67 in quick succession. The laps
that followed were perhaps the most exciting ever clocked in a
Schneider Trophy race, both teams giving a brilliant display of
flying, very low and at astonishing speeds. The Italian pilot Lieutenant Cadringher in particular made perfect vertical turns that
drew the admiration of all who saw them. At last, he was forced
to land after fumes had entered the cockpit of his machine, and
about the same time the other M.67 also dropped out with a
faulty oil pipe. The lovely Supermarine monoplanes continued to
scream relentlessly around the course, followed by the mighty
thunder of their superb Rolls Royce engines, heralding a whole
new era in high speed aviation; ahead lay the Spitfire and Hurricane, Meteor and Lightning, the dawn of supersonic flight.

The Contest ended with Flying Officer Waghorn the winner,

having achieved an average speed of 328·63 m.p.h. The shy, retiring young R. J. Mitchell had triumphed again, for his S.6 had in one race garlanded itself with honours by breaking the existing World Speed Record on the first lap, then breaking that record after another lap and finally creating a new World Record. Never before had Britain's star been so in the ascendancy in racing aviation circles; and if only her supremacy could be retained with a third successive victory, she would have secured the Schneider Trophy for all time.

Yet it was only by a hairbreadth that Great Britain managed to enter the decisive 1931 Contest. The cost of preparation for the races had increased to such an extent that the Socialist Government of that time, under the leadership of Ramsay MacDonald, decided to withdraw its support. In retrospect, such an action may seem incredible, but it was little more than normal policy in the early thirties; lack of money was forcing the abandonment of too many aviation and other important programmes. Nevertheless, there was a great public outcry against the Government which had shown such scant regard for national prestige in the air. "Enough thousands can surely be saved from the weekly financial waste in this country . . . to give us a dominant position in the air from the start of this 'Flying Age', " commented one newspaper.

More than a year passed, seventeen wasted months during which it was understood that France, Italy and perhaps the U.S.A. would be taking part in the Contest. Then, almost at the last moment, the eccentric millionairess Lady Houston, who had an intense dislike of all Socialism, learned of the British predicament and offered the Royal Aero Club a gift of £100,000 to cover all expenses. With only seven months remaining before September 1931, and the day of the Contest, it was quite impossible for Supermarines—or any other company—to produce entirely new designs in time; but R. J. Mitchell's remarkable S.6 type was extensively modified to include vastly improved water-cooling, oil-cooling and fuel systems. Meanwhile, Rolls-Royce had been working on development of their successful 1929 Contest engines, and were able to supply them of the same weight and size, yet with the horsepower output increased to 2,300 h.p. Great Britain could thus finally enter two new Supermarine monoplanes—basically S.6s, but modified in design and therefore known as S.6Bs—and two of the original S.6s with the improved engines. The R.A.F. High Speed Flight formed for the 1931 Contest was under the command of Squadron Leader A. H. Orlebar, the pilots being Flight Lieutenants J. N. Boothman and F. W. Long, and Flying Officer L. S. Snaith. A triangular course had been selected off Spithead to be flown by the competitors seven times, commencing and finishing at Ryde Pier.

The date of the Contest—12th September—arrived only too soon, but a gale of wind and rain in the Solent rendered all flying impossible, and the race was therefore postponed for twenty-four hours. However, despite fine weather, Sunday 13th September brought little of the expected neck-and-neck excitement of previous Contests to the great crowds of spectators on shore and aboard the innumerable yachts and other craft around the course. For various reasons the challengers from Europe and America had failed to have their machines ready in time, and Great Britain—ironically only able to compete herself by nothing short of a £100,000 miracle—thus became the only country taking part in the race after all. The starting-gun broke the silence of the sunlit afternoon with its report, and Flight Lieutenant Boothman took off in the gleaming new Supermarine S.6B soon to hurtle like a blue-and-silver bullet over the heads of the people thronging the Southsea and Isle of Wight coastlines; very fast and terrifyingly low, often down below 200 ft., resolving in a matter of seconds from a tiny dot into a powerful, angry little monoplane.

Without any difficulty, Boothman completed the course at an average speed of 340·08 m.p.h. to win the Schneider Trophy outright for Great Britain. "Weather conditions were good, visibility excellent, and over the sea the air was smooth . . ." he said afterwards. "During the fifth lap my legs began to get slightly cramped, owing to the small cockpit. I rested my knees on the side of the fuselage. However, I quickly moved them when I found that the cockpit walls were blistering hot, and decided that cramp was the lesser evil!" This was, of course, a typical problem of high-speed flight, and one that was to remain unsolved for many years. "During the last lap the engine was still giving the same healthy note and the aircraft was still flying perfectly . . ." continued Flight Lieutenant Boothman. "With the final closing of the throttle a left-hand gliding turn, and an alighting, the last Schneider Trophy Contest was over."

Two hours later, Flight Lieutenant Stainforth, flying the same S.6B, made four high-speed runs along a straight course off the crowded shore of Southampton Water, to raise the World's Speed Record to 407·5 m.p.h. an achievement that remained unbeaten until two years later, when Italy captured the record with a speed of 423·7 m.p.h.

After eighteen years, the Schneider Trophy Contests thus came to an end with the bronze-winged figure symbolising *Speed* established where it has remained ever since—at the Royal Aero Club of the United Kingdom in London. That the Supermarine 'S'-type racing monoplanes led the way for R. J. Mitchell's F7/30 single-seater fighter of 1934, followed in due course by the magnificent Spitfire, is now a well-known story; but the generosity of Lady Houston in putting up the money to save British aviation prestige in 1931 has too often been overlooked in the past. Yet it is acknowledged that the Battle of Britain could not have been won without the Spitfire. Indeed, Lucy, Lady Houston, who died in December 1936, might well be called "the woman who saved London", without diminishing the simple fact that Reginald J. Mitchell, fated to die the following year, left his genius as a legacy destined to save Britain.

7

THE VINTAGE YEARS: 1930–39

∞∞∞∞∞∞∞∞∞∞∞∞∞∞∞∞∞∞∞∞∞∞∞∞∞∞∞∞∞∞

Any comment on flying-boat development between the wars inevitably brings to mind Claudius Dornier's gigantic Do X of 1930, at that time the biggest aeroplane in the world. Completed at Altenrhein on the shores of Lake Constance in 1929, the Do X weighed 52 tons when fully loaded, and was powered by no less than twelve Siemens Jupiter engines, mounted in tandem 'push-pull' fashion on six pylons above the great monoplane wing. She was designed to accommodate between forty and fifty passengers in a hull divided into luxuriously appointed compartments, had an efficient galley capable of providing three-course meals, a cocktail-bar and even cloakrooms fitted with shower-baths. In short, the Do X was large in every possible sense of the word, perhaps a typical German conception, and certainly a striking example of the way in which Dornier's organisation had progressed in less than a decade.

Nevertheless, the Do X failed to live up to expectations, and proved unsuccessful in the task for which she had been designed—that of transoceanic flying passenger liner. In common with so many other multi-engined German aircraft of the period, the Do X suffered from motor troubles, and eventually the Siemens Jupiter engines were replaced by more reliable American Curtiss Conquerors, which generated over 7,000 h.p. and gave a maximum speed of 150 m.p.h. On 21st October 1929 the huge boat took off from Lake Constance with a record total of 169 persons on board, and the following year she set out on a round-the-world tour of some 28,000 miles that brought much welcome publicity and consumed a vast amount of time, without really proving anything. The fact remained that the Do X was ahead of her time, and continued to be fraught with many problems, particularly from her formidable array of twelve engines —the tandem arrangement, for instance, made them a servicing mechanic's nightmare. Her world flight completed, it seemed that the hue and cry over her great size and sumptuous accommodation had no sooner died down than she was quietly retired out of service. For several years, she remained on display in the Berlin Air Museum, a symbol of German achievement and failure, destined finally to be destroyed by Allied bombing during the Second World War.

Looking back over the peacetime years, it is surprising to find so many designers tempted by the apparent advantages of the giant flying-boat—that recurring 'bigger and better than the one before' theme—yet frequently meeting with little or no success. John Porte, with so many remarkable Felixstowe-type boats to his credit, anticipated the Do X by over ten years with his huge triplane flying-boat of 1919, powered by five 334-h.p. Rolls-Royce Eagle VII engines. With a wing span of 125 ft. and a hull length of over 63 ft., the Porte/Felixstowe Fury was the largest British machine to take the air for some years after the Armistice; in fact, there were great doubts that it would rise at all, but Porte himself lifted it gracefully off the water on its maiden flight.

For some time, the Fury was used for experimental work, until finally it quite inexplicably stalled and crashed on take-off, with the loss of all three crew members, not long after John Porte had been invalided out of the Navy as physically unfit for further service. By now he was a very sick man, the tuberculosis that had always haunted him seriously aggravated by too much hard work, but he refused to accept defeat, even from within himself. In August 1919 Porte joined the Gosport Aviation Company, where he renewed an old friendship with the Works Manager, Herman Volk, but there was a post-war slump in orders for seaplanes and the small firm soon closed down. Two months later, at the age of thirty-five, John Porte died at Brighton, with few to mourn the passing of such a remarkable designer and outstanding pilot; undoubtedly the man who gained air supremacy for Great Britain during the North Sea war, 1915 to 1918.

The big flying-boats and amphibians continued to appear on the British scene, evidence of active competition between the three leading firms of Saunders-Roe (commonly known as Saro) Ltd., Short Brothers and the Supermarine Company. There was the twin-engined Short Cromarty of 1921, which preceded a long line of Short flying-boats, including the Singapore series and the Sunderland; the Supermarine Swan amphibian of 1924, designed by R. J. Mitchell; and the Saunders-Roe Severn of 1930. That very successful military version of the Supermarine Swan, the Southampton, first appeared in 1935, initially powered by two 470-h.p. Napier Lion engines, the final (Mark X) models having three Armstrong Siddeley engines. In October 1927 the so-called Far East Flight of the Royal Air Force, under the command of Group-Captain H. M. Cave-Brown-Cave, D.S.O., D.F.C., flew four Southamptons from England to Singapore, than on to Australia, Hong Kong and back to Singapore, a distance of some 27,000 miles. A few months later, a further long-distance record flight was made by Southamptons, this time to Nicobar and the Andamans, covering 19,500 miles.

Short Brothers switched some of the limelight away from the Southamptons when their design team introduced the first of the big, all-metal biplane flying-boats, the Singapore I of 1926. This was the machine loaned by the Air Council to the pioneer aviator Sir Alan Cobham for his memorable 25,000-mile survey flight around Africa, which effectively demonstrated the sturdiness and general efficiency of the type under any conditions. The Singapore II, powered by four excellent Rolls-Royce Kestrel engines followed in 1930, and the last of the Short biplane flying-boats, the historic Singapore III, was also fitted with four Kestrels, but of greatly increased horsepower. Operating with the R.A.F. in some numbers for more than a decade, the Singapores were probably the best military flying-boats anywhere in the world during the 'thirties, and a few were still to be seen on coastal patrol duties around the Far East after the outbreak of the Second World War.

In 1928, Short Brothers had also produced the first of their three-engined S.8 Calcutta flying-boats. This prototype proved so successful from a safety point of view—it could take off in only forty-two seconds with the central engine out of action—that it was obtained from the Air Ministry by Imperial Airways, and inaugurated a trans-Mediterranean service. After completion of the usual tests at Felixstowe, it alighted on the Thames on 1st August 1928, and remained moored near the Houses of Parliament at Westminster for a few days, many aviation personalities and M.P.s welcoming the opportunity to inspect the craft and also consume a record number of cocktails in the luxuriously appointed lounge. Other Calcuttas followed in due course, and operated with regularity and efficiency on the Mediterranean route for a number of years.

Imperial Airways, increasingly anxious to reach out farther and farther around the world, were soon demanding yet more new long-range flying-boats, bringing an unexpectedly halcyon period for the larger manufacturers. The four-engined Short Kents, each with accommodation for a crew of four and sixteen passengers, followed the Calcuttas into commercial service; they featured even more comfortable cabins, well-equipped galleys and enclosed cockpits. Proving to be not only reliable but also versatile craft, two Kent class machines bridged the gap when Imperial Airways urgently needed additional air liners for its cross-Channel route, the tail units and superstructures being simply fitted with modified fuselages and wheeled undercarriages and then delivered. These somewhat ungainly landplane versions of the Kent boats—named *Scylla* and *Syrinx*—were nevertheless extremely comfortable, and had a cruising speed of over 100 m.p.h.

The largest flying-boat to be built in Great Britain since 1919 appeared in 1932. This was the Short R.6/28, later named Sarafand, which had a wing span of 120 ft. and was powered by six Rolls-Royce Buzzard engines. Constructed to an Air Ministry specification calling for a long-range reconnaissance flying-boat with provision for a heavy bomb load, the biplane Sarafand seemed to fulfil all requirements, with its range of 1,450 miles and well-sited defensive positions—including an awe-inspiring one-and-a-half-pounder shell gun. However, after a few years of so-called experimental flying it ended up in the scrapyard; like the colossal N.4 boats and John Porte's ill-fated Fury, its imposing size had eventually condemned it.

Short Brothers now took what turned out to be a decisive step in seaplane development, when their first large monoplane flying-boat, designed to Air Ministry specification R.24/31, appeared in prototype form during 1934. This all-metal, twin-engined machine never went into production, but its arrival on the aviation scene marked the beginning of the end of all biplane flying-boats; indeed, it proved to be the immediate forerunner of the famous Empire class and even more famous Sunderland. Soon commonly known as the 'Knuckleduster' because of the then unusual sharply angled gull wing and rather ugly engine nacelles, R.24/31 had the misfortune to be powered by new steam-cooled Rolls-Royce Goshawk motors, which had shown excellent promise under test but proved disappointing when put into service; and by the time the Air Ministry came round to agreement that better engines were, in fact, needed, Short Brothers were already going ahead with their Empire boats for Imperial Airways.

Meanwhile, the last of the big military biplane flying-boats, epitomised by the Singapores of the Far East squadrons, continued to work out their pleasant peacetime days in R.A.F. service. The three-engined Blackburn Perths used by No. 209 Squadron (and later No. 204 Squadron) had the distinction of being the most heavily armed craft, with three Lewis guns and a one-and-a-half pounder cannon for defence, plus a 2,000-lb. bomb load; Saunders-Roe's Saro Londons, of which forty-eight were to be produced up to the outbreak of war, also had an adequate armament and a useful long-range endurance of twenty hours; while the Vickers Supermarine Stranraers that equipped No. 228 Squadron for some years were at the time of first production (1936) the fastest flying-boats join the Royal Air Force.

Despite their many advantages, all those graceful biplane craft, with their beautifully shaped Alclad hulls and twin or triple engines thundering away between silver wings, would be obsolete by 1940. They belonged to the last years of an era when Britain still had an empire extending over thousands of miles, and no less than the ships of the Royal Navy, they carried the national flag to every corner of the world. Having served that simple, but very necessary, purpose many times, the R.A.F.'s biplane flying-boats faded away, leaving only memories of their vintage summers; warm Mediterranean nights, and Malta like a glittering jewel in the sea; the big duralumin-clad wings passing over the Nile, with the Pyramids swinging past far below; sparkling clear water lapping the hulls moored off Singapore, white sun awnings and tropical uniforms, mess dress and cocktail parties.

A few of the smaller sea-flying biplanes survived the arrival of the monoplane. One of them, destined to perform a thousand different tasks during the Second World War and then linger on into the jet age, appeared in prototype form in 1933. This was the Vickers Supermarine 236 Seagull V amphibian, which went into production as the Walrus, became affectionately known to all who came across the type as 'Shagbat' and will for all time be remembered as one of the most remarkable and versatile aircraft in the history of aviation. Designed by R. J. Mitchell as a ship-borne spotter-reconnaissance machine, the Seagull V evolved by way of his earlier Seagull amphibians of the 'twenties from Supermarine's Sea Lion flying-boats of Schneider Trophy fame. It was not so much ungainly as downright ugly in appearance, wallowed along at a tired 95 m.p.h., made conversation in flight almost impossible with the beating of its Bristol Pegasus pusher-mounted engine—and was so rugged that there was no task beyond it. It also had the distinction of being the first British military aircraft to have a fully retractable undercarriage; the first amphibian in the world to be catapulted from a warship with a full military load; and the first machine with an enclosed cockpit to enter service with the Fleet Air Arm. As a peacetime proto-type, the Seagull V jogged noisily around Britain's harbours, attracting some ridicule and much laughter; but the wartime exploits of the production models—the Walruses—which will be dealt with in some detail later, were to earn everlasting respect and admiration.

Another biplane which refused to become obsolete was the three-seater Fairey Swordfish, designed as a torpedo-spotter-reconnaissance aircraft for the Royal Navy in 1934. A conven-tional fabric-covered sprawling aeroplane, powered by the faith-ful Bristol Pegasus engine, the Swordfish actually looked slow and antiquated when it first entered Fleet Air Arm service, and it seemed even more of an anachronism after a decade of rough-and-tumble achievements; but its handling qualities remained unsurpassed by any carrier-borne aircraft in the world. To the men who sat amid the struts and wires in the draughty open cockpits of the Swordfish, it was known as 'Stringbag'—among a few other less printable names—and they trusted the trundling

biplane to land them safely back on the pitching carrier's deck, in
good or bad weather, at that amazingly slow, controlled speed
which has never been equalled. They were seldom disappointed;
and the Swordfish thus joined the Supermarine Walrus as another intruder into the monoplane age. Nevertheless, in 1935 there
were not a few who doubted the value of the torpedo-bomber as
an air weapon, and a floatplane version of the Swordfish,
intended for catapult spotting duties, was also put into production.

Ever since 1924, when the sadly diminished British naval air
arm of about a hundred machines had been officially named the
Fleet Air Arm, there had been something of a preoccupation
with the idea of launching aircraft by catapult from ships, following upon experiments with a Fairey N.9 seaplane in 1918. The
first successful shipborne catapult, which could be energised by
compressed air or cordite, was designed by an engineer named R.
Falkland Carey, and mounted in the cruiser *Vindictive* for test
purposes. In October 1925 a Fairey III D floatplane, piloted by
Wing-Commander E. J. P. Burling, became the first British naval
aircraft to be catapulted from a warship; two years later the first
air-operated catapult was installed in H.M.S. *Frobisher* and there-
after many variations on the basic principles were introduced
into catapults aboard cruisers and battleships up to the Second
World War. The larger warships had two hangars, each housing
a folded aircraft, which meant that (including the machine at
readiness on the catapult) three spotter seaplanes could be carried. It was extremely unlikely that even a battleship would need
so many 'pairs of eyes' in action, but the fact was not appreciated
until later; nor had the problems of recovery under fire been
taken fully into consideration.

An interesting little special-purpose floatplane to appear in the
late 'twenties was the Parnall Peto, a two-seater reconnaissance
biplane designed to operate from the Royal Navy's only aircraft
carrying submarine, the M.2. Squadron Leader J. J. Teasdale,
R.A.F. (Retd.), who it will be recalled had served in the original
Ark Royal during and after the Dardanelles campaign, vividly
remembers seeing the M.2 on exercises when she was attached to
H.M.S. *Furious* during the 1928 Mediterranean fleet manoeuvres.
"She was the last of three M Class submarine monitors with an

armament of one 12-in. gun and four 18-in. torpedo tubes built during the 1914–18 War for coastal bombardment," he has recollected. "The M.2 was converted to carry a small two-seater floatplane, the 12-in. gun turret being used as the hangar. The floatplane was catapulted from the submarine's deck, and recovered from the sea after flight by means of a light crane fitted atop the hangar."

The first two Peto pilots to serve aboard the M.2 were Lieutenant C. W. Byas and Lieutenant C. Keighley-Peach. "At the time, we considered they were very fortunate indeed," recalls Teasdale, "especially as they were entitled to, and received, both flying pay and submarine pay!"

Despite a number of experiments neither the stainless-steel Parnell Peto or her parent submarine turned out to have more than limited success, the former because of an inadequate speed and ceiling and the latter because of her bulk and general unwieldiness at sea. The M.2 was eventually lost off Weymouth a few years later, probably due to the incorrect carrying out of an order concerning the opening of her hangar doors.

The Hawker Osprey and Fairey Seafox are worthy of mention here as two of the neat little two-seater floatplanes used by the Fleet Air Arm for catapulted spotter-reconnaissance duties during the last years of peace. The Osprey, introduced in 1932, was a naval variant of the ubiquitous Hart day bomber, with an interesting maximum speed of 176 m.p.h.; while the all-metal Seafox, more frequently carried by cruisers, was slightly under-powered, but an otherwise excellent machine. In common with many other British naval aircraft of the 'thirties, the Osprey and Seafox suffered from the disadvantage of trying to perform too many functions at the same time—they were even equipped to carry a few light bombs—and typified the universal policy at that time of having a surprising number of different aeroplane types in service, yet insisting that each be capable of fulfilling more than one role. Both types were eventually superseded by the Supermarine Walrus, and, to a lesser extent, by the floatplane version of the Swordfish.

Many and varied, too, were the types of carrier-borne aircraft serving with the Royal Navy between the wars. By 1939, Great Britain could muster seven carriers, taking some 220 machines to sea, the latest Blackburn Skua monoplanes having just equipped two squadrons in the new, very modern *Ark Royal* displacing 22,000 tons. Of the other ships, the *Furious* and *Argus* inherited from the 1914–18 War have already been mentioned, and the *Eagle* had followed as a welcome addition to the Fleet. Next came H.M.S. *Hermes,* the first British carrier to be designed and built as such from the beginning; then the much larger sister-ships *Glorious* and *Courageous,* each of 26,500 tons and with ample space for forty-eight aircraft. At first sight, the Royal Navy thus seemed to possess a carrier fleet well worthy of the name; but in fact the years of strict economy and penny-pinching had taken a heavy toll.

The new *Ark Royal*—the old one from the First World War had been renamed *Pegasus* and was still in service—could be considered easily as efficient as the latest American carriers, and the *Glorious* and *Courageous,* although originally laid down as battle cruisers, had much to commend them in the carrier role. Nevertheless, the earlier ships were slow, obsolescent, and had many minor disadvantages. For example, the 12,000-ton *Hermes* was much too small for the effective handling of aircraft; and, in any case, she only had hangar space for fifteen machines. Also, H.M.S. *Argus,* in common with the last conversion of *Furious,* carried her smoke-stacks along the sides in order to provide a completely clear flight deck, but the unusual arrangement meant that both ships had red-hot hangar walls when steaming at any speed, and the smoke and soot drifting into the cabins made life intolerable.

However, a ray of sunshine lay over the horizon for the Fleet Air Arm, even though it meant that the years of peace were almost at an end. In 1937, when the angry, raving voices from Berlin were beginning to resound across Europe, Great Britain at last decided to review her scanty defences, and the massive rearmament programme that followed included a greatly increased carrier fleet. Initially, four new carriers were ordered, each of 23,000 tons—these eventually emerged as *Illustrious, Victorious, Formidable* and *Indomitable*—but in 1938 the naval estimates provided for two more, which were to be named *Implacable* and *Indefatigable.* Work on the four ships was commenced at once, but the regular cries of "Disarmament!" had barely been hushed in time; the *Illustrious* did not follow *Ark Royal* into service until 1940.

As peacetime equipment, the old *Furious, Eagle* and *Argus* had originally carried the first successful British carrier-borne torpedo bomber, the Sopwith Cuckoo, replaced in due course by the Blackburn Dart, then the Blackburn Baffin, and finally the Blackburn Ripon. All were conventional biplanes, good steady machines, and some were taken into use with *Glorious* and *Courageous,* to be superseded by the unwieldy Blackburn Shark and later the Fairey Swordfish. This somewhat mixed bag of aircraft in carrier service with the Royal Navy during the early 'thirties also included the Fairey III F and Fairey Seal three-seater reconnaissance machines, and one of the ugliest biplanes ever built, the Blackburn Blackburn.

In the naval single-seater fighter role, the Sopwith Pups and Camels of 1918 had been followed by the Nieuport Nightjar, to depart after only a brief reign in favour of the sturdy little Fairey Flycatcher, which remained the standard Fleet Air Arm interceptor fighter for over a decade. In 1932, the Hawker Nimrod, a very streamlined biplane on much the same lines as the famous Hawker Hart then just going into R.A.F. front-line service, superseded the Flycatcher; and six years later the last biplane fighter to join the Fleet Air Arm, the Gloster Sea Gladiator, replaced the Nimrod.

At the outbreak of war, therefore, British naval aviation was still compelled to rely mainly on various biplane types, many of them outdated and almost all without exception too slow to fulfil anything but the most pedestrian of duties. Yet, oddly enough, in one entirely new category for the Fleet Air Arm a monoplane had been introduced—the two-seater Blackburn Skua, specifically designed as a dive bomber! Powered by a 900-h.p. Bristol Pegasus Perseus XII radial engine, the Skua had all the disadvantages of similar German dive bombers such as the Henschel Hs 123 and Junkers Ju 87; it was too heavy, had very little speed, and made an excellent target when pulling out of the bombing dive or zooming to regain height. A fighter version, named the Blackburn Roc, fitted with a power-driven Boulton and Paul gun turret over the rear cockpit, was introduced in 1938, but only built in limited numbers.

4—AHOMA * *

A number of obsolete biplanes, and a few obsolescent but reliable biplanes; only one operational monoplane type flying out of carriers; and a cumbersome new two-seater fighter monoplane variant with little hope of success. Who could doubt that the Fleet Air Arm had been sadly neglected for almost twenty years? And who could foresee that even under the impetus of war another three years would have to pass before the situation was remedied, and that same Fleet Air Arm become something more than a poor relation of the Royal Air Force?

In the United States, the name of Igor Sikorsky had an increasing influence as an aircraft designer and builder in the early thirties. A young, unassuming but very ambitious Russian engineer, Sikorsky had always shown an interest in very big aeroplanes, and back in 1912 the embryonic aviation industry had been taken by surprise with the appearance of the first of a whole series of giant Sikorsky four-engined biplanes. Arriving in America as a White Russian refugee from the Bolshevik regime, he had soon formed the Sikorsky Manufacturing Corporation, which in 1928 became the Sikorsky Aviation Corporation, actually a struggling little concern situated in an unheated, draughty hangar at Roosevelt Field. At the time, Pan American Airways had just been founded, and a Caribbean network of services was being considered, using flying-boats or amphibians; so Sikorsky hurriedly rushed into production his twin-engined S-36, which led the way for a succession of very advanced amphibians serving what later became the leading United States airline.

From October 1928, when the versatile little S-38, with accommodation for eight passengers, entered Pan American service, flying-boats and amphibians made an outstanding contribution to the rapidly expanding United States civil air routes during the next decade. Loening amphibians continued to be used in some numbers, mainly on the Buenos Aires–Montevideo crossing of the River Plate; a fleet of large 22-seater Consolidated Commodore flying-boats, originally built for the New York, Rio and Buenos Aires Air Line absorbed by Pan American in 1930, operated down the east coast of South America. Meanwhile Igor Sikorsky was working upon the development of both types of sea-flying machine. Perhaps the most successful of all this prolific designer's amphibians was his huge, four-engined S-40, able to carry forty passengers and a crew of six for about 500 miles; if a little slow for long-term economical operation, it was reliable, and so sturdily built as to be almost indestructible.

Soon becoming famous as the first of the 'Clipper' boats of the thirties, the S-40 had scarcely entered regular service when Sikorsky was again commissioned by Pan American Airways to design a large passenger-carrying aircraft, intended for the proposed transatlantic route. He therefore conceived the four-motored S-42, which went into service in August 1934 on the South American run, Great Britain and France having refused to allow landing rights on their soil (or water!) for the original purpose. A big, graceful monoplane flying-boat weighing over 20 tons, the S-42 carried thirty-two passengers in wide, luxurious Pullman-type cabins, and had a high cruising speed of 140 m.p.h. Of paramount importance to Pan American was the range, which Sikorsky had extended in his S-42 to 750 miles.

The following year, Pan American Airways was ready for what at the time seemed an almost impossible undertaking—the commencement of a regular service from California, across the Pacific and so to the Far East, a distance of some 9,000 miles. The first machine to attempt this long, pioneering flight was a Sikorsky S-42 with extra fuel tanks, aptly named *China Clipper* and piloted by Captain E. Musick; without encountering any difficulties, he followed the proposed route to its conclusion in Manila Harbour, calling at Hawaii, Midway, Wake and Guam. Other S-42s were put into service for the shorter legs of the extensive service—New York and Bermuda, Miami and South America, Manila and Hong Kong.

For the new trans-Pacific route, Pan American Airways obviously required even larger aircraft, and soon afterwards the Glenn L. Martin factory at Baltimore satisfied this need with a high-wing monoplane flying-boat, powered by four 830-h.p. Pratt & Whitney radial engines. The Martin M.130 was not unlike the Sikorsky S-42 in general appearance, but unusual in having sponsons, or wing stubs, projecting from the hull—a feature of Claudius Dornier's boats, including the Do X—instead of the wing-tip floats common to Sikorsky machines. To fulfil the requirements of Pan American's long-range Pacific haul, which involved sixty hours of flying time, the M.130 had to be fast but very comfortable, and the main cabin was therefore equipped even more lavishly than the S-42, with armchairs and settees, writing-desks, and off-duty sleeping accommodation for the crew. It was also one of the first flying-boats to carry a flight engineer, all the engine instruments and switches being installed in a separate compartment.

On 22nd November 1935 a Martin M.130 boat also named *China Clipper,* first of the type to undertake the trans-Pacific route, took off from Alameda, carrying only mail and light freight, as it had been decided not to convey any passengers until the new service had been tried and tested under all conditions and every problem ironed out. A year later, after overnight hostels had been built by Pan American Airways on Midway, Wake and Guam, M.130s were at last operating a more sensible schedule, with scarcely an empty seat to be seen on the weekly flights to Manila; and they continued to throb sweetly back and forth over the miles of empty ocean with monotonous regularity until 1940. Nevertheless, Pan American was still looking ahead into the future, seeking a yet larger flying-boat—that recurring 'bigger and better' theme—with an increased range, and capable of carrying many more passengers.

Thus came to be designed the last of the giant pre-war American boats, the Boeing 314 Clipper. A vast, four-engined craft comparable with the Short Empire class machines, it entered Pan American service on their Pacific and North Atlantic routes in the February and June of 1939, and performed sterling work until eventually superseded by the Douglas DC-4 (C-54 Skymaster) landplane of 1945. Generally considered to be the best passenger-carrying flying-boat type ever built, the original Boeing 314 design suffered from a number of teething troubles, but it emerged as a very beautiful monoplane, despite the weight of forty tons, with neat hull sponsons and triple tail fins, the superb accommodation being divided into two decks. The 314 had a top speed of 200 m.p.h. and a maximum range in excess of 5,000 miles, could carry seventy passengers and had a wing span of 152 ft.; a truly magnificent flying-boat, worthy enough for three of the type to be purchased by the British Government for V.I.P. use during the war.

Some mention must be made here on the aircraft produced for the United States Navy in the years immediately preceding the Second World War, including those wonderful little Boeing single-seater biplane fighters that equipped American carriers for over a decade. Commencing with the FB (for Fighter and Boeing) series between 1925 and 1928, the Boeing Company of Seattle turned out many highly successful machines for operation from land bases or carriers, but undoubtedly the most famous was the F4B-4 type which entered service with the U.S. Navy and Marine Corps during 1932. With their bright yellow-and-silver colour schemes and gay squadron markings, reminiscent of the most sunlit days of peacetime aviation, these neat biplanes, having spreader-bar undercarriages and big radial Pratt & Whitney Wasp engines enclosed in Townend ring cowlings, were actually quite normal, ordinary aeroplanes; yet they had an indefinable something in the design that made for perfection, and served for six years as first-line equipment on the carriers *Lexington, Saratoga, Langley* and *Enterprise,* and also at the great base of San Diego.

The F4B-4s were eventually replaced by Grumman F2F and F3F single-seater, very stubby, barrel-shaped biplanes with retractable undercarriages and a pitiful armament of twin forward-firing machine-guns, emphasising the rather odd mixture of modernity and obsolescence so typical of American aircraft at that time. Originally built as a dive bomber, the Curtiss SBC-4 Helldiver two-seater, carrier-borne fighter biplane of the late nineteen-thirties had much the same layout; there was a marked reluctance to admit that the monoplane configuration had come to stay, leading to a curious anxiety to find the best of both worlds. The consequence of so much uncertainty did not become fully apparent until 1941, when the Japanese Mitsubishi A6M Zero-Sen monoplane fighter proved itself capable of flying rings round almost everything the United States could put into the air.

Of the American military flying-boats to emerge during this period, most were conventional biplanes, usually twin-engined, rather slow, but eminently suitable for plodding coastal patrol work. Some of these—the PN (or Patrol Navy) types—were produced by the U.S. Naval Aircraft Factory at Philadelphia, although Boeing brought out a series of successful flying-boats from 1926. Also, the Consolidated Aircraft Corporation, formed in 1923, later built a very advanced high-wing flying-boat designated the PY-1 Admiral, which had the misfortune to make its first appearance in 1929, at the height of the Wall Street stock market disaster. Consequently, no immediate orders seemed to be forthcoming for Admirals from the U.S. Navy, but Consolidated converted the design to a passenger-carrying type, then renamed it Commodore. As already stated, a fleet of twelve Commodores was operated by the New York, Rio and Buenos Aires Line, and later by Pan American Airways; meanwhile, Consolidated forged ahead with development of the P2Y, an improved military version of the same machine.

The P2Y boats, accepted in some numbers by the U.S. Navy, were the direct predecessors of the much more successful Consolidated PBY or Catalina, a strut-braced parasol wing monoplane with a long, sweeping hull, and powered by twin radial engines. The PBY was inadequately armed with two hand-operated machine-guns in large perspex observation blisters, one each side of the boat aft of the main cabin; it was very slow, with a maximum speed of only 130 m.p.h.; and it could be extremely uncomfortable for men forced to spend many hours in the air. Nevertheless, it had a very long range of 3,100 miles, making it a multi-purpose machine able to go almost anywhere in the world, and many hundreds were built during the Second World War. The PBY-5A, an amphibian variant with a tricycle retractable undercarriage, appeared in due course, but was not so widely used, probably due to the loss in general performance occasioned by the weight of the wheel mechanism.

Shipborne, catapult-launched aircraft were, perhaps, not quite so popular in the United States as they were on the Continent and in Great Britain, but some biplane types of two-seater floatplane were produced by the Berliner-Joyce Aircraft Division of North American Aviation Inc. during the early 'thirties for reconnaissance work, and later the Vought-Sikorsky XOS2U Kingfisher and Curtiss SCC-1 Seagull were used by the U.S. Navy in its warships for the same purpose. All these seaplanes had a long central float and small wing-tip floats—a feature of American and Japanese floatplanes for many years. Incidentally, much of the pioneering work for catapult-launched aircraft development in the Imperial Japanese Navy was carried out by the German designer Ernst Heinkel, whose small but thriving post-war company built twin-float spotter biplanes for such battleships as the giant *Nagato* between the years 1925–30.

Heinkel's experience with catapult construction in Japan led to important contracts involving the installation of massive catapults on the *Westfalen, Schwabenland* and *Friesenland,* three ships taken into service by Lufthansa as floating bases for their new South Atlantic mail route. The heavily laden, tandem-engined special Dornier 10-t-Wal flying-boats in use at the time were only able to make such long journeys in two (or sometimes more) stages; and they therefore landed alongside the catapult ship stationed in mid-ocean, were hoisted aboard for refuelling, and then launched on their way once more. Some idea of the very powerful catapult mechanisms needed may be gathered from the weight of the Dornier Wal boats—22,000 lb.

In 1935, Claudius Dornier produced the Do 18, another tandem-engined commercial flying-boat, developed from the Wal and used on the North Atlantic service. A very fast and successful craft, the Do 18 achieved fame flying over a remarkably long route: from Germany to the Azores, refuelling aboard the mother-ship *Schwabenland,* then non-stop to New York, returning the same way. In March 1938, a Do 18 established a World long-distance seaplane record of 5,242 miles. In common with most German civil aircraft at that time, there was a military variant, the Do 18K, with gun positions in the nose and above the wing, between the engines.

The Dornier Do 24 was a larger, three-engined flying-boat, built in some numbers for the Netherlands, and used in the East Indies; although a Luftwaffe version was also produced for coastal patrol work. Like the Do 18 and many other Dornier boats, the Do 24 featured *Dornier-stummel*—or hull sponsons—but otherwise had a surprising resemblance to the Consolidated Catalina. It was followed by the Do 26, another commercial mail-carrying flying-boat, unusual in having its four motors mounted in twin tandem pairs above the wide monoplane wing, with the rear engines pivoted to swing the airscrews up out of the spray when taking off or landing on rough water. Despite its size, the

Do 26 could be successfully operated from catapult ships, and was used on the two-stage South Atlantic mail route.

Meanwhile, the Heinkel company was expanding at a remarkable rate. Twin-float S.1-type monoplanes had earlier been supplied to the Swedish Air Force, and in 1929 a development designated the He 12 was catapulted from the 50,000-ton transatlantic liner *Bremen* on her maiden voyage, arriving with passengers' mail in New York a full day before the great ship steamed majestically into harbour. For the new German Air Force, Heinkel later designed a succession of floatplanes, including the twin-engined biplane He 59, and the smaller He 60; the He 114, a rather curious sesquiplane; and the torpedo-carrying He 115 monoplane, which won a number of speed records in 1938.

However, the best German spotter reconnaissance floatplane at the outbreak of war—and for the next four years—was undoubtedly the Arado Ar 196, a two-seater monoplane developed from the general-purpose Ar 95-see biplane of 1935. Carried in a number of German warships, including the new pocket battleships later to become infamous as raiders, the Ar 196 also became well known for many exploits in squadron strength around the coasts of Axis-occupied Europe. It is perhaps significant that in Germany, not considered to be a seafaring nation, the development of such naval aircraft was encouraged; whereas France was content to struggle along with a handful of obsolete Loire flyingboats and floatplanes, and in Great Britain the Fleet Air Arm continued to be looked upon as a necessary nuisance.

Apart from the purely naval aspect, however, this twilight period between the wars had become a golden era for light civilian aircraft, and numbers of these were adapted as floatplanes at some time during their life. Undoubtedly the most famous of all was the de Havilland D.H. 60 Moth two-seater biplane, a remarkable little machine which revolutionised British private flying in the 'thirties, and was used (in the landplane wheeled version) by Amy Johnson for her record-breaking flight from England to Australia. Another equally redoubtable, but not so well-known, airwoman of this star-studded decade was Lady Bailey, the middle-aged wife of a South African millionaire, and the first woman to fly solo from England to the Cape and back, piloting a Cirrus-engined Moth.

A young Englishman who had spent much of his youth in New Zealand and then returned to Great Britain to take up private aviation as a career was destined to make light aircraft history with his de Havilland Gipsy Moth modified as a float-plane. In 1929 Francis Chichester—now Sir Francis Chichester and famous in later life as a round-the-world yachtsman of great courage and tenacity—had soloed at Brooklands, and after a trial flight around Europe set out in the December to fly himself back to Sydney single-handed. Despite a disappointing accident to his aircraft at Tripoli and numerous other minor setbacks, Chichester arrived safely at his destination on 25th January 1930, having completed the second solo flight to be made from England and successfully challenged the record set up by the more experienced Australian pilot Hinkler. A few months later, back once again in New Zealand, Chichester had made up his mind to attempt the immensely dangerous and lonely flight from Wellington to Sydney, a distance of 1,450 miles across the stormy, treacherous Tasman Sea. He therefore had his Moth *Elijah* fitted out as a floatplane and equipped with extra fuel tanks in preparation for the journey.

Chichester hoped to bridge the vast stretch of water in three stages, by way of two tiny stepping-stones, Norfolk Island and Lord Howe Island, such an astonishing feat of navigation to be undertaken by one man that few experts believed it could be accomplished. Then, while this lean, indefatigable pioneer was still proceeding with his plans, the Australian aviator Guy L. Menzies, piloting an Avro Avian, flew solo across the Tasman Sea west to east, from Sydney to South Island. Nevertheless, Chichester's thirst for new adventure refused to be quenched, and on the morning of 28th March 1931 he took off in his heavily laden Moth floatplane from Auckland and headed for the 'rock dumped in the Pacific' known as Norfolk Island. After many hours of lonely flying over the empty sea, he made a successful landing on a narrow strip of reasonably sheltered water in the lee of the 300-ft. cliffs that form so much of the island. With the willing help of the islanders, refuelling was eventually carried out and some minor engine repairs undertaken, no easy task with the flimsy little aircraft pitching and tossing as she rode the swell.

The first day of April found Chichester circling the bow-shaped, mountainous mass of Lord Howe Island, after a monotonous, uneventful flight over 500 miles of sea. He alighted with some difficulty on the storm-tossed water, and with the assistance of a few islanders who arrived in a launch, moored *Elijah* in the boat pool that formed part of the island's lagoon. But during the night a series of squalls blew up; and Chichester returned to his aircraft in the grey dawn to find it sunk at anchor, twisted and upside down. Despondent and in the lowest possible spirits, he nevertheless began the long, wearisome job of salvaging the Moth and its engine, stripping and cleaning every single part down to the smallest item, and then rebuilding the aeroplane once more; a Herculean task for a man with only limited engineering knowledge and no experience of aircraft construction at all.

However, only nine weeks later, having been assisted by almost the whole population of Lord Howe Island, Chichester felt that the rebuilt Moth would never be more ready for its first flight, and the biplane was launched by the pilot and some of his new-found friends, to rise and fall, once again a thing of fragile beauty, on the green waters of the lagoon. After a series of trials, Chichester considered *Elijah* airworthy enough to attempt the last lap of his flight to Sydney, and took off for the last time from the lagoon of Lord Howe Island. During this final stage of the journey, he was worried by recurring engine trouble, but safely reached the Australian coast some eighty miles north of Sydney, where he was received warmly but with little of the acclaim that had overwhelmed Amy Johnson. In recognition of his great achievement, Chichester was later awarded the Johnston Memorial Navigation Trophy, but the Tasman Sea crossing by no means ended his search for adventure, and he was soon in the air again, undertaking numerous other long-distance flights almost up to the outbreak of war. As already mentioned, this true Elizabethan has more recently attained fame at sea with his racing yacht, aptly named *Gypsy Moth III* to perpetuate the type of biplane that served him so well during the vintage years of private aviation.

Another exponent of the de Havilland Moth was Captain A. J. (now Sir Alan) Cobham, a man who has devoted much of his life to pioneering the air routes of the world. Born in 1894, Cobham served as a pilot in the Royal Flying Corps and later in the Royal Air Force, and upon demobilisation in 1919 decided to make a career for himself in civil aviation. He undertook aerial photography and other work for the de Havilland company, and during the years 1921 to 1925 made a number of long-distance flights in light aeroplanes, including a non-stop journey from Croydon to Zurich, flying the original Moth (G-EBKT) fitted with extra fuel tanks. A tireless champion of private flying, Cobham was also a regular entrant in the King's Cup Races, and during the 'thirties campaigned vigorously for more and better aerodromes.

On 30th June 1926, having already surveyed air routes between England and India and England and Capetown, Cobham took off from the Medway in a De Havilland D.H. 50 floatplane to undertake the most formidable survey task of all—establishing an air link between Great Britain and Australia. With him in the aircraft was his mechanic and close friend, A. B. Elliott. All went well until a dust storm over the Persian Gulf forced Cobham to descend to less than 50 ft. Suddenly there was an explosion in the cockpit and the immediate cry from Elliott of "I'm hit!" sounded startlingly loud in the abrupt silence after Cobham had instinctively switched off the engine. As there was no sign of any fire, the pilot started the engine again and hurriedly passed pencil and paper back to Elliott. The note that was returned by the mechanic indicated, in shaky writing, that it seemed a petrol pipe had burst and wounded him; he was losing a lot of blood and in a very weak condition. There was nothing Cobham could do except make all haste to reach Basra aerodrome.

Elliott died from shock and severe gunshot wounds the following evening. Cobham later found that a rifle bullet, fired up at the low-flying aircraft by some stray Bedouin, had pierced the petrol pipe, passed through Elliott's arm and both of his lungs and embedded itself in his back. Shocked by such a tragic end to his friend's life, Cobham at first considered abandoning the flight, but an R.A.F. mechanic, Sergeant Ward, volunteered to accompany him, and he decided to carry on. Despite severe tropical storms that forced them to land on more than one occasion, the two aviators arrived at Darwin on 5th August, to be greeted by wildly cheering crowds.

Cobham and his mechanic soon afterwards flew on to Melbourne and an even more riotous reception, before making the long return journey to England. On 1st October 1926 he brought the D.H.50 neatly in to land on the Thames opposite the Houses of Parliament, an excited crowd of over a million people and hundreds of shrieking sirens acclaiming the first man to fly from England to Australia and back. For this achievement, Cobham received a well-earned knighthood, but he was no man to rest on his laurels. The following year he was pilot and commander of the 25,000-mile Short Singapore flying-boat survey expedition around Africa already mentioned; and in 1931 he undertook an exploration flight up the Nile to the Congo. Also, he was a pioneer of travelling air displays, and during the 'thirties his colourful 'flying circus' visited almost every major town in the British Isles, attracting many thousands of people to light aviation for the first time.

Shortly before the outbreak of war, Sir Alan Cobham had been experimenting with the problem of refuelling in flight, and after 1948 his improved systems were adopted with great success by the United States Army and Navy Air Forces as well as the Royal Air Force. Now living quietly in the autumn of his years, he can look back on a lifetime spent circumnavigating every continent in the world. "Flying is a luxury nowadays," Sir Alan has commented, "and no longer an adventure."

8

INTO BATTLE: 1939–40

∞∞∞∞∞∞∞∞∞∞∞∞∞∞∞∞∞∞∞∞∞∞∞∞∞∞∞∞∞∞∞∞∞∞∞∞

On 17th September 1939, only two weeks after the British Prime Minister Neville Chamberlain had informed the House of Commons that the nation was at war with Germany—"This is a sad day for all of us, and to none is it sadder than to me"—an enemy submarine, the U.29, sighted H.M.S. *Courageous* in the Bristol Channel, turning slowly into the wind to receive aircraft. A few moments later, the 26,500-ton carrier reeled to the shock of two torpedoes fired in quick succession and sank almost at once, with heavy loss of life. This tragedy, coming within three days of *Ark Royal* and her destroyer escort fighting a running battle with another submarine—the U.39, which fired two torpedoes without result and then crash-dived under a hail of depth charges—caused consternation in Admiralty circles; the small German Navy, under Grand Admiral Raeder, was showing surprisingly fierce teeth very early in the war.

However, the captain of U.39 must have regretted attacking *Ark Royal,* for his boat was so damaged by the depth charges that it was forced to the surface and then sunk by gunfire from the destroyers. At about the same time, three Blackburn Skuas previously flown off from *Ark Royal* sighted the German submarine U.30 and went in to the attack; but two of the aircraft dived too steeply and hurtled into the sea at full speed. Despite heavy machine-gun fire from the surviving Skua, the submarine escaped by crash-diving after taking the two British pilots prisoner of war. It was later learned that both air gunners had been killed, the first casualties to be suffered by the Fleet Air Arm in the Second World War.

Just over a week later, on 26th September, the *Ark Royal* was out again, in company with the battleships *Rodney* and *Nelson* and a large force of destroyers. A flight of Skuas from 803 Squadron took off on routine reconnaissance patrol despite the misty weather, and while circling the British ships the pilots sighted their first German aircraft—three camouflaged Dornier Do 18 flying-boats—very low on the water and obviously shadowing the battle squadron. The Skuas opened fire, damaging two of the Dorniers, which got away; the third dropped heavily into the water and slowly sank, the crew taking to a rubber dinghy. Lieutenant B. E. McEwen and his air gunner, Petty Officer B. M. Seymour, were officially credited with this victory, the first enemy aircraft to be destroyed in the war by any Service.

It turned out to be a memorable day for *Ark Royal* and the sixteen hundred men whose lives were encompassed by her steel walls. No sooner had the Skuas landed back aboard than a twin-engined Heinkel He III roared out of the low cloud, catching the anti-aircraft gun crews unawares; there was a quick hammering of machine-gun fire, then the huge 2,000-lb. bomb came plunging down. Using full helm, the *Ark Royal* swung hard-a-starboard, moments before a great fountain of water erupted alongside the flight deck, making the great ship shudder from stem to stern, her bows rising high into the air. As she wallowed back on to an even keel, the He III reappeared and bullets again whined and ricocheted around the bridge and deck gun positions while below men were climbing shakily to their feet, ears ringing from the shattering concussion. A moment later, the enemy bomber was a speck on the horizon, pursued by the belated thunder of many anti-aircraft guns.

It had been a very near thing; the first of many such narrow escapes for *Ark Royal* and her crew. The pilot of the Heinkel, a young man named Francke, returned to base and reported merely that he had attacked, and probably damaged, a British carrier in the North Sea, but the Goebbels propaganda machine seized the opportunity to invent a great victory, and lurid details were published in the German press purporting to describe the sinking of *Ark Royal*. During the next few months, that same 'success' was repeated over and over again on the enemy radio, until even the announcers must have wearied of broadcasting such obvious lies. As for the bewildered Francke, he received a personal telegram of congratulations from Goering, immediate promotion, and the award of the Iron Cross.

October brought increasing reports of a fast German raider—at first thought to be the pocket battleship *Admiral Scheer*—operating in South Atlantic waters. A number of British warships were therefore ordered to new dispositions in an attempt to encircle the raider and bring her to battle, and *Ark Royal* was detached from the Home Fleet to join the battleship *Renown* as part of Force K based on Freetown, Sierra Leone. Despite the fact that eight groups of British warships, including four carriers, were finally out searching for the raider, she remained elusive and became a serious threat by sinking no less than 50,000 tons of our shipping during the next three months. The Fleet Air Arm reconnaissance Swordfish and Walrus aircraft spent day after day in long, monotonous patrols over vast expanses of ocean; always with nothing to report, no sign of the powerful grey ship—later definitely identified as the pocket battleship *Admiral Graf Spee*—thrusting at top speed through the waves.

Radioed messages from more sinking merchant ships sent *Ark Royal* and *Renown* hurrying to Cape Town, then to lonely St. Helena, but to no avail. At last, on 13th December 1939, Force H, comprising the heavy cruiser *Exeter* and the light cruisers *Ajax* and *Achilles,* with Commodore Henry Harwood flying his flag in *Ajax,* was some 150 miles off the mouth of the River Plate when smoke was sighted on the horizon. From *Exeter* came the long-awaited signal, "I think it is a pocket battleship." Soon afterwards, the top-hamper of the *Graf Spee* came into view, and at 6.14 a.m. the German ship fired the opening salvo from her 11-in. guns.

It was a hard, slogging battle, with the gunnery very accurate on both sides; but the *Graf Spee* quickly concentrated her main armament against her most powerful opponent, *Exeter,* inflicting heavy damage and many casualties. Fires were started; all steering lines were out and communications temporarily lost; and splinters flayed the superstructure. Efforts were made to launch *Exeter's* two Walrus aircraft, but they had to be jettisoned after being hit by shellfire while still on the catapult. Saturated by the terrible weight of explosive from the pocket battleship's 11-in. guns, *Exeter* reeled away, barely under control.

To divide the enemy fire, Commodore Harwood ordered *Ajax* and *Achilles* to close the range, and the light cruisers hammered away so savagely at the *Graf Spee* with rapid salvoes from their small 6-in. guns that she was forced to turn about, hit again and again. The Fairey Seafox carried in *Ajax* was catapulted into the air, with Lieutenant E. D. G. Lewin as pilot and Lieutenant R. E. Kearney as observer; and not only spotted the fall of shot throughout the action, but also passed low over the German ship from time to time, spraying her bridge area with machine-gun fire. The Arado Ar 196 floatplane carried by *Graf Spee* was prepared for launching, but a shell from one of the British ships burst almost on the catapult, knocking it out of action; Harwood's rapid 6-in. fire at close range was beginning to achieve a deadly purpose. Finally, at 6.36 a.m., the harassed pocket battleship retreated westwards under a smoke-screen, hotly engaged by *Ajax* and *Achilles*.

The running battle continued for the rest of the day, with *Graf Spee* heading for the mouth of the River Plate. Her salvoes were still falling with undiminished accuracy; one 11-in. shell bursting alongside *Achilles* wrought fearful havoc in the bridge and gunnery control tower of the light cruiser. Another heavy shell silenced *Ajax's* after turrets, and the superstructure of *Exeter* had long been reduced to a shambles—not that the German pocket battleship was in fit condition for anything than a repair yard. As a final angry gesture, she fired her torpedoes at *Ajax,* but the watchful Seafox still droned overhead, and a word of warning radioed from Lieutenant Lewin made the cruiser swing away from the tell-track white tracks so easily discernible from the air.

At midnight, the *Graf Spee* was in neutral waters, off the brightly lit port of Montevideo, capital of Uruguay, where she was to remain, with the eyes of the whole world upon her, for the next three days. Skilful British diplomacy and the spreading of many rumours led the captain of the pocket battleship, Hans Langsdorff, to believe that a large number of powerful units of the Royal Navy were gathering outside; although in fact only one heavy cruiser—the *Cumberland*—had arrived to reinforce Harwood's battered squadron. It was true that the other British hunting forces were, of course, on the way, including *Ark Royal* and *Renown* but some time would pass before they could arrive on the scene. Meanwhile, Langsdorff had to make up his mind whether to break out and face the heavy opposition he feared lay in wait for him, or hand his ship and crew over to the Uruguayan authorities for internment.

On the evening of 17th December, the *Graf Spee* was seen to weigh anchor and then steam slowly towards the harbour entrance, followed by the *Tacoma,* a German merchant ship also taking temporary shelter in neutral waters. Watched by crowds of excited and puzzled Montevideans, the pocket battleship stopped just outside the harbour, quickly transferred most of her crew to the *Tacoma,* and then got under way once more. For a few moments, a strange, expectant hush fell on the city; then smoke and flame abruptly leapt from the decks of the *Graf Spee* and her grey hull was riven asunder by vast internal explosions. With her superstructure ablaze, the battleship began to settle by the stern, while high above the tilting gunnery control tower *Ajax*'s Fairey Seafox—which had never failed to make reconnaissance flights every day—radioed back to her parent cruiser, with great simplicity, the historic message, "*Graf Spee* has blown herself up."

Thus early in the war came to an inglorious end the career of *Admiral Graf Spee,* one of the latest and most powerful ships in the German Fleet. His command scuttled and crew interned, Langsdorff shot himself three days later, the first of a number of German commanders to choose suicide after defeat, following the ruthless Prussian code of honour that had existed for more than a hundred years. Among various British decorations to commemorate the Royal Navy's victory at the River Plate, Lieutenant Lewin, the pilot of the little Seafox biplane that had performed such admirable service during and after the battle, was awarded the Distinguished Service Order. He was the first Fleet Air Arm officer to receive a decoration in the Second World War.

In less than a week, British sea-flying aircraft were again in the news. On 21st September the tramp steamer *Kensington Court* was torpedoed by a U-boat about seventy miles off the Scillies and sent out urgent distress signals, which were picked up by two Short Sunderland flying-boats of R.A.F. Coastal Command, one from No. 204 and the other from No. 228 Squadron, out on reconnaissance patrol. When the first Sunderland arrived over the merchantman, it was in a sinking condition, with the survivors jammed like sardines in a wallowing, overcrowded lifeboat. The flying-boat therefore alighted on the very rough sea and took aboard some twenty men. As it made the long, slow take-off—rising at last up on the step, all four engines thundering at full power, the spray creaming back in great clouds from behind the hull and wing-tip floats—the second Sunderland touched down, rocking wildly from side to side in the Atlantic waves. The remaining seamen scrambled out of their lifeboat and into the big aircraft; then it, too, was swaying over the water at top speed to finally become airborne. An hour later, the entire crew of the *Kensington Court* had been safely landed in England.

As already mentioned, the development of the versatile Sunderland could be traced back to the Short R.24/31 'Knuckleduster' completed in 1934. The same year, Short Bros. commenced designing a very advanced, large, all-metal monoplane flying-boat intended for Imperial Airways, which showed remarkable faith in the new type by placing an order valued at some £1,750,000 for twenty-eight of the machines, direct from the drawing-board. Thus was born the extremely beautiful prototype of the famous Empire C-Class flying-boats, powered by four 920-h.p. Bristol Pegasus radial engines. Named *Canopus* before its maiden flight on 4th July 1936, this aircraft featured the later well-known deep, double-decked hull, with ample space for the crew, large freight hold, a galley, baggage compartments, toilet facilities, and cabins for twenty-four day or sixteen night passengers. It went into service on the Imperial Airways Mediterranean route less than two weeks later.

The succeeding Empire boats—*Centaurus, Caledonia, Cambria* and the rest—helped to give Great Britain complete superiority on the civil air routes of the world up to the outbreak of war. The later G-Class boats, generally similar to the C-Class but considerably larger, were a development intended for non-stop transatlantic mail services, the only three machines—*Golden Hind, Golden Fleece* and *Golden Horn*—appearing in 1939. They were re-equipped as military flying-boats and used for ocean patrol work during the first two years of war; then fitted out to carry priority passengers and diplomatic mail on the perilous England via West Africa to Lisbon route.

Various experiments were being made at this time in an attempt to overcome the problems associated with high-speed carrying of mail and urgent freight over long distances, some of the research involving the design of a composite aircraft in conjunction with Short Brothers at Rochester. The Short-Mayo machine consisted of a medium-sized, four-engined floatplane named *Mercury* attached above a modified Empire C-Class flying-boat named *Maia,* and was used with some success during 1938. In July of that year, *Mercury* was lifted into the air by *Maia,* separated over Foynes, Ireland, and thus made the first non-stop flight between Britain and Montreal, carrying a payload of 1,000 lb. The following October, *Mercury* was again released from *Maia* for a long-range flight from Dundee to South Africa, setting up a World distance record for seaplanes of 5,998 miles. However, despite many advantages, the Short-Mayo method of long-distance service was expensive and complicated, needing further research; but the outbreak of war prevented the potentialities of such composite aircraft for commercial use being more fully exploited.

Meanwhile, a military development of the Empire class flying-boat had been designed to fulfil the requirements of Air Ministry specification R.2/33, which called for a large four-engined monoplane to replace the biplane craft that had served the Royal Air Force well for nearly twenty years. In October 1937 the prototype Sunderland made its first flight, to be followed during the next two years by the further twenty-one boats completed in accordance with the final specification 22/36. As in the Empire class boats, the hull of the Sunderland was divided into two decks, the lower deck being fitted out with nose mooring equipment, crew rest rooms and a galley. Above was the spacious flight deck for two pilots, flight engineer, navigator and wireless operator; while immediately aft was the large bomb compartment. For the first time in a British flying-boat, power-operated Frazer-Nash gun turrets were fitted in the bow and stern of the Sunderland, later supplemented by single free-mounted Vickers guns in the starboard and port upper beam positions. The standard power plants were four Bristol Pegasus XXII radial engines, giving a maximum speed of 210 m.p.h., and the endurance was just over thirteen hours. During that time, on long ocean patrols, the crew quite literally lived aboard, preparing their own meals and sleeping in hammocks slung within the vast hull during their off-duty periods; while the big Sunderland trundled steadily on over miles of water, easily the most comfortable of all military flying-boats ever to enter service.

During 1939 an order was placed by the Air Ministry for thirty-six more new Sunderlands—741 would, in fact, have been built when production finally ceased in October 1945—and soon afterwards the first four Sunderland squadrons, Nos. 204, 210, 228 and 230, were ready for operational service. The *Kensington Court* episode was followed by a rather curious incident on 30th January 1940, when the captain of a German submarine scuttled his boat upon sighting a Sunderland of No. 228 Squadron diving towards him; but three months later another of the big flying-boats demonstrated its wonderful defensive capabilities by successfully tackling six attacking Junkers Ju 88 long-range fighters, shooting one down in flames and forcing another to crash-land in Norway.

On 9th April 1940, when the so-called Phoney War came to an abrupt end with the German attack on Denmark and Norway, flying-boats on both sides were soon playing an invaluable part in the campaign; Sunderlands being used to convey senior officers, including the commander of Allied Forces in Central Norway, Major-General Carton de Wiart, to their advanced headquarters. The German forces, penetrating against heavy opposition to Oslo, Kristiansand, Stavanger, Bergen, Trondheim and Narvik, used large numbers of three-engined Junkers Ju 52/3mW monoplanes—floatplane versions of the ubiquitous Ju 52/3m troop-carrying landplane in extensive service with the Luftwaffe—and a few of the curious, twin-boomed Blohm und Voss Bv 138 flying-boats originally produced for long-range reconnaissance duties.

The Fleet Air Arm also soon found itself plunged headlong into the hopeless struggle to save Norway. On 10th April sixteen Blackburn Skuas of Nos. 800 and 803 Squadrons took off in the bitter cold of early morning from their wind-swept base at Hatston in the Orkneys and crossed the North Sea, flying very low as they approached the Norwegian coast. The two squadrons flew up Bergen fiord, the aircraft rising and falling to clear the high mountains on either side; then abruptly the harbour was spread out below them, with the 6,000-ton German cruiser *Königsberg* lying at anchor outside. Led by Lieutenant W. P. Lucy, the first squadron gained height, then the dive-bombers heeled over in rapid succession and fell with roaring engines towards the target. As anti-aircraft guns around the fiord and on the enemy warship crashed into action, the 300-lb. bombs left their racks, the Skuas zoomed up through the flak and smoking tracer, and the second squadron, under Captain R. T. Partridge, R.M., came sweeping in over the harbour.

As the last Skuas raced for home, almost invisible against the towering mountains, a tall pillar of black smoke, tinged with crimson, erupted from the *Königsberg;* she had been directly hit by three bombs, and a fourth had exploded just alongside, opening up her hull below the waterline. Still at anchor, the stricken ship slowly settled and after fifty minutes capsized, though without great loss of life among her crew. To the Skuas of Nos. 800 and 803 Squadrons thus went the honour of sinking the first German warship by air attack in the Second World War; and a week later the same aircraft returned to Bergen fiord, sank the supply steamer *Bahrenfels* at anchor, and set a flying-boat ablaze. Other Fleet Air Arm machines, initially from the carrier *Furious,* bombed and strafed the German invasion areas again and again, sinking seaplanes at their moorings, destroying tankers in harbour, and burning down many of the harbour wooden buildings, scattering enemy troops and vehicles.

It was a lost cause; a disastrous campaign for the Allied forces from the very beginning. The aircraft-carrier *Glorious,* hurriedly recalled from the Mediterranean, flew off a squadron of R.A.F. Gloster Gladiator biplane fighters to operate from the frozen surface of Lake Lesjeskog, but within two days the temporary airfield had been rendered untenable by repeated attacks from German bombers. On 24th April *Ark Royal* also arrived in the Norwegian theatre of operations, and her Swordfish and Skua aircraft ranged far and wide in support of the British expeditionary force, despite having to battle against tremendous odds. At last, only Narvik could be considered still in Allied hands; and that was an isolated, tenuous hold, likely to be broken at any moment.

On 13th April, three days after the savage battle between five British and eight German destroyers in Narvik harbour that brought the first Victoria Cross of the war to the mortally wounded British commander, Captain B. A. Warburton-Lee, the great battleship *Warspite* led a flotilla of destroyers into the fiord. She had previously catapulted off one of her floatplanes, a Fairey Swordfish Piloted by Petty Officer F. C. Rice, with Lieutenant-Commander W. L. M. Brown as observer and Leading Airman M. G. Pacey as air gunner; and the big, unwieldy biplane, flying at mast-head height, preceded the battle squadron between the high mountains, heading, it seemed, right into the lion's mouth. At least seven enemy destroyers were known to be in the fiord, together with a number of supply ships and some flying-boats and transport craft, while around the shore were two battalions of mountain troops under the command of General Eduard Dietl.

The *Warspite* opened fire, and the mountains echoed and re-echoed to the rolling thunder of her mighty 15-in. guns. The radioed reports from the Swordfish circling overhead at once proved to be of immense value, relaying the exact positions of lurking German destroyers, spotting the fall of shot and giving urgent warning when enemy torpedoes were fired. Majestically, *Warspite* continued up the long Ofot Fiord, firing regular salvoes, the terrible effect of her guns at such comparatively short range recalling similar actions in the Gallipoli campaign of that other, earlier war. All the German destroyers were destroyed, set on fire or beached; some of the merchantmen were left in a sinking condition; and many of the shore batteries were knocked out. Meanwhile the battleship's Swordfish ventured up the dangerously narrow Herjangs Fiord, coming unexpectedly upon an enemy submarine, the U.64, which was bombed and sunk before it could take evasive action. "I doubt if ever a shipborne aircraft has been used to such good purpose as it was during this operation . . ." commented the British commanding officer, Vice-Admiral W. J. Whitworth, in his despatch to the Admiralty after the battle.

For some hours, Dietl and his men were completely disorganised by the *Warspite*'s action, but too much time was lost while the Allied forces hesitated where to land reinforcements, and the Germans retained their bridgehead. With the Luftwaffe reigning supreme in the air over what soon became a whole series of embattled fronts—on 10th May Hitler's blitzkrieg had blasted a path of fire and steel across France and the Low Countries—the situation in Norway deteriorated until it became impossible to hold out any longer. It was therefore decided to effect an evacuation, and more R.A.F. fighters were hurriedly committed to the area in order to cover the withdrawal. On 18th May the carriers *Glorious* and *Furious* arrived with these and other aircraft, flying off sixteen Gloster Gladiators of No. 263 Squadron to operate from a bleak, snow-covered airstrip at Bardufoss, north of Narvik, and also disembarking a number of Royal Navy Supermarine Walruses at Harstad for communications and other duties.

In reply to this renewed Allied air activity, the Germans threw in still more squadrons of Heinkel He 111 bombers and Messerschmitt Bf 109 fighters, and seaplanes of all types—Dornier Do 24s and Do 26s, Heinkel He 115s and the inevitable Junkers Ju 52/3mWs, even the big, four-engined Blohm und Voss Ha 139 transports, of which only three had been built, just before the war. On 26th May a squadron of R.A.F. Hawker Hurricanes was flown off *Glorious* to reinforce the Gladiators heavily engaged at Bardufoss; and for a few days the flood of enemy aircraft was stemmed, the German bombers and troop transports suffering badly at the hands of the fast, eight-gun monoplane fighters. On 28th May two Dornier Do 26s attempting to disembark mountain troops near Narvik were both shot down by roving Hurricanes; one of the flying-boats, piloted by the well-known German exponent of seaplane development, Oberleutnant Graf Schack, making a forced landing just outside the town. The same day, the Allies began destroying iron ore and other works in the Narvik area, immediately prior to evacuation.

Thus ended the unfortunate Norwegian campaign. At last, the time came to withdraw the R.A.F. fighters, sadly reduced in numbers, but still operating from the bomb-torn, makeshift runways of Bardufoss. The Gladiators and Hurricanes had, of course, to be landed back aboard the aircraft-carriers that had brought them; no easy task for trained naval airmen, and a terribly hazardous feat for the R.A.F. pilots, who had no experience of deck landing operations at all. Nevertheless, the ten surviving Gladiators were successfully taken aboard *Glorious,* and soon afterwards the Hurricane pilots surprised the Admiralty deck-flying experts by landing their monoplanes on the carrier neatly and without any trouble, the first time this had been achieved with such modern, high-speed aircraft. Watched by the men of *Ark Royal,* now also returned to Norway to assist in the evacuation, *Glorious* turned for home, her escorting destroyers *Acasta* and *Ardent* rising and falling in the stormy arctic seas.

Meanwhile, the German battleships *Scharnhorst* and *Gneisenau,* with the heavy cruiser *Admiral Hipper* and four destroyers, had left Kiel bound for north Norwegian waters, with orders to sink any British ships they encountered, and finally bombard the Allied base at Harstad. On the afternoon of 8th June this powerful squadron sighted *Glorious,* not long after *Hipper* had been detached to intercept British convoys returning to Britain; and both battleships at once opened fire with their main 11-in. armament, closing to 20,000 yd. Direct hits were scored on the bridge of the carrier and her hangars were soon put out of action, salvo after salvo plunging with deadly accuracy on the reeling warship, in bitter contrast to the brave reply from her pitiful little outranged guns. Meanwhile, *Acasta* and *Ardent* raced into the fray, attempting to lay a smoke screen, but the *Glorious* was soon well ablaze, her flight deck opened up and her super-structure reduced to wreckage.

The German battleships now switched their well-aimed fire on to the two destroyers, which replied with guns and torpedoes, but a hail of shells, falling squarely on to *Ardent,* sank her within minutes, shortly before *Glorious* turned over to starboard and went down. The gallant little *Acasta,* battered by a fearful weight of gunfire, headed directly for the *Scharnhorst* and fired a last salvo of torpedoes, which struck the enemy battleship near her aft turret, resulting in severe damage. All the time, *Gneisenau* continued to slam shells into *Acasta* at point-blank range, and in the early evening the destroyer sank, her task as escort having been performed to the letter, and with complete devotion to duty regardless of the consequences.

On 11th June, a Norwegian fishing-smack picked up thirty-eight survivors from the *Glorious* and one man from the *Acasta;*

all that remained of the vast complement that had expected to reach home from ravaged Norway. Every one of the Gladiator pilots had been lost, together with their fighters; indeed, not a single aircraft was saved. There remained one small entry on the credit side of a tragic account—*Scharnhorst*'s extensive damage had caused the abandonment of the sortie, and she had been forced to put into harbour at Trondheim. In a desperate attempt to sink the crippled battleship at anchor, *Ark Royal* immediately flew off sixteen Blackburn Skuas, which dived through appalling weather and a wall of anti-aircraft fire to drop their bombs, but without success. German fighters took to the air in large numbers, and nearly half of the Skua force was destroyed.

It was a sombre homecoming from Norway for all the British ships, with Allied fortunes at their lowest ebb, darkened by the fall of France, and brightened only momentarily by the miracle of Dunkirk. Nevertheless, at last the tired Chamberlain government had collapsed, and Winston Churchill was in power: "I felt as if I were walking with Destiny, and that all my past life had been but a preparation for this hour and for this trial," he was to write afterwards. Yet in the first of his historic fighting speeches the new Prime Minister had "nothing to offer but blood, toil, tears and sweat"; it was a grim warning that a long and weary struggle lay ahead.

9

TARANTO AND MATAPAN: 1940-41

Having waited until Belgium and the Netherlands had surrendered, and ensured that the Allied armies in France were broken
beyond repair by the German armour thrusting forward to the
Channel coast, the dictator of Italy decided at last to enter the
war on Hitler's side. On 10th June 1940 Benito Mussolini
officially opened hostilities against France, sending thirty-two
divisions into action on the Alpine front; a week later, the same
troops had still failed to tidy up a mere six French divisions of
exhausted infantry, and the Germans eventually moved in from
the rear to do the job for them. Within another week, France had
capitulated, but Hitler allowed Mussolini only the few yards of
territory Italian troops had actually conquered, leaving the Duce
"very much embarrassed", according to the diaries of his
diplomat son-in-law, Count Ciano. In truth, as Mussolini must
have feared, Hitler had had the last word.

From the British point of view, Mussolini's tardy intervention
in the war implied trouble in the Mediterranean at an early date
from the powerful Italian Fleet and the Italian Air Force—the
Regia Aeronautica. In common with his German ally, Mussolini
had from the beginning appreciated the value of air power,
encouraging the steady growth of his air arm until by 1940 it
consisted of about five thousand machines, including over a
thousand bombers. Undoubtedly the best Italian bomber—and
almost certainly the most efficient land-based torpedo-bomber to
appear during the Second World War—was the three-engined
Savoia-Marchetti SM 79 Sparviero, built in large numbers, and
widely used in the Mediterranean and other areas. Also in service
was the much slower and more unwieldy Savoia-Marchetti SM
81 Pipistrello; the twin-engined and twin-tailed Fiat BR 20

Cicogna medium bomber; and Italy's only heavy bomber, the Piaggio P.108B, a big, four-engined machine not unlike the American B-17 Flying Fortress in general appearance.

The Italian fighter force was numerically large enough to seem a dangerous opponent, but the strength was an illusion, consisting as it did of too many obsolescent Fiat CR 42 Falco biplanes and sadly under-powered Fiat G.50 and Macchi C.200 Saetta monoplanes. Of the Italian marine aircraft in service at the time, mention need only be made of the Cant Z.506B Airone floatplane, a large, three-motored machine equipping two groups of the Regia Aeronautica; and the single-engined Cant Z.501 Gabbiano flying-boat, used for patrol duties by some fifteen squadrons until the 1943 Armistice.

On 11th June—the day after Mussolini had declared war on Great Britain and her Allies—Italian Savoia-Marchetti SM 79 and Fiat BR 20 bombers, without any fighter escort, attacked Malta, dropping a number of bombs on Valetta. They were met by the island's defending fighter force of six Gloster Sea Gladiator biplanes, and although none of the attackers were shot down, a second wave of bombers later in the day was accompanied by Fiat CR 42 and Macchi C.200 fighters. Thus began a whole series of heavy raids by the Regia Aeronautica on Malta during the summer of 1940, although much of the Italian bombing was inaccurate and the resulting damage negligible compared with the havoc wrought by Kesselring's large-scale Luftwaffe attacks two years later. The little flight of Sea Gladiators flew hundreds of sorties against this flood of enemy aircraft, admittedly without shooting down many bombers, but certainly harassing the Italian pilots; and on more than one occasion driving off the escorting fighters. However, servicing difficulties and the rough-and-ready landing conditions finally reduced the Gladiator force to three airworthy machines—the same biplanes later to become famous as *Faith, Hope* and *Charity* and remembered with affection as symbols of the air defence of besieged Malta. In July a Hurricane squadron arrived to reinforce the ageing, battle-scarred Gladiators, and for the next three months the attackers suffered increasing losses.

Meanwhile, in April 1940, the first of the Royal Navy's armoured fleet carriers had been commissioned for service. The

23,000-ton *Illustrious* was equipped with a fighter reconnaissance squadron made up of Fairey Fulmar and Blackburn Skua aircraft, and two squadrons of Fairey Swordfish torpedo-bombers; the Fulmars being new and extremely promising eight-gun two-seater fighters which it was hoped would be able to meet the latest German and Italian aircraft on equal terms. Operating in the Mediterranean were now two powerful British naval forces: the Eastern Mediterranean Fleet, based on Alexandria, which included H.M.S. *Eagle,* the long outdated carrier of the 'twenties, with a handful of Swordfish aircraft; and Force H, based on Gibraltar, and composed of the battle-cruiser *Hood,* the old battle-ships *Valiant* and *Resolution,* the aircraft carrier *Ark Royal,* two cruisers. and eleven destroyers. At the end of August, *Illustrious* was also directed to the Mediterranean theatre of operations, thus becoming a most valuable asset to the Commander-in-Chief there, Admiral Sir Andrew Cunningham.

Despite her age, *Eagle* had already proved that she was still a first-class carrier, when the Italian Fleet, consisting of two battle-ships, sixteen cruisers and a large force of destroyers, was sighted on 9th July, roaming at will in the central Mediterranean, and apparently prepared to risk battle. Admiral Cunningham ordered his fleet to alter course and intercept the enemy ships, while *Eagle* flew off two successive striking forces of Swordfish, which attacked through heavy anti-aircraft fire and badly damaged an Italian cruiser. Soon afterwards the British warships opened fire at extreme range, but the enemy fleet at once withdrew at high speed to its home base at Taranto, coming under the protection of many land-based fighter and bomber squadrons.

Also in the July, Force H, commanded by Admiral Sir James Somerville, had taken part in one of the most unhappy incidents of the Second World War—"this melancholy action", as Mr Winston Churchill was to call it—against the French Fleet at Oran and Mers-el-Kebir. After the fall of France, it had been hoped that her strong 'fleet in being' could be prevented from becoming a welcome addition to the small German Navy, and British proposals were in due course put forward making arrange-ments for the French warships to join the Allied forces. All suggestions, including a final request that his ships be scuttled within six hours, were rejected by the French commander-in-

chief, Admiral Gensoul; and on 3rd July Force H arrived, grey
and menacing, off Oran.

Captain C. S. Holland, in command of *Ark Royal,* spent much
of the day trying to persuade Admiral Gensoul to change his
mind, but the French commander remained unmoved, and Holland sadly returned to his ship. There was a last signal from the
Admiralty to the British flagship, stating, "French ships must
comply with our terms or sink themselves or be sunk by you
before dark," but Somerville had received much the same instructions the previous day, and been told, "You are charged with
one of the most disagreeable and difficult tasks that a British
Admiral has ever been faced with, but we have complete
confidence in you. . . ." He had already given the order to open
fire.

Directed by spotting Swordfish from *Ark Royal,* the mighty
guns of *Hood, Valiant* and *Resolution* simultaneously belched
smoke and flame, their salvoes sinking the old battleship *Bretagne*
and damaging the flagship *Dunkerque,* which was forced to run
aground. Two destroyers were also sunk, and a number of
similar lightly armoured ships damaged; not an outstanding
example of accurate shooting from 15-in. guns firing on station-
ary targets, without opposition. Meanwhile, five other Swordfish
from *Ark Royal* were at work dropping mines in the entrance to
Mers-el-Kebir harbour, effectively sealing in the few French ships
anchored there.

In the gathering dusk the modern battleship *Strasbourg,* with an
escort of six destroyers, slid quietly out of Oran harbour and
headed eastwards at full speed. Six Swordfish armed with bombs
took off from *Ark Royal* in pursuit, and sighted the French
warship as darkness fell, but failed to secure any hits on her. A
squadron of Swordfish carrying torpedoes also met with no success; without any previous experience of night torpedo attack
procedure against heavily-screened capital ships, the pilots
dropped their torpedoes from too great a distance, and the *Strasbourg* got clean away. There was little more that could be done in
this unfortunate business except make certain that *Dunkerque,* at
least, would remain immobilised for some considerable time. On
6th July three flights of Swordfish, again from the overworked
Ark Royal, came in very low over Oran harbour and dropped

their torpedoes, which ran perfectly on course to the target. Four out of six of the deadly missiles struck home; and the useful life of the French battleship was ended.

Admiral Cunningham's Mediterranean Fleet had still to deal with the dangerous force of Italian warships divided between Naples and Taranto naval bases; a hazardous operation, but one that had been considered by the Admiralty for some years before the war. Although the Fleet Air Arm pilots lacked experience in making torpedo attacks against fast-moving, heavily escorted battleships, exercises had long been carried out involving such attacks on anchored ships in defended harbours, more particularly by aircraft of H.M.S. *Glorious* at Malta. By 1939 the most likely enemy target in the event of war had already been envisaged as the Italian Fleet, possibly lying in the wide expanse of Taranto harbour; and the following year Admiralty plans only needed bringing up to date for the great sortie to take place. It was true that the gallant *Glorious* had gone for ever, but *Illustrious* was there, with Rear-Admiral A. L. Lyster—who had served as captain of *Glorious* until 1939—flying his flag in the new carrier.

It had been decided that the operation would be mounted on the night of 21st October 1940—the 135th anniversary of Nelson's victory at Trafalgar—but the attack was delayed when a serious fire broke out in the main hangar of *Illustrious* and damaged most of her aircraft, some beyond repair. The carrier pilots had to sit back and wait for three weeks until the next moon period, it being impossible to risk such a low-level sortie in total darkness. Meanwhile, R.A.F. Martin Maryland reconnaissance aircraft from Malta kept an eye on Taranto to see if any changes occurred in the dispositions of the Italian ships lying there. The photographs showed clearly that of the main fleet, five out of six possible battleships and nearly all the Duce's cruisers and destroyers lay in the harbour, protected by anti-torpedo nets and barrage balloons, and surrounded by hundreds of anti-aircraft guns of all calibres. On 10th November the sixth Italian battle ship arrived at Taranto, to set the stage for one of the most remarkable attacks by carrier-borne aircraft in the history of naval aviation.

The following day, the carrier *Illustrious,* with an escort of four cruisers and four destroyers, was detached from the Mediterranean Fleet to take up a position some 180 miles from Taranto. She was heavily laden with aircraft, having transferred five Swordfish and crews from the weary old *Eagle,* which had proved too aged and bomb-shattered to join in the action. Two striking forces from Nos. 815 and 819 Squadrons were to be directed against Taranto: one composed of twelve Swordfish led by Lieutenant-Commander K. Williamson; the other consisting of nine Swordfish under the command of Lieutenant-Commander J. W. Hale. All these aircraft carried only pilots and observers, a special extra fuel-tank being fitted in the third cockpit of each machine to increase the somewhat limited range.

At about 8.30 p.m. the first striking force took off from *Illustrious,* slowly gained height and disappeared in neat formation into the moonlit night. An hour later eight aircraft of the second striking force trundled down the deck of the carrier and became airborne; the ninth suffered a slight accident while moving forward to take off, and had to be taken below for repairs. However, the pilot, Lieutenant E. W. Clifford, was determined not to miss the operation, and finally took off just before 10.0 p.m., the big Pegasus engine of his Swordfish pulling the heavily laden biplane gamely along in an effort to make up for lost time. Meanwhile, Lieutenant-Commander Williamson's force was approaching Taranto, and soon afterwards he detached his two flare-carrying aircraft. After laying a line of flares along the harbour, they dropped some bombs, setting an oil storage depot alight and causing other damage.

Led by Williamson and his observer, Lieutenant N. J. Scarlett, the torpedo-carrying Swordfish went in to the attack through a curtain of anti-aircraft fire, jinking to avoid the deadly balloon barrage wires, heading for the long, grey shapes of the Italian battleships dimly seen behind the spurting flame from hundreds of guns. At point-blank range the torpedoes were released, and in quick succession the Swordfish swung up and away, leaving below them the white tracks streaking towards their targets. Somewhere in the confusion, unseen amid the drifting cordite smoke, blinding flashes and interlacing lines of tracer, Williamson's aircraft was lost, the only machine which failed to return out of the first striking force.

The second striking force was now coming in sight of Taranto, no longer in darkness, but brilliantly lighted by anti-aircraft fire and the beams of searchlights. As before, two Swordfish were detached to drop flares, and they also dive-bombed the burning oil storage depot to spread the fires. Then the torpedo-carrying aircraft went down to the attack, flying into the outer harbour at a height of less than 150 ft., through a fearful box barrage from multiple automatic batteries firing from both sides. Again, one Swordfish was hit—it was seen to spin into the sea—before the flame-stabbing hulls of the enemy warships loomed up in front of the thundering radial engines, and the torpedoes fell away. On through the boiling cauldron of tracer and high explosive, over the masts of cruisers and destroyers hurling up a vivid umbrella of shot and shell, past the balloon barrage cables and the murderous flak ships at the harbour entrance, frantically reaching for height, the Swordfish left Taranto. As they disappeared into the night the solitary biplane manned by Lieutenant Clifford and his observer, Lieutenant G. R. M. Going, arrived over the harbour almost unnoticed, like the last guest at a successful party; it had been a cold and lonely flight, but the target had been reached after all.

Clifford dived the Swordfish, swung to port—thus avoiding the tracer-streaked outer harbour—and headed for the *Mar Piccolo,* or inner harbour, which contained a number of cruisers and destroyers in line, at anchor. He dropped a stick of bombs neatly along the enemy ships, turned to drop the remainder of his bombs on the cruisers, and then raced for the open sea, pursued by heavy but inaccurate anti-aircraft fire. Two hours later, Clifford was back aboard *Illustrious* making his report, and the carrier was steaming at a good 20 knots to rejoin Admiral Cunningham's Mediterranean Fleet. Back at Taranto the guns fell silent and the searchlights went out one by one; but the fires continued to burn fiercely, casting flickering shadows over the darkened harbour where heeling ships lay in pools of their own fuel oil.

The following morning, R.A.F. Maryland aircraft from Malta flew a reconnaissance over Taranto to take photographs and report on the state of the Italian Fleet. The pictures revealed that startling results had been achieved during the night by two handfuls of elderly biplanes: the 23,600-ton battleship *Cavour* so badly

Above, H. C. Baird, *left,* pilot of the winning floatplane in the 1925 Schneider Trophy contest with the designer, R. J. Mitchell; *below,* the Supermarine S.6B, three times winner of the Schneider Trophy

Above, Germany's Dornier Do.X, in 1930 the largest aircraft in the world; *below,* a Dornier Wal flying-boat being catapulted from the "Schwabenland" Atlantic island

damaged that she would later have to be beached; the battleship *Duilio* also disabled, and already beached; the battleship *Italia* hit and down by the bows, gushing oil; and the cruiser *Trento* thoroughly bombed out of commission. Also, two destroyers had been damaged, two supply ships sunk, the Taranto seaplane base knocked out for some time, and the oil storage depot virtually burned down. For the loss of only two Swordfish the effective strength of the Italian Fleet had been more than halved, and would remain thus seriously diminished for almost a year; many months were to pass before the *Duilio* and *Italia* left harbour, and the *Cavour* took no further part in the war. "It is hoped that this victory will be considered a suitable reward to those whose work and faith in the Fleet Air Arm made it possible," wrote Captain (later Rear-Admiral Sir) Denis Boyd of the *Illustrious,* some time later.

As a direct consequence of the victory at Taranto, it became possible to risk more convoys through the Mediterranean to Port Said and Alexandria; the first of these, which included ships for beleagured Malta, being despatched under the escort of Force H, commanded by Admiral Somerville. Early on the morning of 27th November aircraft out on reconnaissance patrol from Malta sighted almost all that remained of the Italian Fleet—two battleships, seven cruisers and about sixteen destroyers—just south of Sardinia, and closing the convoy. To keep an eye on the enemy ships two Swordfish were flown off by *Ark Royal,* while Force H prepared for battle. About noon, as previously arranged, the squadron was joined by the old battleship *Ramillies,* the cruisers *Newcastle, Berwick* and *Coventry* and a screen of destroyers, all detached from the Mediterranean Fleet, and a welcome sight to Admiral Somerville.

At extreme range the British warships opened fire. Meanwhile, a striking force of eleven aircraft took off from the *Ark Royal* and in brilliant sunshine dived to attack the enemy battleships, the *Vittorio Veneto* and *Guilio Cesare,* both of which took violent evasive action and turned away. Nevertheless, hits were made on the *Vittorio Veneto,* the Fleet Air Arm pilots flying so low through the intensive flak thrown up by the warship that return fire from the British rear gunners shattered windows along her bridge and forward superstructure. The Italian cruisers also

5—AHOMA · ·

retired under a smoke-screen, and soon afterwards Admiral
Somerville, with the responsibility for his convoy in mind,
decided to break off the action; although a second striking force
from *Ark Royal* overtook the retreating enemy squadron and
attacked, claiming two cruisers damaged. Meanwhile, the British
convoy continued on course for Alexandria.

Nothing more was seen of the Italian Fleet until March 1941,
and by that time Admiral Cunningham had received two valuable
additions to his battle squadron—the carriers *Formidable* and *Indomitable,* sister ships of the *Illustrious,* equipped with the latest
Fairey Albacore torpedo-carrying aircraft and Fulmar fighters.
The Albacore was unusual in being one of the very few biplanes
to be designed in a monoplane age; it was, in fact, a contemporary of the Blackburn Skua. Intended as a replacement for the
ageing Swordfish, the Albacore had a comfortable, enclosed
cabin for a crew of three, a windscreen wiper and other refinements, and was slightly faster than the earlier aircraft, with a
maximum speed of 161 m.p.h. at 4,000 ft. It has been called 'a
gentleman's aeroplane'—as indeed it was—but most Fleet Air
Arm pilots perversely tended to prefer the Swordfish, and in the
event that faithful old biplane outlasted its intended successor in
service! As for the two-seater Fulmar, the first Fleet Air Arm
fighter with an eight-gun armament, it was a very manoeuvrable
aircraft with an excellent rate of climb, but it lacked speed, and
served to highlight the growing need for a carrier-borne single-
seater fighter.

At dawn on 27th March, then, four Albacores and a Swordfish
from the *Formidable* were out on reconnaissance over the central
Mediterranean seeking a number of Italian warships that had
been sighted by an aircraft from Malta the previous evening,
heading eastward. Before noon, two groups of enemy heavy
cruisers had been spotted, and also a very powerful battle squadron including the battleship *Vittorio Veneto,* the three forces
making giant pincers that seemed likely to close—perhaps
unwittingly—on the British cruisers, under the command of
Vice-Admiral Pridham-Wippell. It was quite impossible for
Admiral Cunningham's battleships to intervene in time, and
he therefore decided to mount an attack against at least one of
the enemy squadrons with Fleet Air Arm machines.

The first striking force to be flown off H.M.S. *Formidable* consisted of six Albacores with an escort of two Fulmars. Led by Lieutenant-Commander W. H. J. Saunt, the formation soon came in sight of the main Italian battle fleet, and the Albacores went in to the attack against the *Vittorio Veneto* while the Fulmars tackled a pair of Junkers Ju 88 twin-engined German fighters that threatened to make trouble. Alarm klaxons howled a warning on board the enemy warships, and anti-aircraft fire began to splotch across the sky. Surrounded by her scurrying destroyers the *Vittorio Veneto* thundered forth a frightful barrage, with her huge, 15-in. guns depressed to fire into the sea and throw up great fountains of water in front of the Albacores; but the frail biplanes rocked and swayed through the reeking spray to successfully release their torpedoes. At least one of the missiles struck home, and the battleship turned sharply away, losing speed, the escorting destroyers clustering helplessly around her.

Although the British fleet was making all haste to catch up with the enemy ships, it was essential to slow the *Vittorio Veneto* even more before nightfall, and a second striking force was ordered by Admiral Cunningham to be flown from the *Formidable*. These aircraft—three Albacores and two Swordfish, with an escort of two Fulmars—trundled down the carrier's deck in the early afternoon, and just over an hour later sighted the limping battleship in full retreat. Led by Lieutenant-Commander J. Dalyell-Stead, the five biplanes attacked at low level, and three hits were scored, against the loss of Dalyell-Stead's Albacore, which crashed into the sea after being struck by anti-aircraft fire. Now surrounded by her cruiser squadrons, the *Vittorio Veneto* continued to plod gamely homeward, her speed reduced to a mere 13 knots.

A third striking force was at once despatched from the over-worked *Formidable,* consisting of six Albacores and two Swordfish. As they dived to the attack, again led by Lieutenant-Commander Saunt, all the Italian ships opened up a desperate, overwhelming fire from every gun they possessed—"The sky was filled with streams of tracer ammunition of various colours . . ." in the words of Admiral Pridham-Wippell, watching from twelve miles away—and the aircraft dispersed, taking independent action. Despite these individual attacks being pressed home at the closest possible range, no torpedoes hit the *Vittorio Veneto* but the 10,000-ton cruiser *Pola* was struck and brought to a complete standstill. Two other cruisers, the *Zara* and *Fiume*, were detached to stand by and assist the *Pola* while the remainder of the Italian squadron took advantage of the onset of darkness to get away.

Thus ended Fleet Air Arm participation in the Battle of Cape Matapan, at first sight appearing unremarkable but in fact much more successful than might have been expected, in view of the intense anti-aircraft fire from the enemy ships. All three attacks had been notable for great personal gallantry by the pilots concerned. The Fleet Air Arm policy of 'find, fix and strike' that was so simple in conception and yet not so easy to effect in practice had been carried out to perfection; and there had been excellent co-ordination between the air and surface forces. Two out of three of the attacks had effectively served their purpose by drastically reducing the speed of the *Vittorio Veneto,* and even the third sortie could not be considered a failure—Admiral Cunningham's battleships had caught up with the cruisers *Pola, Zara* and *Fiume* during the night, and sank all three ships with heavy loss of life. Also, two simple but important facts cannot be overlooked when measuring the value of the Fleet Air Arm actions at Matapan: first, Admiral Pridham-Wippell's cruisers might well have suffered badly under the guns of the Italian squadrons if two successive air strikes had not radically altered the situation; and, secondly, without those same air attacks the British main fleet would not have been able to bring the enemy to battle at all.

The Battle of Cape Matapan was over, but the Battle of the Mediterranean went on, increasing in ferocity as the Luftwaffe began to dominate the sky in support of Rommel's *Afrika Korps* hammering away at General Sir Archibald Wavell's hard-pressed army in the Western Desert. The previous September, Grand Admiral Raeder had advised Hitler, "Gibraltar must be taken. The Canary Islands must be secured by the Air Force. The Suez Canal must be taken," and it seemed that the Fuehrer was making a great effort to carry his worried Italian ally along to a Mediterranean victory. With German troops flooding through tortured Greece, Wavell at last in retreat towards the Nile and Malta besieged by endless waves of enemy bombers, the whole theatre of operations would soon be ablaze from end to end; but Mussolini was destined to find that his partner's powerful intervention brought no reward for him—or Italy—except ignominious defeat and complete disaster.

10

THE GALLANT COMRADES: 1941–42

In the early morning of 24th May 1941 the 42,100-ton British battle-cruiser H.M.S. *Hood,* the pride of the Royal Navy and for nearly twenty years the largest warship in the world, was exchanging 15-in. gun salvoes with the most powerful modern battleship in commission, the mighty *Bismarck,* at a range of some 13 miles. In order to bring his after turrets to bear on the distant German ship, Admiral L. E. Holland, flying his flag in the *Hood,* ordered a turn to port of 20 degrees; but only a moment later the battle-cruiser was hit squarely by the *Bismarck*'s accurate, plunging fire. A giant pillar of smoke and flame fountained from the depths of the *Hood,* taking up to the sky great fragments of the ship; there was a momentary glimpse of the bows and stern leaping out of the water, with the midships disintegrated and pieces falling; then nothing remained except scattered, floating wreckage. The splendid ship that had commenced building in 1916, been launched in 1918 and finally completed in 1920 at a fantastic cost of over £6,000,000 was gone in the twinkling of an eye, leaving only pitiful debris and three survivors out of her complement of 1,300 men.

The events leading to that short, tragic action in the North Atlantic only briefly involved the Fleet Air Arm, but British carrier-borne aircraft were to play an important part in the terrible retribution that soon hounded *Bismarck* to a relentless doom. Nevertheless, it was a twin-engined Martin Maryland of No. 771 Naval Air Squadron at Hatston in the Orkneys, piloted by Lieutenant N. E. Goddard, R.N.V.R., with Commander G. A Rotherham as his observer, that braved the heavy rain and thick cloud on 22nd May to fly very low around the Norwegian coastline, skimming the grey waves to penetrate Grimstad and Bergen fiords, where the 42,000-ton *Bismarck* and a heavy cruiser, the *Prinz Eugen,* had lain at anchor, taking aboard supplies, It was a routine reconnaissance that had to be undertaken regardless of weather conditions, and on this day the great risk to aircraft and crew was rewarded by vital news: the two German warships had put to sea.

In anticipation of such a serious eventuality—and it was serious indeed, to all who realised that a new, extremely modern battleship like the *Bismarck* could sink many thousands of tons of Allied shipping in a very short time—the Admiralty had placed at the disposal of Admiral Sir John Tovey, commanding the Home Fleet at Scapa Flow, a number of heavy ships. They included the newly commissioned battleship *Prince of Wales,* the battleship *King George V* and the battle-cruiser *Hood,* with cruisers and destroyers; the battleships *Rodney* and *Ramillies,* on Atlantic convoy duty; and also Admiral Sir James Somerville's Force H, comprising the battle-cruiser *Renown* and the aircraft carrier *Ark Royal,* heading northward in all haste from Gibraltar. Admiral Tovey badly needed a carrier much nearer at hand, but the truth was that he did not have a single one available at Scapa Flow. The old veterans *Furious* and *Argus* were fully employed taking aircraft to Malta and the embattled Middle East theatre of operations, and the new carriers *Illustrious* and *Formidable* had suffered so heavily in the Mediterranean from continuous bombing attacks that they were undergoing extensive repairs. However, at the last moment Tovey was able to take to sea with his squadron the latest of the *Illustrious*-class carriers, the brand-new and untried *Victorious,* intended to join a Middle East convoy, but now urgently required for more immediate duties.

Through the outer submarine defences of mist-enshrouded Scapa Flow moved the dim shapes of Tovey's fleet, while the *Bismarck* and *Prinz Eugen* battled northwards around Iceland in mountainous seas. In the early evening of 23rd May the two German warships were sighted in the Denmark Strait by the heavy cruisers *Suffolk* and *Norfolk,* under the command of Rear-Admiral Wake-Walker, and all that night the grim, tense business of keeping contact by radar went on while the *Hood* and *Prince of Wales* steamed at full speed on a course of interception. At about 5.30 a.m. the following morning Admiral Gunther Lutjens, flying his flag in the *Bismarck,* received the message from his look-out, "Two ships on the port bow!" and soon afterwards gave the order to open fire. Many miles away, the 15-in. guns of the British warships thundered in response; the brief, ill-fated first clash of steel with *Bismarck* had begun.

The duel ended with the *Prince of Wales* swinging hard a-starboard to avoid floating wreckage from all that was left of a 42,000-ton ship; and in the War Room at the Admiralty men sat in stunned surprise, shocked into silence by the simple, urgent signal, "*Hood* has blown up." Both the German ships now directed an avalanche of gunfire on to the *Prince of Wales,* already at a disadvantage with increasing mechanical teething troubles—she was so newly fitted out that she had sailed with a number of civilian workmen still aboard—and almost at once the battleship vanished behind a curtain of smoke and shell splashes. As she emerged, Rear-Admiral Wake-Walker in *Norfolk,* now the senior British officer taking part in the action, ordered an immediate withdrawal, and *Prince of Wales* turned away, heavily hit and on fire forward. But the battleship and her two cruisers did not retire very far; they intended to keep *Bismarck* in sight if possible until the bitter end.

All that day the shadowing warships retained contact with *Bismarck,* despite thick fog and heavy seas. It was monotonous, trying work, enlivened only when the enemy battleship turned abruptly upon the *Suffolk* and fired a few angry salvoes; whereupon smoke was hurriedly made by the cruiser as she opened the range. In fact, Admiral Lutjens was giving *Prinz Eugen* an opportunity to slip away in the mist, and the German heavy cruiser thus escaped the vast net being spread by the Admiralty, arriving at Brest ten days later. Meanwhile, Tovey's Home Fleet and Somerville's Force H were on their way to close the iron ring; the elderly battleship *Revenge* had sailed from Halifax; and *Rodney* and *Ramillies* would soon be ordered to break away from their Atlantic convoy duties to take part in the chase.

The following day brought a rising gale and sleeting rain, with all the warships heaving and plunging in very rough seas. It became of the utmost importance to disable or at least slow down *Bismarck* before nightfall; and with some reluctance, because she was such a new and unprepared carrier, Admiral

Tovey ordered *Victorious* to fly off a torpedo striking force. As her hangar had originally been piled high with crated fighters for the Middle East, the *Victorious* was only equipped with nine Fairey Swordfish and six Fulmars, and in the early evening the whole of No. 825 Squadron, led by Lieutenant-Commander Eugene Esmonde, taxied down the lurching flight deck of the carrier and took to the air. In due course they sighted *Prince of Wales, Suffolk* and *Norfolk,* and finally the *Bismarck,* all four ships little more than grey streaks in the gathering dusk, glimpsed through rain-streaked goggles. Descending to low level, the Swordfish came in at varying angles to drop their torpedoes, while the *Bismarck* took violent evasive action and opened up a rapid, defensive fire. She avoided all the torpedoes except one, which exploded on her starboard side, between the bridge and bows. Then the Swordfish were climbing steeply away, pursued by the barrage of anti-aircraft fire from *Bismarck,* to make the long return flight to their storm-tossed parent carrier. It is to the great credit of Esmonde and his inexperienced crews that all nine biplanes had successfully been landed back on *Victorious* by midnight.

Nevertheless, it soon became painfully obvious that the single hit on *Bismarck* had not reduced her speed, and to make matters worse, four hours later *Suffolk* lost radar contact with the enemy battleship in the storm. Suddenly, *Bismarck* was no longer a definite target carefully plotted on the Admiralty charts in Whitehall, with powerful forces closing in upon her; instead, she became a mere dot somewhere inside a widening circle, with Tovey's Home Fleet still far to the north-east and Somerville's Force H hopefully racing up from Gibraltar. Aircraft from *Victorious* were sent out up to their maximum range to roam the miles of turbulent ocean in a frantic search for the vanished battleship, but without success.

By great good fortune, on 26th May a Royal Air Force Consolidated Catalina flying-boat of No. 209 Squadron, Coastal Command, flown by Pilot Officer D. A. Briggs, sighted the *Bismarck* briefly through a break in the clouds, the battleship identifying herself beyond any doubt by the accuracy and intensity of her anti-aircraft fire. She was about 750 miles west of Brest, and obviously heading for that port; within twenty-four hours her present course and speed would bring her within range of massive Luftwaffe air cover from France. Before that time elapsed, the *Bismarck* had to be brought to a standstill and destroyed, by warships still a good distance away from her and beginning to run dangerously low on fuel oil. Everything now depended on Admiral Somerville's solitary battle cruiser, the *Renown,* together with the carrier *Ark Royal* and escorting cruisers and destroyers, the only force not actually chasing the enemy battleship from astern; she was all unwittingly steaming to within air striking distance of the Gibraltar-based squadron.

But it was going to be no easy task for *Ark Royal* to fly off aircraft. Her flight deck was rising and falling more than 50 ft. as she plunged through the rolling seas, and the Swordfish that were brought up into the lashing gale of wind and rain had to be held down by the handling party. Nevertheless, *Bismarck* had to be found—it was not yet known on the carrier that she had already been located—and at 8.30 a.m. the ten ubiquitous old biplanes somehow rocked and swayed into the air. Two hours later the *Bismarck* had been sighted, now being shadowed by a Catalina flying-boat of No. 240 Squadron, R.A.F. Coastal Command, and two Swordfish also took station over the German battleship, hanging on grimly despite the storm. Meanwhile the cruiser *Sheffield* was detached from Force H to make all speed towards the *Bismarck* and regain contact by radar; the enemy was not going to be allowed to escape again.

At 2.50 p.m. a striking force of fourteen torpedo-carrying Swordfish successfully took off from *Ark Royal,* gained height and disappeared into the mist. An hour later they were going into long, shallow dives, heading for the grey shape only just visible through the thick cloud of driving rain, flying very low to drop their torpedoes; but an urgent signal was coming through in plain language from *Ark Royal,* "Look out for *Sheffield*! Look out for *Sheffield*!', And of course the target was indeed that unfortunate cruiser, swinging hard over to avoid the streaking torpedoes, some of which proved to be defective and exploded while still on course. By a remarkable exhibition of seamanship, *Sheffield* managed to evade the remainder, and the Swordfish crews sadly made their way back to *Ark Royal* to report their failure. All the aircraft touched down safely, although the wet and slippery flight deck was now pitching to almost 60 ft. at times.

A second striking force, composed of fifteen Swordfish of No. 818 Squadron, led by Lieutenant-Commander T. P. Coode, took off from *Ark Royal* in the early evening and in due course located *Bismarck* in the swirling fog. Formation was lost, and the aircraft attacked singly or in twos and threes from port and starboard sides, small-calibre gunfire flickering along the battleship's hull and superstructure. In spite of the appalling flak barrage—one Swordfish was hit no less than 175 times—all the torpedoes were successfully dropped at close range. Only two, however, struck home on the battleship, but one of these hits proved to be decisive; the *Bismarck*'s rudders were jammed, her steering-gear damaged, and propellers twisted.

A shadowing Swordfish radioed back the great news to *Ark Royal* that the *Bismarck* was virtually out of control, heading in a northward direction. During the night a most gallant torpedo attack was carried out on the battleship by a destroyer force under the command of Captain Philip Vian of *Altmark* fame, but no hits were scored, owing to the accuracy of *Bismarck*'s return fire; and about the same time, Admiral Lutjens received a signal from Hitler: "All our thoughts are with our victorious comrades." The reply from *Bismarck* indicated that Lutjens knew only too well his ship was doomed: "We shall fight to the last shell. Long live the Fuehrer!"

In the grey, stormy Atlantic morning, the British heavy units came upon the scene, and at a range of 25,000 yd. the battleships *King George V* and *Rodney* opened fire. At once *Bismarck* replied, showing magnificent gunnery control, but it was impossible for her to compete against such overwhelming odds, and she quickly became surrounded by the giant splashes from 15- and 16-in. shells. Then salvo after salvo began to crash directly on to the German ship, destroying her main battery director, wiping out the admiral's bridge, littering the main bridge with dead and wounded. The guns continued to pound monotonously away, precise, directed fire, until the *Bismarck* was nothing more than a blazing wreck, all her upper works, funnels, everything, gone; yet still she floated, until the British battleships and their heavy cruisers were all around the burning hulk, slamming shells into it at such short range that secondary armaments were also being used. At last, there came the somewhat forlorn signal, "Cannot get to sink her with gunfire," a last, unconscious tribute to the quality of Krupp armour plating, amounting on *Bismarck* to 16,000 tons dead weight.

The Swordfish pilots from *Ark Royal,* circling over the area in case they were needed, saw Admiral Tovey's battleships break off the action, and the cruiser *Dorsetshire* close in on all that was left of *Bismarck*. At a range of two miles, three torpedoes were fired in quick succession, and the gutted enemy ship slowly turned turtle, floated keel upwards for a few moments, then disappeared beneath the waves, her ensign still flying. The historic signal, "*Bismarck* sunk", sped on its way to the War Room of the Admiralty, and the faithful Swordfish returned to *Ark Royal* and Force H, which would soon be steaming back to Gibraltar. Already many miles away, the mighty ships of the Home Fleet were on their way home, with scarcely enough fuel left to reach Scapa Flow.

It was all over. The pride of the German Navy had sunk the ageing, but greatly loved and respected, pride of the Royal Navy and a relentless, terrible vengeance had been exacted. Without the intervention of the Fleet Air Arm the *Bismarck* would, under the most favourable circumstances, have been at large for a much longer period of time; in such hopeless weather conditions, it is very doubtful if she could have been caught at all. "It was evident that she had too great a lead for H.M.S. *King George V* to come up with her unless her speed could be further reduced," wrote Admiral Tovey in his despatch on the action. "Our only hope lay in torpedo attack by the aircraft of H.M.S. *Ark Royal.*"

Sad to relate, the carrier that brought about the *Bismarck*'s destruction had only a few more months of life remaining before she, too, was sunk. On 13th November the *Ark Royal* was landing on her aircraft about 30 miles from Gibraltar when she was hit amidships by a single torpedo fired from either U.81 or U.205, two submarines that it was later learned had been shadowing the carrier for some time. Only one man had been killed by the explosion, and the rest of the crew, including all the Fleet

Air Arm personnel, were quickly and efficiently transferred to the carrier's escorting cruisers and destroyers. The *Ark Royal* stayed afloat for fourteen hours, listing more and more to starboard, the Swordfish and Fulmar aircraft in her empty hangar sliding about with a great crashing and splintering of wings and fuselages; then, as if too weary to stay above water any longer, she quietly turned right over and went down, leaving only a little scattered debris. Her end was witnessed by Admiral Somerville, who had arrived in a launch from Gibraltar to see the last moments of the fine ship already sunk so many times by the venomous Goebbels propaganda machine.

As for the Fairey Swordfish, it had been brought to the zenith of a long and memorable career by the *Bismarck* episode; and only one other outstanding torpedo attack was to be made by the type before it faded gracefully away into the twilight of second-line service. But the six Swordfish destined to undertake that last, courageous sortie were to go out in a great blaze of glory; as did their crews, every pilot, observer and air gunner; and no star shone more brightly in the falling than Lieutenant-Commander Eugene Esmonde, from Drominagh, Tipperary: a very gallant Irishman. If it is impossible to speak of the Fleet Air Arm without recalling to mind the Swordfish, surely it is equally difficult to visualise that lovable, antiquated biplane without remembering the name of young 'Winkle' Esmonde? And who can doubt that both will remain immortal in the annals of British naval aviation?

The day of ultimate sacrifice for Eugene Esmonde and his squadron proved to be 12th February 1942. In the English Channel that grey, misty morning, the 30,000-ton battle cruisers *Scharnhorst* and *Gneisenau* were attempting what appeared to be not only impudent but downright impossible; in company with the heavy cruiser *Prinz Eugen* and seven destroyers, they would soon be passing through the Straits of Dover in a daring breakout from the uncertain security of Brest Harbour. Although it was not generally realised until many months later, the truth was that Hitler had suddenly begun to fear an Allied invasion of Norway, and he wanted his two battle cruisers back in Scandinavian waters without delay, to join the battleship *Tirpitz* at

Trondheim. While it was appreciated in Whitehall that the German warships in Brest might put to sea at any time—even the possibility of a Channel passage had been considered—it was taken for granted that, whatever the route, most of the enemy movement would take place during the hours of darkness. But Hitler, always the inveterate gambler, simply reversed the obvious timing for such an attempt, despite cries of protest from his naval commander-in-chief, Admiral Raeder; and on the night of 11th February the German battle flotilla slid quietly out of Brest under cover of yet another British air raid.

The events that followed were like tragic stepping-stones on the road leading to Eugene Esmonde's last rendezvous with fate over the Channel. A British submarine patrolling off Brest with orders to report on movements of the enemy ships missed their break-out in the darkness; the early morning R.A.F. reconnaissance patrol also failed to spot them; and not until 10.30 a.m. did a pair of Spitfires, flown by the Battle of Britain veterans Group Captain Beamish and Wing Commander Boyd, sight the German fleet. By that time the battle cruisers had been at sea for nearly fourteen hours, and were past the narrowest part of the Channel, between Dover and Calais. Vice-Admiral Ciliax, flying his flag in *Scharnhorst*, began to feel increasingly fearful that his enduring good fortune could only be a forerunner of disaster—what was the British trap that must be lying in wait somewhere ahead?

High above the warships circled Admiral Ciliax's insurance against air attack, a continuous, moving umbrella of Messerschmitt Bf 109 and new Focke-Wulf Fw 190 fighters, operating under an elaborate plan designed to provide alternate waves of aircraft overhead throughout the daylight hours. In order to repel attacks by British light naval units, the battle cruisers were now close-screened by their destroyers and a large force of E-boats; and shortly after noon these ships were being heavily engaged by motor torpedo boats from Dover. Racing at full speed, all guns firing back at the German escort craft, the Dover boats managed to pierce the screen and launch their torpedoes, but without success. Riddled by cannon and machine-gun fire they dropped astern and withdrew under cover of two gun-boats also sent out from Dover.

Meanwhile, at Manston R.A.F. station, Lieutenant-Commander Eugene Esmonde, late of the aircraft carriers *Victorious* and *Ark Royal* and more recently transferred with his squadron from the naval air base at Lee-on-Solent in anticipation of this very crisis, had just been ordered to take his two sub-flights of Swordfish in to the attack. As top cover and close escort—the difference between life and death when striking at such heavily defended targets—Esmonde had been promised five squadrons of Spitfires from No. 11 Group, Fighter Command. Soon afterwards he was told that a few of the fighters might be a little late. In fact the unexpected daylight passage of the enemy fleet through the Channel, together with the astonishing delay in detecting the German ships, was creating confusion and a certain lack of co-ordination between the various Commands; there should have been a number of modern Bristol Beaufort torpedo bombers on hand, but the only squadron within reach had just landed at Coltishall, having been caught in the midst of transferring from Leuchars; while the heavy, four-engined machines of Bomber Command were taking far too long in coming up to a state of readiness.

The telephones continued to jangle in Whitehall and Dover and in the operations rooms of R.A.F. stations all over the southeast coast, but to little apparent purpose, while time passed and the enemy fleet moved steadily on toward home waters. Clear as crystal, one fact emerged; Esmonde's handful of biplanes comprised the only air striking force immediately available. When he hurried out with his crews to the six Swordfish which stood armed with torpedoes and dispersed ready for immediate take-off, the fighter escort had still not arrived, and yet every moment delayed was a moment wasted. Walking across the field, glancing up at the grey empty sky which should have been alive with Spitfires, Esmonde realised that a routine, if very dangerous sortie against a force of powerful German warships was turning into a suicidal mission that could only have one ending. According to Wing Commander T. P. Gleave, the station commander at Manston, who saw Esmonde take off, the young Irishman had suddenly assumed "the face of a man already dead. I had always known him as a vital man, alive and eager for anything. Now his eyes were dulled, his face grey, almost haggard . . . It shocked me as nothing had done before nor has done since."

The six Swordfish biplanes taxied down the field, turned into the wind, and took smoothly to the air; recalling other, similar take-offs to face overwhelming odds over the Flanders trenches in an earlier war. As they gained height and slid neatly into formation, there was still no sign of any escort fighters. Esmonde now knew, beyond any doubt, that the furnace lying ahead in the Channel could consume them all, he and the seventeen others who also no longer had any illusions, but were ready to follow him to the bitter end. Nevertheless, the final decision had already been made; and Esmonde was not a man to dither or change his mind. The two sub-flights disappeared into the heavy cloud, flying eastward—towards the enemy fleet.

As the Swordfish reached the coast, they were met at last by a few welcome Spitfires from Biggin Hill that immediately streaked out over the sea in an attempt to break up the deadly German fighter umbrella. Plodding along behind them, the naval biplanes dropped into line astern and went down to 50 ft., moments before the first shark-nosed Bf 109s flashed past with guns blazing. High above the formation, the Spitfires weaved and twisted in desperate running battles with dozens of German fighters, but more flights of the black-crossed monoplanes came in very low, punching cannon fire into the lumbering Swordfish at close range. Fabric tore back in the slipstream from riddled fuselages, wings shook to the impact of bullets and 20-mm. shells, but the squadron flew relentlessly on.

Because there were so few survivors of the Channel attack, we have only glimpses of the events that followed Esmonde's first sighting of the enemy ships, long grey destroyers lying dead ahead across the sights, with the great bulking might of the battle cruisers beyond, wreathed in acrid smoke. A devastating barrage of anti-aircraft fire from guns of all calibres crashed out to meet the first sub-flight of Swordfish, heavy shells exploding all around them, multi-coloured tracer from the E-boats, destroyers and darting enemy fighters interlacing through the bullet-holed formation. Huddled down in his cockpit like a man making his way forward against a driving snowstorm, Esmonde remained on course, passing through the fearful wall of flak from the outer screen of destroyers, heading directly for *Scharnhorst*. In these final moments, with every man intent only on the objective, there were tiny acts of heroism in plenty, sprinkled like stars through the whole gallant attack: Esmonde's gunner, Leading Airman W. J. Clinton, completely out of his cockpit and astride the fuselage, beating at the burning fabric with his gloved hands; Sub-Lieutenant Edgar Lee, observer in the second Swordfish, standing upright in a blizzard of steel to shout warnings of individual attacking fighters to his pilot, because the gunner was dead and only the swiftest evasive action could save them; and, in the third aircraft of the sub-flight, Leading Airman D. A. Bunce also stood up to fire burst after burst of Lewis into the Bf 109s and Fw 190s streaking past on either side.

The heavy 11-in. guns of the battle-cruisers now opened fire almost in Esmonde's face, their shells striking the water just ahead of his Swordfish to make a carpet barrage in which the disturbed sea fell back like a solid wall on to the staggering biplanes. The pilot of the second Swordfish, Sub-Lieutenant Brian Rose, was hit by a burst of fighter cannon fire; and a moment later the lower port wing of Esmonde's machine abruptly disappeared, carried away by a deflected shell. Wrestling desperately with his controls, Esmonde miraculously kept the Swordfish in the air, the vast, flame-outlined bulk of *Scharnhorst* looming up ahead. Then, with the observer and gunner behind Esmonde both dead, an enemy fighter moved in very close and flayed the tattered fuselage of the biplane with tracer. Esmonde fell forward, terribly wounded in the head and back; probably his last act in this world was to pull up the nose of his aircraft and release the torpedo.

As Esmonde's destroyed machine crashed into the sea, the second Swordfish was coming in very low through the smoke and flame to attack *Gneisenau*, with Sub-Lieutenant Lee still leaning over to shout directions at his barely conscious pilot slumped down in his ruined cockpit, Rose responded instinctively to the urgent, demanding voice in his ear, and fired the torpedo. The Swordfish flew on, right into the muzzles of the battle-cruiser's blazing guns, until Rose at last reacted to Lee's screamed, "Up Brian! Up fast!" and pulled the machine up and over the enemy warship. Somehow he brought his observer through the outer

screen of destroyers and E-boats once more, even gaining a
little strength, before the Swordfish lost height and belly-landed
on the sea. Rose and Lee were later rescued by the motor torpedo
boats from Dover, and both men survived.

The third Swordfish of the sub-flight struggled over the enemy
destroyer screen. Hit again and again, it burst into flames and all
three of the crew were wounded, but the pilot, Sub-Lieutenant
Colin Kingsmill, nevertheless battled forward to only 2,000 yd.
from his target—the cruiser *Prinz Eugen*—before releasing his
torpedo. Then the riddled old Swordfish limped gamely over the
German battle fleet and dropped into the sea. As a Dover-based
motor torpedo boat raced forward to save the crew, the second
sub-flight of three Swordfish, led by Lieutenant J. C. Thompson,
came in to the attack, flying in V formation, under continuous
and increasingly more accurate gunfire.

Seen briefly through the smoke and deluging water from the
carpet barrage, the biplanes crossed the outer destroyer screen,
harried by snub-nosed Fw 190 fighters with undercarriages
lowered and flaps down to reduce speed and so keep the lumbering targets in their sights; but of what happened during the
next few minutes we know nothing, because not one of the three
Swordfish was ever seen again. Somewhere beyond the belching
guns of *Scharnhorst* and *Gneisenau* machines and men simply vanished as if they had never existed, gone to join Eugene Esmonde
in the great sacrifice. Flying at wave-top height over a sea alive
with powerful, heavily armoured enemy warships, trying to
remain aloft in a sky filled with enemy fighters, they never had a
single chance of success; and the measure of their devotion is
that they nevertheless attempted the impossible, although their
squadron leader had fallen.

Unharmed, the German battle fleet steamed on, leaving behind
on the rising water only a few fragments of debris to mark the
spot where Eugene Esmonde had died, so far from the lovely
wooded countryside of his native Tipperary. Later posthumously
awarded the Victoria Cross—the first member of the Fleet Air
Arm to receive that decoration in the Second World War—he
had once unconsciously expressed the reason why, for him, there
could be no other way. "I can think of no greater honour," he
had written while serving in the carrier *Furious,* "nor a better way

of passing into Eternity than in the cause for which the Allies are fighting this war." At a time when there is so much talk of discontinuing our annual Day of Remembrance, it does no harm to pause here for a moment and reflect on those words of the 'small meteor' named 'Winkle' Esmonde. Surely, if only recalled to mind on one day of the year, the memory of this young Fleet Air Arm officer and those many others like him who went forth to battle with the terrible certainty in their hearts that they would not return, should be allowed to remain with us?

Too late by many hours, the various Commands of the Royal Air Force assembled their forces and hurled them into the smoke and flame surrounding Admiral Ciliax's squadron. While Hurricanes, Spitfires and even twin-engined Whirlwinds tangled with the vast air umbrella over the German warships, and dogfights unwound from coast to coast across the Channel, two successive strikes by Bristol Beaufort torpedo bombers of Coastal Command failed to halt or even damage the battle-cruisers, although at least six aircraft succeeded in releasing their torpedoes. During the afternoon and early evening, three waves of Bomber Command aircraft of various types struck at the enemy ships, but the increasing rain and thickening mist was against them, and many bombers failed even to find the targets. Of those that did, fifteen were shot down; the German fighter cover was virtually impregnable that day.

Only twice did the battle-cruisers come near to meeting with real disaster. At about 2.30 p.m. the *Scharnhorst* struck a mine that greatly reduced her speed, Admiral Ciliax and his staff transferring to a nearby destroyer, the Z-29; and later, when that ship developed engine trouble, moving on to another destroyer, the *Hermann Schoemann*. However, within an hour *Scharnhorst* had managed to effect temporary repairs, and in due course caught up with the main fleet. All went well until the warships were almost in home waters, when *Gneisenau* also struck a mine, and a great rent was opened in her bottom near the stern. Temporarily patched up with steel collision mats, she limped into Heligoland Bight shortly after midnight.

As a final stroke of bad luck for Admiral Ciliax within the space of a few hours, *Scharnhorst* had no sooner passed the Frisian Islands than she hit another mine and again came to a standstill.

The exhausted battle-damage repair parties went to work once more, and by midnight the battle-cruiser was able to proceed independently, making a slow but sure 12 knots to Wilhelms-haven. Meanwhile, anchor chains were rattling off the Elbe; the 'Ugly Sisters' fleet—as the German warships were known in R.A.F. circles—had come home at last, after a long, hard day.

"The enemy betrayed his surprise to the advantage of our formation by throwing in his air forces precipitously and without plan," wrote Admiral Ciliax later, in his personal report to Hit-ler. "For the failure of the enemy Air Force to reach the target during the afternoon and evening in spite of the extreme deter-mination shown in their first torpedo attack, we have to thank the shipborne flak and the fine services of our fighter cover. After this, there was a gap of some two hours or more without any attacks from the enemy and which gave us a decisive brea-ther during which we increased our distance from the enemy and the weather deteriorated. There is no explanation from our side for this delay in the enemy's actions."

And no good explanation from any other side. The Channel dash of 12th February 1942 remains a remarkable German achievement, but one that should never have been allowed to take place. One effect of the immediate public outcry in Great Britain was to highlight the pressing need of the Fleet Air Arm for more modern aircraft, a situation that had been virtually ignored since the outbreak of war. The thunderous reverbera-tions of the Channel affair resulted in Admiralty permission to develop a naval version of the Supermarine Spitfire single seater fighter, to be known as the Seafire. Later, there would follow the Fairey Barracuda and Firefly monoplanes, and a host of Amer-ican-built naval aircraft—the Grumman Martlet, Wildcat and Hellcat fighters, the three-seater Avenger torpedo-bomber, and many more—but much valuable time was to be lost before these new machines entered service. When it came to the question of priorities, naval aviation always seemed to be somewhere at the bottom of the list.

We are left with the words, already quoted, of Vice-Admiral Ciliax, including his tribute to the last sortie by Esmonde's squad-ron, and "the extreme determination shown in their first tor-pedo attack . . ." At about the same time, the Flag Officer

Commanding at Dover, Vice-Admiral Ramsay, was writing in his official report: "In my opinion, the gallant sortie of these six Swordfish constitutes one of the finest exhibitions of self-sacrifice and devotion to duty that the war had yet witnessed."

Agreement between opposing commanders that a job had been well done; Eugene Esmonde and his young crews would have asked for nothing more.

PEARL HARBOUR TO SINGAPORE: 1941-42

Some 400 miles north of Pearl Harbour a powerful Japanese naval striking force, composed of the battleships *Hiei* and *Kirishima*, the six aircraft carriers *Akagi, Kaga, Hiryu, Shokaku, Soryu* and *Zuikaku*, three cruisers and nine destroyers, pitched and rolled in wintry seas. On the flight decks of the heaving carriers, thousands of officers and men watched an aged battle-flag rise to *Akagi*'s masthead, and stood rigidly, unmoving, at attention; for this was the actual flag flown by Admiral Heihachiro Togo at the great Japanese naval victory of Tsushima in 1905.

There were tears in many eyes, and more than one heart beat faster as the sailors pondered upon the stirring words of their beloved Commander-in-Chief, read out to all ships' companies only a few moments before. "The moment has arrived!" thundered Admiral Isoroku Yamamoto's call to arms. "The rise or fall of our Empire is at stake. Everyone will do his duty to the utmost . . ." Then the flag broke in tattered, fluttering glory at the carrier's masthead, and cheers and cries of "banzai" rang out across the darkening Pacific waters. Engine-room telegraphs clanged as quick orders were given to increase speed and change course southwards, and within minutes the men had dispersed as the force plunged on through the stormy December night.

Exactly when the decision to attack the important American naval base at Pearl Harbour was made is uncertain; but there can be no doubt that for some years prior to the Second World War the Japanese naval air arm had increased in strength and quality far beyond Allied calculations, and by 1941 was composed of extremely modern fighters and bombers, manned by crews who had gained valuable battle experience in China. The fall of France and the entry of Italy into the war in Europe had ensured that

British interests in the Far East continued to be sadly neglected, and there was a pressing need for a strong fleet operating from Singapore. However, the United States, particularly deficient in air power in the Pacific—although that was a situation gradually being remedied—chose to retain her main battle fleet as a 'display of force' at Pearl Harbour, considering such a formidable array of capital ships to be more than sufficient warning to the Japanese, who were, after all, more than 3,000 miles from Hawaii.

But in Tokyo the fanatical Japanese Premier and Minister of War, General Hideki Tojo, had long been bent on the conquest of virtually all the Far East, despite the reluctance of his military and naval advisers, who feared a war with America; and now he seized his chance, at a time when relations between the two countries were already unsettled. A broad plan for a number of simultaneous assaults was drawn up, including two important proposals put forward by the Commander of the Combined Fleet, Admiral Yamamoto: first, that the attacks should be made by surprise, launched in conjunction with, or immediately before, a declaration of war; and secondly, that the dangerous United States Pacific Fleet would have to be destroyed at anchor in Pearl Harbour.

The outstanding British success with carrier-based aircraft against the Italian Fleet at Taranto the previous November prompted the Japanese strategists in 1941 to consider using masses of torpedo bombers and dive bombers against the main American targets, with the intention of operating on a large scale from carriers. For such attacks, Japan was, in fact, particularly well equipped, possessing the *Akagi* and *Kaga,* each displacing over 35,000 tons, and two of the largest carriers in the world; the smaller, 17,500-ton carriers *Hiryu* and *Soryu* and, most up-to-date of all, the 30,000-ton *Zuikaku* and her sister-ship *Shokaku,* only just taken into service. It was finally decided to take the risk of using all six carriers in the attack on Pearl Harbour, flying off some 350 aircraft, mostly of Aichi, Nakajima and Mitsubishi manufacture.

A comparatively heavy, but nevertheless highly manoeuvrable, low-wing monoplane, the Aichi D3A (later code-named Val under the Allied identification system) was designed in 1936, and went into production the following year as a carrier-borne dive bomber. A two-seater aircraft, fitted with a spatted, fixed under-carriage resembling that of the infamous Junkers Ju 87 Stuka, and powered by a 1,300-h.p. Mitsubishi Kinsei 54 radial engine, the Aichi D3A had by 1940 established itself as an extremely effective machine, superior in range and bomb load to such Western contemporaries as the British Blackburn Skua or the American Douglas Dauntless. Indeed, the Aichi Val, in an improved version, remained in full production until 1944, and was one of the few really successful dive bombers to emerge during the Second World War.

Japan's most widely used light bomber and torpedo bomber for operation from carriers was the Nakajima B5N2, code-named Kate, the prototype of which flew for the first time early in 1937. It was a conventional, low-wing, two-seater monoplane in much the same class as the Fairey Battle, but more adaptable, although it had all the British machine's fatal vulnerability to fighter attack. As the war progressed, the Nakajima Kate was therefore relegated to second-line duties, but in 1941 it could be considered a good, sound machine, comparable with the best American aircraft of similar type then in service.

One of the most remarkable aircraft in the history of aviation, and a fitting contemporary of that superlative trio of single-seater fighters, the Spitfire, Hurricane and Messerschmitt Bf 109, the long-range Mitsubishi A6M Zero-Sen revealed only too well the failure of British and American experts in correctly estimating Japanese ability to produce first-class machines. Conceived by a team working under the leadership of a brilliant designer, Jiro Horikoshi, the A6M Zero-Sen (code-named Zeke by the Allies) made its maiden flight on 1st April 1939, went into production the following year, and was used with great success in China. Featuring a 1,130-h.p. Nakajima Sakae radial engine—at a time when in-line engines were strongly favoured by most of the Western air forces—and having a maximum speed of 350 m.p.h. and an armament of two Oerlikon-type 20-mm. cannon and two wing-mounted machine-guns, this extremely light and versatile naval fighter was destined to be produced in greater numbers than any other wartime Japanese aircraft, nearly 11,000 of all variants being built up to the end of hostilities.

Such were the main types of naval aircraft being assembled on the Japanese carriers' flight decks when the striking force under the command of Admiral Chuichi Nagumo reached its flying-off point, 270 miles north of Pearl Harbour, at dawn on 7th December 1941. On the lumbering flagship *Akagi,* Commander Mitsuo Fuchida, who was to lead the first wave, composed of forty Nakajima B5N2 Kates, each armed with an 18-in. torpedo, fifty more Kates fitted out as high-level bombers, fifty Aichi Val dive bombers and an escort of fifty Mitsubishi Zero-Sen fighters, climbed into the cockpit of his machine. Solemnly, he accepted the traditional gift of a white cloth *hakamaki* headband—symbolising preparation for glorious death—while propellers spun and engines thundered into life all around him. Then the six carriers turned slowly into the wind, pitching heavily in the southern seas. Signal flags were run up to the mastheads, a green light blinked in the darkness and the fighters and bombers were on the move, taking off, one by one, into the lightening sky. Fifteen minutes later, 183 machines—all the first wave—were circling over the fleet to gain height before setting course for the target, lying peaceful and all unsuspecting under the rising sun.

Ninety minutes later Commander Fuchida glanced down through a gap in the clouds and glimpsed the white surf breaking along the shore of Kahuku Point, Oahu, with beyond, dimly seen through the early-morning mist, Pearl Harbour and Honolulu. In and around the sprawling American naval base that Sunday were some ninety ships, including eight battleships, two heavy cruisers, six light cruisers and twenty-nine destroyers. By great good fortune, and to the everlasting regret of Admiral Yamamoto and his advisers, not a single aircraft-carrier remained at Pearl Harbour; the mighty *Enterprise, Lexington* and *Saratoga* had all to put to sea, engaged on various precautionary duties. Nevertheless, the so-called Battleship Row seemed crowded with the masts and foretops of capital ships—"the whole U.S. Pacific Fleet in a formation I would not have dared to dream of in my most optimistic dreams," in the words of Commander Fuchida—as the Japanese formation prepared to attack, circling over the sleepy, unstirring target; while little civilian aeroplanes bumbled happily around over Honolulu in the sunshine.

The time was 7.55 a.m. when the first bombs fell on Pearl

Harbour. At the military airfields, dozens of American fighters and bombers were lined up literally wingtip to wingtip, as if on parade, and the Aichi Val dive bombers plunged like eagles towards Hickam Field and Ford Island, bombing and machine-gunning the rows of parked aircraft into burning wreckage. Within minutes, clouds of black smoke were drifting up from the seaplane base at Kaneoke Bay, where another squadron of Vals had dived on a large number of PBY Catalina flying-boats moored there, leaving only three undamaged. The sky was suddenly filled with roaring Zero fighters, streaking at roof-top height across Wheeler Field, with guns blazing; below the hurtling wings, men scattered frantically in all directions, little spurts of dust jumping at their heels.

Meanwhile, the Nakajima Kate torpedo bombers, led by Lieutenant-Commander Shigeharu Murata, were heading directly for the main objective—Battleship Row. Before a gun could be fired in defence, their torpedoes were on the way, dropped at point-blank range, with every pilot determined that the United States Pacific Fleet must be wiped out; and the appalling results of the attack made Commander Fuchida, for one, certain that success had been achieved. The flagship of Vice-Admiral W. S. Pye, the mighty *California,* was hit at once by two torpedoes, and began to list heavily to port; also struck by armour-piercing bombs, she was at first abandoned, but later boarded again and the many fires subdued. During the next three days the stricken *California* settled slowly and inexorably to the bottom of the harbour, until only her superstructure showed forlornly above water. Astern of her, the battleship *Maryland* occupied an inside berth, and was missed by the torpedo bombers, although she was damaged by a huge, armour-piercing bomb. Her unfortunate outer companion, the *Oklahoma,* was, however, hit by three torpedoes in quick succession, followed by two more as she reeled over to port, and within twenty minutes lay capsized in the mud, entombing over four hundred men.

Disaster piled upon disaster in the smoke and flames now raging across Pearl Harbour. The battleship *Tennessee* had escaped the torpedoes, but was damaged by bombs and flying debris; the *West Virginia,* hit by at least six torpedoes, burned as she settled to the bottom, with more than 150 casualties. Astern, the *Ari-*

zona shook under a deluge of armour-piercing projectiles from the Japanese high-level bombers, and began to list; then a great fountain of black smoke, crowned with red flame, erupted 500 ft. into the air as she blew up. Some 1,100 officers and men were killed, including Rear-Admiral Isaac C. Kidd and Captain Franklin Van Valkenburgh, the senior officers aboard. The repair ship *Vestal,* close alongside *Arizona,* was reduced to a shambles by the explosion, and later had to be beached.

The battleship *Nevada* was saved from complete destruction by quick thinking on the part of more than one member of her crew. As enemy torpedo bombers hurtled in to the attack, they were met by a flurry of accurate light anti-aircraft fire which destroyed at least three machines, and only one torpedo struck home on the warship, near the port bow. While damage-repair parties worked in the acrid smoke and fumes below decks to patch up the great, gaping hole in her hull, Lieutenant-Commander Shigekazu Shimazaki led the second wave of Japanese aircraft—fifty-four Nakajima Kate high-level bombers, eighty Aichi Val dive bombers and thirty-six Mitsubishi Zero-Sen fighters—over Pearl Harbour, through a sky now splotched with hundreds of bursting shells. A flight of Val monoplanes peeled off and fell, screaming, almost vertically towards *Nevada,* hitting her twice with armour-piercing bombs before pulling out and swooping low around the foretop, spraying machine-gun fire. Then, to the surprise of all who saw her, the battleship swung ponderously out of her berth and got under way, heading for the harbour entrance; the senior officer aboard, Lieutenant-Commander Francis J. Thomas, was attempting a desperate break-out to the open sea.

Steadily, in slow majesty, *Nevada* steamed down the channel, past the burning wreckage of many ships, inching clear of the gutted *Arizona;* under attack from almost the first moment she moved by an increasing number of enemy aircraft. With all her high-angle guns putting up a fearful bombardment, huge columns of water from bomb bursts rising around her, the battleship drew level with the Navy Yard, where the flagship of the Pacific Fleet, the *Pennsylvania,* lay in dry-dock, together with two destroyers. Both capital ships seemed to disappear at times under the hail of bombs, but in the event *Pennsylvania* survived with only slight damage, although both the destroyers were wrecked.

Hit again and again—one particularly violent explosion was seen to hurl debris up to masthead height—the *Nevada* finally went out of control, turned around and slid to a standstill in the mud of Hospital Point. Later, after the Japanese attacks had ended, tugs were sent to the battleship's aid, and she was beached at Waipio Point, in comparative safety. Extensively reconstructed and repaired, *Nevada* would rejoin the fleet two years after her gallant sortie against tremendous odds at Pearl Harbour, one of the few ships worth salvaging out of the United States Pacific Fleet after 7th December 1941—President Roosevelt's "date which will live in infamy"—had slipped away.

Ninety minutes after the first grey-green Japanese bombers had streaked across Hickam Field and Ford Island the raid on Pearl Harbour was coming to an end. Commander Fuchida, who had long since ordered his radio operator to signal Admiral Nagumo's flagship the single, repeated code word, "Tora, tora, tora," indicating that the surprise attack had been completely successful, circled slowly over the ruined naval base, taking photographs and endeavouring to assess the damage. One of the last pilots to leave the target, he landed back on *Akagi* at 1.0 p.m. with only a few gallons of fuel left in his tanks. Below, a very different message had been sent to Washington and all American forces at sea by Rear-Admiral Patrick N. L. Bellinger and repeated a little later by the Commander in Chief of the Pacific Fleet, Admiral Husband E. Kimmel: "Air raid on Pearl Harbour—this is no drill"; causing many others besides U.S. Navy Secretary Knox to exclaim, "My God! This can't be true!"

Unfortunately, it was only too true, and to prove it the United States had eighteen ships sunk or seriously damaged, 188 aircraft destroyed, over two thousand men killed and a thousand wounded, against the loss of only twenty-nine Japanese aircraft. Nor was that all. Within the next twenty-four hours, Clark Field and Nichols Field, the main American air bases at Manila, would be all but wiped out by a great force of twin-engined Japanese medium bombers, the opening phase of many weeks of bitter fighting destined to end with the Philippines in enemy hands; Malaya was already under attack from large invasion forces; and Hong Kong had begun the courageous resistance so savagely to be overcome before the end of the year. Suddenly, like a giant torch, the whole of South East Asia was ablaze, and although the British Prime Minister, Winston Churchill, was to write long afterwards, "To have the United States at our side was to me the greatest joy," the two countries had joined hands against the Axis powers at the time of a whole series of staggering calamities.

To hold the Malayan Peninsula, the British government was relying faithfully on the so-called 'fortress' of Singapore, supported by the battleship *Prince of Wales* and the battle-cruiser *Repulse,* hurriedly despatched there in lieu of the fleet that was so urgently needed. On 8th December, these two powerful ships, under the command of Admiral Sir T. S. V. Phillips, put to sea with the intention of opposing the Japanese landings at Singora on the western coast of Malaya, but without the benefit of any fighter protection—there were only about 150 aircraft to defend the whole of Malaya. In view of the grave danger from enemy torpedo bombers, Admiral Phillips therefore turned back for Singapore under cover of darkness.

While still heading north, the British battle squadron received news of a reported Japanese landing at Kuantan, some 120 miles north of Singapore, and altered course to investigate; a fatal decision, as it turned out, for in fact the warships had already been sighted by an enemy reconnaissance aircraft. A large formation of Japanese machines—thirty-seven high-level bombers and sixty-one torpedo bombers—took off from bases in Indo-China, and at 11.0 a.m. on a beautiful sunlit morning attacked out of a cloudless sky. Quickly and efficiently the *Prince of Wales* and *Repulse* swung into action, throwing up a tremendous barrage of high-angle anti-aircraft fire; but without air cover both ships were inevitably doomed. For some years it had been feared that the battleship might be too vulnerable to air attack—a new factor in modern war already demonstrated by the American General 'Billy' Mitchell in the early 'twenties, when he proved that well-aimed bombing could sink the mightiest leviathan ever to leave harbour. Now all doubts were about to be resolved, and the reward for many wasted years of indecision reaped in the pitiless waters of the South China Sea.

The Japanese high-level bombers, in two waves, passed over

the warships, hitting *Repulse* but inflicting only minor damage; then three waves of torpedo bombers, pressing their assault home with such determination that the anti-aircraft batteries were completely overwhelmed, hit hard at the battle squadron. Despite violent evasive action, the *Prince of Wales* was struck almost at once by two torpedoes, and turned in a wide circle, out of control. The *Repulse* now had to bear the full brunt of the enemy attack, and at last was shaken by a torpedo hit which brought her almost to a standstill. Four more torpedoes crashed home on the stricken battle-cruiser, and the order to abandon ship was given. Only ninety minutes after the first enemy aircraft had been spotted, *Repulse,* her anti-aircraft guns piled high with empty shell cases and surrounded by dead, capsized and sank, with the loss of over five hundred men.

Half a mile away the crippled *Prince of Wales* was fighting back successive waves of Japanese high-level and torpedo bombers, flown with great skill and courage by men hitherto considered by many Western experts of little consequence as pilots—partly because they were all said to have poor eyesight. Hit by another four torpedoes, the battleship finally slid beneath the waves, taking with her 327 officers and men, including Admiral Phillips and her commander, Captain J. C. Leach. For a moment the great, grey bow was seen jutting out of the water, then the *Prince of Wales* was gone after less than a year of active life, leaving hundreds of men struggling in a sea covered with fuel oil and scattered wreckage. As a decisive weapon, the torpedo bomber—provided it was a modern, efficient machine and not the outdated equipment of a neglected air arm—had been more than vindicated.

"In my whole experience, I do not remember any naval blow so heavy or so painful as the sinking of the *Prince of Wales* and the *Repulse* on Monday last," Mr Winston Churchill told a shocked House of Commons. "These two vast, powerful ships constituted an essential feature in our plans for meeting the new Japanese danger as it loomed against us in the last few months ... The naval power of Great Britain and the United States was very greatly superior—and is still largely superior—to the combined forces of the three Axis powers. But no one must underestimate the gravity of the loss which has been inflicted in Malaya and

Hawaii, or the power of the new antagonist who has fallen upon us, or the length of time it will take to create, marshal and mount the great force in the Far East which will be necessary to achieve the absolute victory." Any hopes of stopping the Japanese flood of conquest within a few months were thus quenched by a man who knew only too well what dark days lay ahead; it looked like another long, weary struggle, against a dedicated and fanatical enemy, with the end not even remotely in sight.

On 15th February 1942 Singapore fell, and by the end of the month the Japanese octopus was preparing to swallow up the myriad islands of the Dutch East Indies before reaching out for the glittering prize of Australia. To take Java, a large invasion force of over a hundred ships was assembled, under the protection of the heavy cruisers *Haguro* and *Nachi,* the light cruisers *Jintsu* and *Naka,* and an escort of destroyers; more than sufficient in view of the only Allied opposition in the area—a somewhat curious collection of battle-damaged cruisers and destroyers of various nationalities, under the command of a Dutch admiral named Karel Doorman. These two fleets clashed on 27th February in the engagement later to be known as the Battle of the Java Sea, which resulted in a total victory for the Japanese commander, Admiral Takagi, after two days of bitter fighting, with no quarter asked or given. The Allied losses were nothing less than catastrophic: the British cruiser *Exeter* (of *Graf Spee* fame) sunk; the Australian light cruiser *Perth* sunk; the United States cruiser *Houston* sunk; the Dutch cruisers *De Ruyter* and *Java* sunk; six destroyers and one sloop also sunk. In fact, out of the whole fleet, only four elderly American destroyers had escaped to reach Australia. Despite the most gallant resistance, Java's doom was inexorably sealed; in a matter of hours, enemy troops were landing on the island.

Slowly but surely the stage was being set for a far more important naval engagement, and one in which carrier-based aircraft were to be vitally concerned—the Battle of the Coral Sea. Meanwhile, Admiral Yamamoto and his staff had spent many hours in conference on the new battleship *Yamato* anchored in Hiroshima Bay; and at the end of March a powerful Japanese battle fleet, composed of four battleships, five carriers, three cruisers and nine destroyers, entered the Indian Ocean. Admiral Nagumo,

again flying his flag in the carrier *Akagi,* intended to seek out and
destroy the British Far Eastern Fleet and attack—possibly even
capture—Ceylon; on the face of it, an operation fraught with
staggering risks in waters so far from Japan, but actually one
well within the capabilities of such a strong force.

It could well have been the Java Sea tragedy all over again.
The British Far Eastern Fleet, commanded by Admiral Sir James
Somerville, was a hastily assembled assortment of ships, gathered
together and rushed out to the Indian Ocean; it included five
battleships, but only one—the *Warspite*—that had been moder-
nised, the other four—*Revenge, Resolution, Ramillies* and *Royal
Sovereign*—being veterans of the First World War. However,
Admiral Somerville also had in his force two modern cruisers,
the *Cornwall* and *Dorsetshire* and, by no means least in importance,
two new aircraft-carriers, the *Indomitable* and *Formidable,* and an
elderly light carrier, the *Hermes.* On paper, therefore, he could
muster quite a powerful little battle squadron and an air striking
force of about eighty machines. Unfortunately, the British carrier-based aircraft—mostly Fairey Albacore torpedo bombers and
Fulmar fighters—were far outclassed by Admiral Nagumo's
Aichi Vals, Nakajima Kates and Mitsubishi Zekes in overall performance.

The bright dawn of 4th April found the Japanese fleet some
500 miles from the coast of Ceylon, where it was sighted by a
patrolling Consolidated Catalina flying-boat that radioed the
enemy's position back to Colombo. Admiral Somerville hurriedly prepared to take his force to sea from the base he had
established at Addu Atoll, and the handful of Hawker Hurricanes and Fairey Fulmars that made up the fighter defence of
Ceylon were placed at immediate readiness. When a great formation of heavily escorted bombers from Admiral Nagumo's five
carriers arrived over Colombo the following morning, they were
thus hotly engaged almost within minutes, and a series of running dogfights developed over the harbour area, the Hurricanes
battling grimly with the nimble little Zero-Sen fighters. Meanwhile, the enemy high-level and dive bombers—about 150 aircraft under the command of Mitsuo Fuchida—commenced a
systematic attack on railway and other installations around
Colombo, but so spirited was the defence that only minor

Above, Mayo composite aircraft: the smaller plane, the Mercury, was carried pick-a-back and launched out at sea to expedite mail and freight delivery. An expensive project, it was used only during 1938; *below,* one of the most effective military flying-boats between the wars was the Short S.19 Singapore III

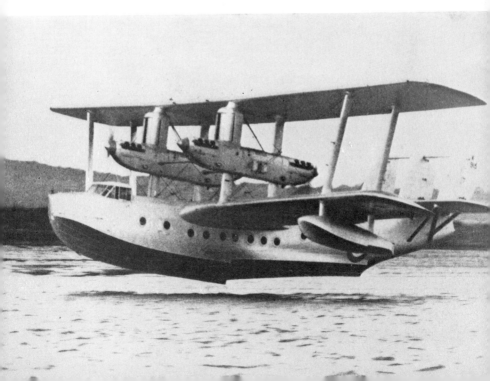

Above, Sikorsky S.42 Clipper, most famous of the China Clipper passenger flying-boats; *below,* the Vickers Supermarine Walrus, used in many peacetime roles and during the Second World War

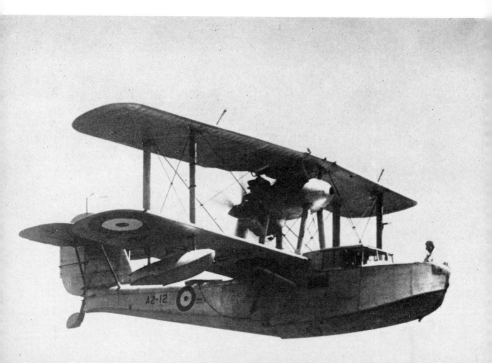

damage was inflicted. About twelve Japanese machines were shot down, and a number of British aircraft destroyed, including an unfortunate torpedo striking force of six Fairey Swordfish biplanes from Trincomalee that strayed into the battle and paid the price for their obsolescence.

The Colombo raid came to an abrupt end when Commander Fuchida picked up a message from a Japanese spotting float-plane, reporting that two British heavy cruisers, perhaps the van-guard of a large squadron, had been sighted steaming south towards Nagumo's fleet. As he led his formation back to the parent carriers, a wave of Aichi D3A Vals under the command of Lieutenant-Commander Takashige Egusa, most brilliant of all Japanese dive bomber pilots, had taken off from the deck of *Soryu*; the executioners of *Cornwall* and *Dorsetshire* were on the way.

At 1.30 p.m., Commander Egusa sighted the two 10,000-ton cruisers, and the dive bombers screamed down to hurl their bombs at the reeling, terribly exposed ships, hitting them again and again. Within minutes, the *Dorsetshire* had been struck no less than seventeen times, and was sinking in a great pool of oil. Soon afterwards *Cornwall* followed her to the bottom, while the escorting destroyers raced frantically around amid the debris, picking up survivors. At Egusa's signal, the Japanese aircraft climbed triumphantly away, untroubled by any opposition; not a single machine had been lost.

For the next three days Admiral Somerville's Far Eastern Fleet and Admiral Nagumo's carrier squadron roamed the vast wastes of the Indian Ocean without crossing swords, although on at least one occasion part of the Japanese force was sighted by Fleet Air Arm Albacores. In fact, Nagumo was trying to persuade his British adversary into a daylight engagement, and thus make full use of his superior air power; whereas Somerville had been taught a bitter lesson by the loss of *Cornwall* and *Dorsetshire,* and sought only a night action. It amounted to simple statistics, well appreciated by both admirals: Nagumo had more, and better, aircraft; Somerville had the biggest guns.

At last Nagumo wearied of the cat-and-mouse game so far from his home waters, and decided to attack the British naval base at Trincomalee in Ceylon, a last sharp thrust with his air weapon before returning to Japan. On the morning of 9th April, Commander Fuchida approached the coast with over a hundred bombers and fighters, to be met by scattered anti-aircraft fire and about twenty courageous Hurricanes and Fulmars; newly installed British radar had successfully detected the waves of raiders. Nevertheless, the scanty Trincomalee defences were quickly overwhelmed, and considerable damage was done around the base, three small warships also being sunk at anchor in the harbour.

By a strange coincidence, the events of 4th April were now to be almost exactly repeated. As the Japanese pilots turned back for their carriers, Admiral Nagumo was reading a signal from one of his spotter-reconnaissance machines, informing him that a British aircraft carrier and her escort had been sighted in the Bay of Bengal. Again, Commander Egusa and his élite crews hurried out to their machines, and just over an hour later the big radial-engined Val monoplanes were circling over the carrier, soon identified as the ageing *Hermes*. Naked to air attack, the helpless British ship was sending out desperate messages to Trincomalee for fighters, unaware that the airfield there had been temporarily put out of action by Commander Fuchida's raiders.

The dive bombers fell like hawks out of the heedless sky. Despite her evasive action, even though her multiple anti-aircraft guns at once opened fire, the *Hermes* had no chance; hit at least nine times in succession, she was soon crippled and brought to a standstill. Within thirty violent minutes she rolled over and sank, while the Japanese pilots turned their attention to the escorting Australian destroyer *Vampire* and corvette *Hollyhock*, both of which also quickly went down under a deluge of heavy bombs.

Commander Egusa and his jubilant crews landed back on *Soryu* to be greeted as heroes, but Admiral Nagumo knew that enough was more than enough; the time had come to set course for home. Unscathed, except for the loss of a few aircraft, his proud carrier fleet made the long journey back from Ceylon, through the Straits of Malacca and past Singapore to Japan, satiated with many victories. Most decisively at Pearl Harbour, and then more recently against Admiral Phillips' battle squadron in the South China Sea, together with the sinking of *Cornwall*, *Dorsetshire* and *Hermes*, it had been demonstrated that naval air power need not merely be the subordinate arm of a fleet, but could be a powerful weapon on its own account. Also, Admiral Yamamoto had proved beyond doubt what Hitler well appreciated before he risked sending *Scharnhorst* and *Gneisenau* through the Channel; modern battleships could operate successfully, even in the most heavily defended enemy waters, provided they had adequate air protection. Without fighter cover—as attempted in the Far East—capital ships were useless, and a fast, efficient carrier fleet was now of infinitely more value than a squadron of battle cruisers.

With good reason, the *sake* flowed freely in the admirals' cabins of the mighty ships in Hiroshima Bay, but the headier wine of success was about to trickle out for the Japanese warlords—though it was not apparent to them or the Allies at the time. Admiral Yamamoto's 'hit-and-run' surprise tactics had indeed more than served their purpose since December 1941, but after six months his technique was no longer unfamiliar, but half expected, and therefore capable of being thwarted. It will be recalled that America's carrier force had been fortunate enough to escape the disastrous attack on Pearl Harbour; and these were the ships destined to play a major part in halting the Japanese bid for a new empire. In 1942 the Coral Sea amounted to little more than a peaceful, glittering tropical paradise, and Midway was only another remote island in the Pacific Ocean, but both were to give their names to the naval battles that first turned the tide against the Rising Sun.

12

SEA FLYERS AT WAR: 1942-44

∞∞∞∞∞∞∞∞∞∞∞∞∞∞∞∞∞∞∞∞∞∞∞∞∞∞∞∞∞∞∞∞∞∞

Out of the seven hundred and forty-one Short Sunderland flying-boats of all Marks and variants produced during the Second World War, only a few crashed for reasons not directly attributable to enemy action; but in one such accident a man was killed whose death came as a great shock not only to his family but to all the people of Great Britain. On 25th August 1942 a Sunderland Mark III, serial numbered *W4026* and piloted by Flight Lieutenant Frank Goyen, was en route from Invergordon naval base to Iceland when, for reasons still not properly explained, it moved off course. Instead of hugging the Scottish coastline, as planned, the big white flying-boat headed slowly but surely more inland, dangerously near high, rocky ground, passing with a great roaring of engines over the scattered farms and cottages of that remote area.

In thick cloud the Sunderland descended to a very low height, narrowly missed a 900-ft. pinnacle beyond the little village of Berriedale known as Eagle's Rock, ,and then struck the ground at full speed, disintegrating with such great force that nothing but fragments remained. Of the fifteen people aboard, only the tail gunner, Andrew Jack, was left alive; after wandering the countryside in a dazed condition for some time, he found shelter in a small cottage, and eventually recovered. Among the bodies littered around the smoking wreckage lay that of a handsome man wearing the badges of rank of an air commodore. In fact, the officer was His Royal Highness the Duke of Kent, fourth son of King George V, killed on active service just as surely as any prince of medieval times. A great tragedy had come to peaceful Oban, at a time when the whole world was already weighed down by many tragedies.

With Allied shipping losses mounting in the Atlantic, and the Far East ablaze from Singapore to Pearl Harbour, it was becoming increasingly difficult for the Royal Air Force effectively to patrol the vast stretches of water involved, and Short Sunderlands were being employed on many duties, aside from anti-submarine and reconnaissance work. In the Mediterranean theatre of operations alone the flying-boats had already proved invaluable, safely evacuating many hundreds of men from Greece and Crete; on more than one occasion individual aircraft successfully took off with between sixty and seventy troops aboard. Two overworked Sunderland squadrons, operating from Bathurst, Freetown and Lagos under the worst possible conditions of malaria, humid heat and tropical rain, meanwhile waged a continuous war against the U-boats menacing the Cape convoys, and over the colder, misty waters of the North Sea and mid-Atlantic other Sunderlands roamed for many hours at a time, also seeking the telltale periscopes. But the great hunting-ground for enemy submarines and their protective fighter cover in 1943 remained the Bay of Biscay, scene of many savage air battles between Sunderlands and the Arado Ar 196s and Junkers Ju 88s out from Bordeaux.

Over the Bay of Biscay the Sunderlands had to fight for their very existence; and the big flying-boats never failed to enhance the reputation they had achieved in 1940. On 30th July 1942 a Sunderland of No. 461 Squadron fought a typical engagement with three cannon-firing Ar 196 floatplanes, shooting down one of the enemy machines and damaging another, then turning on the third with such concentrated fire from all guns that it dropped to wavetop height and fled. Another Sunderland of No. 461 Squadron, riddled from bow to tail with cannon shell and machine-gun bullet holes, made a successful landing on a beach; but even this accomplishment was outshone by a Short boat of the same type which had a great gap stove in the hull by heavy seas and crashlanded on the aerodrome at Angle, in South Wales.

Undoubtedly, the most memorable air battle involving a Sunderland took place in the early summer of 1943, following upon many months of increasing enemy activity in the Bay of Biscay. Apart from the problems created by more and more U-boats intent on breaking out into the Atlantic—and now no longer diving to escape when sighted, but so heavily armed with anti-aircraft weapons that they were prepared to fight it out with attacking aircraft on the surface—the Sunderland squadrons were having to cope with whole formations of Ar 196 floatplanes or Ju 88 medium fighters operating from forward bases in France. On 1st June a B.O.A.C. Douglas D.C.3 airliner, flying on the Lisbon to England route with thirteen passengers on board, including the famous actor and film star Leslie Howard, was intercepted over the Bay by eight Ju 88s of *Kampfgruppe* 40 and shot down in flames. There were no survivors. The next morning a Short Sunderland, again from No. 461 Squadron, was on patrol in the area when it was also attacked by eight Ju 88s, probably of the same Luftwaffe unit, from Kerhouin-Bastard airfield near Lorient. Coming in from each beam, the heavily armed fighters determinedly set about shooting the Sunderland to pieces.

Captained by Flight Lieutenant Walker, with an Australian crew, the flying-boat jinked and weaved, fighting back attack after attack, taking a fearful amount of punishment, but refusing to go down. The port outer engine was hit and set on fire; bursts of 20-mm. cannon fire raked the flight deck; the wings and hull were shot through and through with bullet holes. Then the front gunner caught one of the Ju 88s with an accurate burst as it hurtled past at close range, and the fighter flicked wing over wing into the sea, a mass of flames. The rear turret of the Sunderland was struck by cannon fire and the tail gunner badly wounded; but crossfire from the front and midships turrets met in the cockpit of a second Ju 88, shooting it down. Still the battle continued, until the flight deck of the Short boat had been reduced to a shambles, littered with wreckage from the destroyed radio compartment and shattered instrument panel. The so-called 'galley gun'—actually a ·303-calibre gas-operated Vickers K gun fitted by No. 461 Squadron armourers on a swivel mounting to fire through the galley hatches—was put out of action, and the gunner killed. Three more crew members were wounded by flying splinters; it seemed that the gallant Sunderland was doomed.

Then the rear gunner recovered sufficiently to man his multiple Brownings, and hit a Ju 88 which flew unsteadily on to be met by the concentrated fire from the Sunderland's nose turret.

Streaming flames and black smoke, the fighter exploded into the sea. Another Ju 88 reeled out of the battle, badly damaged; and yet another retired with an engine on fire. At last, only two enemy fighters remained, and they merely hammered out a few more futile bursts before disappearing in the direction of France, leaving the Sunderland battered but triumphantly alone in the arena.

Showing great skill, and although in pain from wounds, Flight Lieutenant Walker nursed the crippled flying-boat back to England on three engines, slowly losing height. Three hundred yards from the Cornish coast another engine failed, and the Sunderland dropped heavily into the sea, to be broken to pieces against the rocks within a few hours. Nevertheless, Walker and his crew had returned home, after destroying three enemy fighters, probably destroying two more, and damaging the other three, out of a formation of eight machines—a magnificent achievement.

After 2nd June 1943 the Short Sunderland was viewed with even more respect in Luftwaffe circles than before; indeed, a special Intelligence report was requested by Berlin for the historic engagement fought over the Bay of Biscay on that day. Finally it was decided that the Sunderland involved must have been heavily armed with 20-mm.—or even perhaps 37-mm.—cannon, thus making it virtually impregnable. About the same time as this report was made, or possibly because of it, the Sunderland type became known as the *Stachelschwein,* or Porcupine, among the German airmen, who had good cause to fear its amazing ability to fight back against the most overwhelming opposition.

It was true, of course, that only increased fire power for the Sunderland could provide the answer to the more intensive enemy fighter and U-boat activity in the Bay of Biscay, and during 1943 various armament modifications were carried out, including more ·303-calibre Browning guns in the bow turret, four fixed ·303-calibre Brownings in the nose to be fired by the captain, and additional Vickers K guns. Also, the fitting of galley guns became approved, standard practice; and the Sunderland Mark V was to be further reinforced by two ·5-in. Browning guns in beam positions. The Luftwaffe might well already consider the most famous of all Short boats to be "a very dangerous aircraft"; for the next two years, it was going to prove equally harmful to the German submarine service.

The increased armament of the Bay of Biscay Sunderlands, particularly the fixed battery of nose guns, turned out to be even more effective than had been anticipated, and many a U-boat commander regretted attempting to fight it out with his attacker on the surface once the modifications had come into general use. Typical of many sharp encounters between Sunderlands and enemy submarines was the engagement involving a flying-boat of No. 10 Squadron, R.A.A.F., piloted by Flying Officer Roberts, who dived to attack a U-boat on the surface when patrolling over the Bay. The submarine, which was the U.426 outward bound from Lorient, immediately opened fire with a 37-mm. cannon and a battery of 20-mm. cannon mounted in the conning tower, supported by machine-guns deployed fore and aft, but Roberts remained unswerving in his low-level approach and at 1,200 yd. pressed the firing button of his nose guns. Momentarily, the tracer from the Sunderland intermingled at point-blank range with the enemy cannon fire; then the German weapons spun uselessly on their mountings as the gunners collapsed, their legs mown from under them. Roberts pulled the control column back, banking the Sunderland around to make a second attack. Coming in very low from the starboard quarter, he saw the U-boat wallowing in the bullet-frothed water, with her conning tower now cleared of men, and dropped six depth charges, which erupted just alongside the long, grey hull. As he passed over the submarine a third time, Roberts had the satisfaction of seeing it go down by the stern in a pool of oil, with the crew jumping overboard; a successful conclusion to a textbook attack, frequently to be repeated by other Sunderlands right up to 4th May 1945, when Grand Admiral Doenitz called upon all his U-boats to cease hostilities.

Much more could undoubtedly be written about the work of Short Sunderlands between the years 1939 and 1945, and, for that matter, Avro Ansons, Lockheed Hudsons, Consolidated Liberators and Catalinas, and all those other splendid aircraft of R.A.F. Coastal Command manned by crews who endured all the hardships of their predecessors of the First World War with equal courage and patience. One recalls the Lockheed Hudson of No. 269 Squadron, flown by Squadron Leader James Thompson, which was on patrol off Iceland when a U-boat was sighted and attacked with depth charges. Damaged beyond immediate repair, the submarine U.570 surrendered by waving a white flag from the conning tower, and was later towed to Iceland by the Royal Navy, eventually to join British service. As for the Avro Anson—old 'Faithful Annie'—suffice it to say that the type remained in continuous production for seventeen years, and although considered obsolescent by 1940 three of the machines successfully repulsed nine Bf 109 fighters and shot down two of them over the English Channel in June of the same year. In common with the Lockheed Hudson, the larger four-engined Consolidated B-24 Liberator was supplied to Great Britain by the United States under the Lend-Lease agreement, and served with Coastal Command in large numbers, especially on patrols over the Atlantic and Bay of Biscay. A striking example of the type in action, reminiscent of many similar exploits by Sunderlands, took place in August 1943, when Flying Officer L. A. Trigg, R.N.Z.A.F. piloting a Liberator of No 200 Squadron, attacked an enemy submarine which remained on the surface and hit back with massed cannon and machine-gun fire. Mortally wounded, and with his aircraft in flames, Flying Officer Trigg nevertheless destroyed the U-boat before crashing into the sea; a courageous member of the Commonwealth fated to die far from his native islands, he was posthumously awarded the Victoria Cross.

Of British and American manufacture, twin- and four-engined, anti-submarine bomber or reconnaissance amphibian, let the Short Sunderland flying-boat symbolise all the varied aircraft of Coastal Command. It served with the Royal Air Force from 1938, into and beyond the darkest days of the Second World War, and faithfully endured a host of modifications, from the Mark II of 1941 to the last Mark V completed by Short Brothers in June 1946. The Sunderland represented the successful culmination of flying-boat development since the days of T. O. M. Sopwith's Bat Boats, followed by the huge biplane craft conceived in the brain of John Porte at Felixstowe; and it is a little sad to reflect that only one example of the type remains in the United Kingdom today, non-flying, but kept in perfect condition by a handful of enthusiastic volunteers at Pembroke Dock. Surely two or three of the Sunderlands allowed to moulder away in the great scrapyard at Seletar in the post-war years could have been saved, if only to keep the memory green of what they had achieved?

"The time has come", the Walrus said, "to talk of many things," according to Lewis Carroll; and if the Vickers Super-marine Walruses used during the war could have exchanged stories of their experiences they would indeed have had many a long and interesting discussion. Mention has already been made of the catapulted shipborne aircraft involved in the Battle of the River Plate, and other Walruses were soon performing a great variety of tasks in many theatres of operations, including the Atlantic, Mediterranean, Red Sea and Indian Ocean. During 1941 the ambling biplanes, launched from such cruisers as the *Shropshire, Glasgow, Capetown, Australia* and *Canberra,* were particularly active in searching for the pocket battleship *Admiral Scheer* and the equally elusive merchant raiders—*Atlantis, Pinguin, Kormoran* and the rest. Undoubtedly the most successful of the German merchant auxiliary cruisers, or Q-ships, was the 7,860-ton *Atlantis,* commanded by Captain Bernard Rogge, which sunk or captured a total of 145,697 tons of Allied shipping in twenty adventurous months at sea; she was eventually sent to the bottom by the heavy cruiser H.M.S. *Devonshire* in November 1941, after being sighted and shadowed by a Walrus catapulted from the British warship.

The bringing to battle of the merchant raider *Kormoran,* commanded by Captain Theodor Detmers, was to end in disaster for both sides, perhaps because a Walrus was not more quickly launched to do its job. On 19th November 1941 the 9,000-ton former Hamburg-Amerika Line ship was in the Indian Ocean, disguised as the Dutch steamer *Straat Malakka* and steaming a N.N.E. course, when the Australian light cruiser H.M.A.S. *Sydney* was sighted, closing fast. When challenged to identify herself, the *Kormoran* hoisted the correct recognition signal of the *Straat Malakka* and also radioed a general alarm that she was being stopped by an unknown cruiser. Obviously still very suspicious, the *Sydney* came nearer, until she was less than a mile away, her 6-in. guns ready to open fire.

Captain Detmers could see the cruiser's Walrus aircraft on its catapult with the engine running, apparently about to be launched. "At any moment it would be catapulted into the air," he writes in his book *The Raider Kormoran*,[1] "and once the observer spotted us from above he would recognise us at once for what we were, an auxiliary cruiser . . . It might be possible to conceal the range-finding crew with their apparatus before the plane arrived, but the camouflage of the guns in Hatches 2 and 4 was not so perfect that it could stand such close scrutiny." However, the *Sydney* did not launch her Walrus, but instead signalled: "Give your secret sign," which was, of course, unknown to Detmers. The Australian warship was by now moving very slowly almost parallel to *Kormoran* at a range of about 1,000 yd; her main turrets and port torpedo tubes were still trained on the raider, but stewards were at the rails, gazing across the gap more with curiosity than suspicion.

"Give your secret sign!" urgently repeated the *Sydney,* and Captain Detmers knew his bluff was at an end. At his quick command, the German battle ensign broke at the foretop of the *Kormoran,* the rails dropped, hatch covers crashed down and the main and secondary armament hurled a devastating broadside into the Australian cruiser, all within the space of a few seconds. Hit in the superstructure, bridge and fire director tower, the *Sydney* nevertheless immediately replied with a full salvo, which passed over the *Kormoran*; then the raider was slamming salvo after salvo into her. Both ships fired torpedoes, and one hit the *Sydney* abaft of A turret, exploding a magazine; the Walrus was destroyed, and B turret blown out of its barbette over the side. Within minutes the cruiser was burning from stem to stern, but two of her turrets came into action again, and the *Kormoran* was struck amidships and in the engine-room.

Brought to a standstill, *Kormoran* nevertheless kept up a rapid and continuous fire, sweeping the stricken *Sydney*'s starboard side until nothing moved above decks, and she was drifting helplessly away, down by the bows, a mass of flames. When the range had lengthened to over 10,000 yd., Captain Detmers gave the order to cease fire, leaving the cruiser to depart in peace. For some time

[1] By Theodor Detmers (William Kimber, 1962).

she could be seen glowing in the oncoming darkness, then there was a momentary brightening of the light on the horizon, as if from a violent explosion. Nothing more was ever seen or heard of the *Sydney* or her crew of 645 officers and men.

With his ship badly damaged, and much of the superstructure well ablaze, Captain Detmers was in the curious situation of a man who had simultaneously won a victory and yet lost a battle. The *Kormoran* was beyond salvage or repair, and her commander could do no more than order the placing of scuttling charges and see his men safely into the lifeboats. In the early hours of 20th November they rowed sadly away, and soon afterwards *Kormoran* blew up with a tremendous detonation that hurled a fountain of flame over 1,000 ft. into the air. Huge fragments of debris rained down all around the boats, then the raider lifted her bows for the last time and was gone. Captain Detmers and most of his crew were eventually picked up by Allied ships and taken to Australia, where they remained as prisoners of war until 1947. Often lonely, they were kept cheerful by the memory of an incredible achievement in naval warfare; a thinly plated, virtually unarmoured, converted passenger steamer armed with six 5·9-in. guns and four torpedo tubes had sunk a modern, very fast light cruiser, despite all her advantages in up-to-date fire control and superior armament.

Meanwhile the Supermarine Walrus amphibians, catapulted from many British warships—some smaller than the gallant *Sydney* and some much larger, but all relentlessly searching out the enemy regardless of the consequences—were droning noisily around to scour the seven seas. On at least one occasion, in 1940, a Walrus had been put to work as a dive bomber against the fortified town of Dante, in Italian Somaliland; and another of the ubiquitous three-seater biplanes was sent to trundle amiably in wide circles over Genoa on a February morning in 1941, spotting the fall of shot from the battleships *Malaya* and *Renown* and the cruiser *Sheffield,* all of which subjected the Italian city to a heavy and concentrated bombardment for over half an hour. Yet another Walrus alighted in Tobruk harbour at night to deliver urgent medical and other supplies for the 8th Army troops—the famous 'Rats of Tobruk'—besieged in the fortress by General Rommel's armoured divisions.

The Supermarine Walrus Mk. II, with a wooden hull, was produced almost exclusively by Saunders-Roe Ltd. from 1941 onwards, mainly for air-sea rescue work, and proved invaluable in that role with the Royal Air Force. During the great fighter battles over the Channel in 1943 and the round-the-clock heavy bomber offensive against Germany through 1944 into 1945, many British, American and German airmen survived only because a Walrus was standing by ready for any emergency; and more than one 'Shagbat' alighted to pick up a ditched pilot, despite warnings of enemy aircraft or E-boats in the vicinity. A typical example of the kind of situation that could easily arise took place on 16th June 1943, when a Walrus of No. 277 Squadron, piloted by Flight Lieutenant J. A. Spence, R.C.A.F., took off from Hawkinge to locate a British airman reported down in the Channel. The tiny dinghy was soon sighted, with a Spitfire circling protectively overhead, and Spence made a successful landing in spite of very rough seas. With great difficulty he managed to taxi almost alongside the survivor, Sergeant Ticklepenny, who was finally hauled aboard the Walrus after six attempts had been made. However, a take-off proved to be impossible.

Taxiing on the choppy water, Spence commenced the long journey back to the English coast, grateful for the company of two R.A.F. motor launches from Dover that had arrived on the scene. Meanwhile the watchful Spitfire overhead had been joined by two more; but a few moments later a formation of about twenty Focke-Wulf Fw 190s dropped out of the sun, and a savage, whirling dogfight unreeled across the Channel.

At last Spence reached Dover, having ploughed the sturdy Walrus home through seas that would have broken up many a larger craft. Above his head the air battle had died down, after four of the German fighters and two Spitfires had been destroyed, but Spence knew nothing of all the excitement and confusion; intent on steering his machine back to England, he had been completely unaware of what was happening outside the cockpit windows.

In 1944 the Supermarine Sea Otter entered service with the Fleet Air Arm as a replacement for the Walrus. Although somewhat similar to the Walrus in appearance, except for a more conventional Bristol Mercury tractor engine, the Sea Otter never quite gained the same deep affection from naval airmen as its illustrious predecessor, and only outlived the Walrus by a few years. In fact, the later aircraft had a more powerful engine than the Walrus, a faster speed and almost twice the range; but the air-sea rescue amphibian biplane, as a type, was dead by 1945. The Sea Otter proved to be the last of a long and distinguished line of Supermarine biplane amphibians, the last biplane to enter squadron service with the Fleet Air Arm and to be used by the Royal Air Force.

Of course, there was—and will always be—only one Walrus amphibian; the type was virtually indestructible and persuasively irreplaceable. "The engine makes a steady roar, but sufficiently above and behind us to make conversation possible," writes Terence Horsley in his history of the Fleet Air Arm.[1] "On a rough day the Walrus behaves more like a cow than a bus—a very friendly cow, however. She wallows in the trough of the rough airs as a heifer knee deep in a boggy meadow . . ." And that just about sums up in a few words the most loved aircraft in the Fleet Air Arm, with the possible exception of the Fairey Swordfish; slow and cumbersome, noisy and inclined to be draughty, not easy to fly, but always dependable.

In the decade that the Walrus was in full production, 741 machines were built, of which 453 were sub-contracted and manufactured by Saunders-Roe, Ltd. Today it is believed that only one example of the type remains in flying condition, used for private purposes by its Australian owner. But how many other Walruses have been neglected and left to rot away on deserted airstrips and beaches all over the world in the intervening years, forgotten and abandoned, the characteristic beating of those open-exhaust Pegasus cylinders never to be heard again?

[1] *Find, Fix and Strike* (Eyre and Spottiswoode, 1944).

13

THE CORAL SEA: 1942

~~~~~~

In his youth, Lieutenant-Colonel James H. Doolittle had been a member of that exclusive little band of happy-go-lucky, barn-storming, stunt-flying airmen who thrilled and delighted fairground crowds in the rural communities of the American mid-Western states. In time of war, at the age of forty-five, Doolittle was perhaps a little less reckless, more matured, but still abrim with energy; a man whose active brain teemed with far-sighted, unusual aviation ideas. Early in 1942 Doolittle was preparing for what seemed to many of his superior officers an impossible venture to undertake less than six months after Pearl Harbour—a bombing raid on the Japanese capital city of Tokyo.

As Tokyo was many thousands of miles from the nearest American air base, it followed that only carrier-borne aircraft could be used in the proposed attack; but the comparatively limited range of all normal United States naval striking bombers at that time prohibited Doolittle from even considering them. He needed a sturdy machine with an overall range of well over 2,000 miles, capable of carrying a bomb load of at least 2,000 lb. and yet able to take off from the deck of an aircraft-carrier, perhaps in the roughest of seas. Finally, the twin-engined North American B-25 Mitchell medium bomber was selected, although it was a fairly large aircraft with a wing-span of 67 ft., and twin-motored types had never before been operated from carriers. Once the difficult decision had been made—the Martin B-26 Marauder having also been carefully considered—Doolittle went to work training his special volunteer aircrews.

The prototype North American B-25 flew for the first time in January 1939, and later the same year the first production batch of 184 machines was leaving the Inglewood, California, assembly lines. Some time in 1941 the type was officially named Mitchell, after the brilliant, outspoken American colonel of the twenties who had displayed such remarkable, if individualistic, views on air bombardment; and by the time of Pearl Harbour it was becoming established as easily the best United States medium bomber to enter service for some years. Large numbers of B-25s had also been supplied to Russia and Great Britain under the Lend-Lease agreement, and many variations on the basic theme were to appear before the end of the Second World War, including the B-25G version armed with fourteen 0·5-in. machine-guns and a 75-mm. cannon, produced mainly for use against ship and ground targets.

For three hard months Lieutenant-Colonel Doolittle prepared his volunteer crews from the squadrons of the 17th Bombardment Group and the 89th Reconnaissance Squadron to take part in the raid; twelve weeks of alarmingly short take-offs, perilous, low-level flying and the study of dozens of maps and pictures. At last the energetic, demanding air commander was satisfied, and embarked with his men and sixteen B-25B Mitchells on the aircraft-carrier *Hornet,* commanded by the famous Admiral William F. ('Bull') Halsey, Jr. The bombers were too large to be stowed in the carrier's hold in the usual manner, and had to be lashed down on the flight deck, of necessity exposed to the elements except for canvas covers.

While the carrier force was at sea Doolittle continued to put his crews through their gunnery and navigation paces, although no actual flying could, of course, be carried out. His original plan called for the bombers to take off in the late afternoon of 18th April, when the *Hornet* was about 400 miles from Tokyo, and thus arrive over their target during the night. They would then have just sufficient fuel left to reach the Chinese bases selected to receive them. However, shortly after dawn the carrier was sighted by the Japanese patrol boat *Nitto Maru* while still 800 miles from Tokyo, and although the enemy ship was sunk almost at once, it was feared that a radio warning had been sent out. After a hurried conference on board the *Hornet,* it was decided to fly off the B-25s within the hour, which meant that the raid would now be carried out in daylight, but with any luck before the Japanese could muster large fighter forces over their capital.

At 8.20 a.m. Lieutenant-Colonel Doolittle, in the leading B-25, gave the twin Wright Cyclone engines full power, and the big, dun-coloured machine rumbled down the heaving deck of the *Hornet* to dip slightly at the stern, then rise up and away. He was successfully followed by the other fifteen bombers, which joined formation, then raced at full speed for the Japanese coast, skimming the storm-tossed waves. In the event, the sudden change of plan proved to have been well worthwhile; the enemy defence system was taken completely by surprise. "We approached our objectives just over the house-tops, but bombed at 1,500 ft.," commented Doolittle afterwards. "The target for one plane was a portion of the navy yard south of Tokyo, in reaching which we passed over what apparently was a flying school, as there were a number of planes in the air." Hits were observed on various military objectives, including installations at Kobe, Yokohama and Nagoya, and "the rear gunners reported seeing columns of smoke rising thousands of feet into the air," to quote Doolittle's own words again.

Heading for Chinese territory through increasingly stormy weather, the B-25s became scattered, and one by one they ran out of fuel. Most of the crews baled out in the darkness; eight men landed in Japanese-occupied areas, but the majority were fortunate enough to come down in China. At least one B-25 made a landing in Russia near Vladivostok, and the crew members were interned. Despite many hazardous adventures, of the eighty aircrew involved in the first Tokyo raid, seventy-one in due course arrived home, a not unhappy ending to an attack in which all the bombers had been lost.

"This inhuman attack is causing widespread indignation among the populace!" trumpeted the Tokyo radio, adding with some truth that the material damage was inconsiderable. Nevertheless, the blow to Japanese morale, made more severe by the uncertainty as to which American base had been used by the B-25s, caused great consternation in enemy high circles. At a press conference two days later President Roosevelt revealed some details of the raid, and, with his famous twinkling smile, mentioned that the bombers had operated from Shangri-La! Apparently only a very few Japanese or Germans had read the novel *Lost Horizon* by James Hilton, for the statement was repeated with complete sincerity by the enemy radio stations; from Berlin, the announcer commented: "Doolittle carried out his air attack from the base Shangri-La, which was not otherwise described by Roosevelt."

Long before the shock of Colonel Doolittle's 'thirty seconds over Tokyo' reverberated around Japan, Admiral Yamamoto and his staff had settled upon the next phase of General Tojo's overall plan of conquest in the Pacific—the invasion of the Solomons and New Guinea, followed by the capture of the important American base of Midway Island. During the first week in May, therefore, a large fleet of some seventy ships, including the 30,000-ton aircraft-carriers *Shokaku* and *Zuikaku* and the 12,000-ton light carrier *Shoho,* was converging at top speed on the Solomon Islands. Vice-Admiral Shigeyoshi Inouye, in command of the whole powerful force, had been informed that heavily escorted American carriers were also in the South Pacific, moving on a course to intercept his ships; but he was confident that if it came to a battle the Japanese, with their superior aircraft, would be the victors.

The United States carriers in the area were, in fact, the *York-town,* with five cruisers and a destroyer screen, under Rear-Admiral Frank Fletcher, and, sent out in haste from Pearl Harbour, the *Lexington,* in which flew the flag of Rear-Admiral Aubrey W. Fitch. On 3rd May American reconnaissance aircraft sighted the large concentration of enemy shipping in the Coral Sea, with the small Solomon Islands harbour of Tulagi thronged with troop transports and destroyers. It soon became apparent that Tulagi had already fallen without any difficulty to Admiral Inouye, and his carrier fleet was on the way to attack Port Moresby, the stepping-stone to Australia; but Admiral Fletcher nevertheless decided to mount a series of air strikes in an attempt to destroy the enemy invasion force in the Solomons.

During 4th May three attacks were made on the Japanese ships in Tulagi harbour by some forty Douglas TBD-1 Devastator torpedo bombers and SBD Dauntless dive bombers from the *Yorktown,* regrettably with only limited success. The new genera-tion of American naval airmen lacked none of the courage and determination that their fathers had displayed in the First World War, but when the Battle of the Coral Sea opened they badly needed more experience in action. Also, the Devastator, slow and with inadequate defensive armament, was already obsolescent by 1942; and the Dauntless, although a most versatile aircraft in many ways, never quite succeeded in the dive bomber role. Many torpedoes were launched, more than seventy heavy bombs dropped and thousands of rounds of machine-gun ammunition expended at Tulagi, in order to drive one enemy destroyer aground, sink two or three minesweepers and landing-craft, and destroy a flight of seaplanes at anchor. Three American aircraft were lost.

Two days later *Yorktown* made a satisfactory rendezvous with the *Lexington* force, and refuelling was carried out before proceeding on course for the New Guinea coast. By now Admiral Inouye's fleet was well into the Coral Sea, with spotter aircraft out searching for the American ships; both groups of carriers were thus almost within striking distance of each other, but by pure chance still not making contact. Finally a B-17 Flying Fortress from Port Moresby sighted the spearhead of the Japanese invasion convoy, which included the light carrier *Shoho* and four heavy cruisers. Admiral Fletcher at once detached three of his cruisers, with an escort of three destroyers, to intercept the enemy force. This American support group under Rear-Admiral J. G. Crace was soon spotted by a Japanese reconnaissance machine, and Admiral Inouye despatched thirty-three medium bombers, escorted by eleven fighters, from Rabaul to attack it.

Meanwhile, an aircraft on patrol from the *Yorktown* sighted the Japanese light cruisers and some gunboats, but due to an error in decoding the pilot's radioed report, Admiral Fletcher was led to believe that two enemy carriers and four cruisers had been seen. The elusive *Shokaku* and *Zuikaku* seemed at last within striking distance, and the American commander ordered an air attack of maximum strength from both *Yorktown* and *Lexington*. Within an hour, seventy-five torpedo and dive bombers, with an escort of eighteen fighters, were in the air. Not surprisingly, no important Japanese units were at first to be seen, but by great good fortune Lieutenant-Commander W. L. Hamilton, flying one of the *Lexington*'s aircraft, suddenly noticed ships on the horizon—two enemy cruisers and a light carrier. Minutes later alarm bells were

ringing frantically on board the *Shoho* as the American bombers
hurtled down to attack her.

Weaving through heavy, if rather excitable, anti-aircraft fire,
the Devastators released their torpedoes, while the *Shoho* swung
into the wind in a vain attempt to launch some of her fighters.
Then the Dauntless dive bombers were hitting the carrier hard;
one bomb exploded close alongside and blew a number of aircraft overboard, another destroyed the steering gear, and a third
set the flight deck ablaze. More bombs and torpedoes crashed
home on the staggering *Shoho*, which continued to swing in a
circle, listing and out of control. Thirty minutes after after being
sighted by Lieutenant-Commander Hamilton, she went down,
the first Japanese carrier to be sunk by American airmen.

Admiral Inouye had no sooner been informed of the *Shoho*'s
loss than more bad news was received; his attack on Admiral
Crace's cruiser squadron by shore-based aircraft had been a complete failure. Thanks to expert evasive action, all the American
warships had escaped unscathed through a deluge of bombs and
torpedoes, and five of the raiders would never return to Rabaul—
proving once again that experienced carrier-borne naval airmen
always stood a far greater chance of success when operating
against targets at sea. The Japanese now decided to cut their
losses, and withdrew the Port Moresby invasion force in the
hope that it might still evade the *Yorktown* and *Lexington* groups.
At the same time, a squadron of torpedo bombers was flown off
by the *Shokaku* in an attempt to locate the United States carriers.

Despite rain squalls and increasingly heavy cloud, the Japanese
pilots, led by Lieutenant-Commander Kuichi Takahashi, sear-
ched for their targets far into the night, until all the crews were
completely exhausted. Then, without realising how close they
were to success, the bombers passed directly over a mist-
enshrouded *Lexington*; but the carrier's radar detected their presence, and Grumman Wildcat single-seater fighters took to the
air. In the short, sharp dogfight that ensued, nine of the Japanese
machines were shot down, a disastrous ending to what had
proved to be an unfortunate day for Admiral Inouye and his
subordinate commanders.

Nevertheless, the American carriers had at last been found, less
than a hundred miles away from the nearest Japanese ship, *Sho-*

kaku. Early on the morning of 8th May, Lieutenant-Commander Takahashi again took off, leading thirty-two Aichi Val dive bombers, eighteen Nakajima Kate torpedo bombers and eighteen Mitsubishi Zero-Sen fighters into action. Meanwhile, Admiral Fletcher's reconnaissance aircraft, out since dawn, had sighted the Japanese carrier fleets, and soon after 9.0 a.m. fifty-two Dauntless dive bombers, twenty-one Devastator torpedo bombers and fifteen Wildcat fighters were launched from the *Yorktown* and *Lexington.* The Battle of the Coral Sea—the first naval engagement in history fought entirely between carrier-based aircraft, with surface units taking no part—had begun.

In a steady tropical rainstorm the American striking force dived from 17,000 ft. to attack the *Shokaku* and *Zuikaku,* which were both hurriedly launching their fighters. Flying through driving squalls, the Devastators and Dauntlesses lost *Zuikaku* in the mist, but *Shokaku* had to bear the full brunt of the United States attackers, and was soon hit again and again. Two 1,000-lb. bombs, falling in quick succession, pierced her flight deck, causing an intense petrol-fed fire; and while damage-repair parties were still fighting the blaze, another wave of dive bombers scored more direct hits that sent columns of black smoke towering high into the air. Then the *Zuikaku* was glimpsed for a few moments, and a number of Devastators released their torpedoes at her before she dodged away into the low cloud once more, escaping without damage.

Meanwhile, the *Yorktown* and *Lexington* were valiantly defending themselves against waves of determined Japanese attackers. Commander Takahashi, diving through the intense barrage of anti-aircraft fire from *Yorktown,* was killed when his aircraft was blown to pieces by a direct hit, and the two bombers immediately following were also destroyed. A heavy bomb struck the carrier amidships and passed through three decks before exploding with devastating effect in the confined space below, but she successfully avoided the many torpedoes directed at her. Nine of the Nakajima Kate torpedo bombers came in very low to attack the *Lexington*—"I could see American sailors staring at my plane as it rushed by," reported one Japanese pilot afterwards—and the big ship heeled over as she quickly swung to starboard. Torpedo tracks criss-crossed on either side; the stern of the *Lexington* came frantically around; then two violent explosions erupted on her port bow, near the bridge. Simultaneously a tight formation of Aichi Vals fell in almost vertical dives, hitting the carrier twice with bombs that put her aircraft lifts out of action, broke numerous fuel pipes and flooded three boiler rooms. However, the damage seemed to be more spectacular than serious, and the many small fires were soon being brought under control.

By noon, the sound and fury of battle had died away. The surviving Japanese aircraft returned to their parent carriers to find the *Shokaku* still blazing and unable to accept landings, while the *Zuikaku* was trying desperately to cope with almost twice her normal complement of machines. This was obviously quite impossible, and a number of the bombers and fighters were forced to land on the sea and be abandoned. At last the twin carrier fleets were ready for the slow, limping journey back to Japan; they had hardly been completely defeated, but not by any stretch of the imagination could there be any excuse for another victory celebration in Tokyo Bay.

The American forces were also out of luck that warm Pacific afternoon. No sooner had the last enemy raider disappeared than men were swarming all over the stricken *Lexington,* repairing damage and fighting fires; within an hour she was back on an even keel. Then, suddenly, the carrier was shaken by a tremendous explosion from deep within her vitals; fuel seeping from a fractured pipe had been ignited by a spark from a running generator. The fires roared through the decks with renewed vigour, spreading along the ship from stem to stern, until all landing on of aircraft had to be abandoned. Nevertheless, despite the raging heat all around them, *Lexington*'s exhausted crew continued to fight the flames throughout the long, weary afternoon, until driven back by a whole series of violent detonations from exploding ammunition.

In the early evening, cruisers and destroyers began taking aboard boat-loads of men from the doomed '*Lady Lex*'—as the big 33,000-ton carrier was affectionately known in the United States Navy—and three hours later she was deserted, 2,735 of her company having been rescued. A vast, burning hulk, with intermittent explosions hurling debris up to masthead height, the *Lexington* still floated, and the destroyer *Phelps* was ordered to sink her with torpedoes. Just before 8.0 p.m. the carrier went down with a great hissing of steam and the deep rumble of a final detonation, which seemed to many who watched her tragic end a last cry of despair against such an ironic destruction.

Badly damaged, and still troubled by fires below decks, the *Yorktown* headed for Hawaii and a repair yard. Admiral Inouye, disturbed by the loss of *Shoho* and the heavy casualties in men and machines sustained by the *Shokaku,* had already broken off the action, and his ships were retiring at speed to their home ports, thus bringing to a close the Battle of the Coral Sea. What, then, had been achieved—or lost—on either side?

From the Japanese point of view, Admiral Yamamoto could feel that his forces had not fared too badly in this first clash between carriers, especially as most reports encouraged him to believe that both the *Lexington* and *Yorktown* had been sunk; but the damage to the *Shokaku* made it painfully obvious that the tide was beginning to turn in favour of the United States for the first time since Pearl Harbour. As for the Americans, they had been taught some bitter lessons, and gained invaluable battle experience—though admittedly at the cost of a large, modern carrier. Of far greater importance, their successes against the *Shoho* and *Shokaku* had shown them that the Japanese naval air arm was by no means invincible. The destruction of the *Lexington* had robbed the United States commander-in-chief in the Pacific, Admiral Chester W. Nimitz, of a tactical victory in the Coral Sea; yet strategically there was no doubt who had won the day, and the precise, blue-eyed Texan knew that at last he was ready to face the enemy on more equal terms.

Although the *Shokaku* and *Zuikaku* lay in Kure naval yard, recovering from their untimely venture into the Coral Sea, Admiral Yamamoto and his staff remained convinced that Japan still possessed more than enough carriers to implement the ambitious Midway plan. During the last two weeks in May dozens of warships were assembled into battle fleets, and many elaborate rehearsals were carried out in preparation for the great invasion. One by one, the huge fleet carriers *Akagi, Kaga, Hiryu* and *Soryu* gathered at Hashira anchorage near Hiroshima, under the flag of Admiral Chuichi Nagumo, veteran of Pearl harbour; and also in

Hashira, the mighty battleships *Yamato, Nagato, Mutsu, Ise, Hyuga, Fuso* and *Yamashiro* daily awaited the signal to raise anchor. Almost all the Japanese Imperial Navy—a vast armada of two hundred ships totalling over a million tons gross weight— was to be committed against the single, lonely, uninviting Pacific atoll at the end of the Hawaiian chain.

Yamamoto's scheme offered an open invitation to the American fleet to come forth and accept battle; which was exactly what the Japanese admiral hoped would now take place. He had correctly surmised that the United States, with her enormous potential for ship repair and production, would recover fairly quickly from the set-back at Pearl Harbour, and he wanted a second chance to knock out the troublesome enemy carriers—especially after the unexpected Doolittle raid on Tokyo. Also, the capture of Midway would provide Japan with a vital, almost impregnable base from which to operate against the American mainland, and Yamamoto knew very well what his capital ships could achieve against American morale, apart from material successes, by repeated bombardment of the sprawling west-coast cities such as San Francisco and San Diego.

Unfortunately for the Japanese naval experts, Admiral Chester Nimitz had for some time suspected that they might attempt to take Midway with a large striking force, and while the carriers of both sides were still fighting it out in the Coral Sea a coded enemy message was deciphered by United States intelligence confirming Yamamoto's intentions, and outlining the main details of his Midway plan. Yet, despite these advantages, Nimitz was a man beset by many problems; for his Pacific fleet was sadly lacking in numbers to cross swords with the largest assembly of ships in the history of naval warfare. After the sinking of *Lexington,* the American commander-in-chief could muster only four carriers, the *Yorktown, Saratoga, Enterprise* and *Hornet.* Of these, the *Yorktown* was under repair at Pearl Harbour, and *Saratoga* had just completed modernisation and still lay in harbour at San Diego; only the *Enterprise* and *Hornet,* recently returned from the Doolittle raid, were immediately available for Pacific duties. As for Nimitz's battleships, they were too slow and ponderous to risk sending into action with fleet carriers, and he rightly judged they would be of little use to him.

Then Nimitz learned that by little short of a miracle the *York-town* was seaworthy. It had been estimated that her battle damage would take at least three months to put right, but when she limped into Pearl Harbour more than 1,400 men worked around the clock for two full days and nights in order to complete the repairs; to Nimitz's surprise and delight the carrier sailed triumphantly for Midway only a few hours after the main American fleet. Steaming at full speed, the *Yorktown* in due course joined *Enterprise* and *Hornet,* the three ships, under the command of Rear-Admiral Frank J. Fletcher, forming Nimitz's main defence against the Japanese armada. "Those three carriers," remarked the U.S. commander-in-chief to a subordinate, "are all that stand between the Japanese fleet and the American coastline."

On 30th May 1942 the Japanese invasion force was on course for Midway, and out of the Inland Sea. It was divided into five tactical groups: the Advance Expeditionary Force, which included the light carriers *Ryujo* and *Junyo*; Nagumo's Carrier Striking Force, comprising *Akagi, Kaga, Hiryu* and *Soryu*; the Midway Occupation Force of troop transports, escorted by two battleships, with heavy cruisers and destroyers; the Main Body, or battleship squadron, centred around Yamamoto's 73,000-ton flagship *Yamato,* supported by *Mutsu* and *Nagato*; and a Northern Area Force, intended to move into the North Pacific and provide a diversion towards the Aleutian Islands. In summary, Admiral Yamamoto's plan called for an initial attack by ships and bombers of the Advance Expeditionary Force, followed by a heavy bombardment from Nagumo's carrier-borne aircraft, which would also, if necessary, strike at the American Fleet. Then the huge battleships of the Main Body would arrive on the scene to finally destroy all opposition; and the Occupation Force could land its five thousand troops without further hindrance.

On the afternoon of 3rd June, Ensign Jack Reid, flying a PBY Catalina flying-boat out on reconnaissance patrol 700 miles west of Midway, sighted a number of Japanese troop transports, heavily escorted by cruisers and destroyers. He also thought that battleships were in the convoy, and therefore signalled back to base, "Enemy Fleet in sight," continuing to keep in touch for the next two hours. Nine Midway-based Boeing B-17 Flying Fortress bombers then made three separate high-level attacks on the

Japanese ships—which were, in fact, part of the Occupation Force—but without success. That evening four Catalinas, also from Midway, dived through scattered clouds in the bright moonlight to launch their torpedoes at the enemy convoy, and scored one hit on a troop transport, causing only slight damage.

Thus ended the night and the opening rounds of the Battle of Midway, which had included the first torpedo attack to be delivered by flying-boats in the history of naval aviation.

14

CLIMAX AT MIDWAY: 1942

~~~~~~

When Admiral Nagumo's Carrier Striking Force was some 250 miles north-west of Midway the *Akagi, Kaga, Hiryu* and *Soryu* swung into the wind under the encircling protection of their battleships and cruisers. On the flagship, *Akagi,* the commanding admiral was briefing his pilots in no uncertain terms—"Although the enemy is lacking in fighting spirit he will probably come out to the attack as our invasion proceeds"—and on the flight decks of all four carriers aircraft were lined up, with warming engines just turning the propellers over. Everywhere there was a hum of activity, concealing suppressed excitement and the deep fear that comes before action; it was like the morning of Pearl Harbour all over again.

In the dawn twilight of 4th June the first attack wave against Midway, a total of 108 machines, took off with the quiet but rapid efficiency that had always been a hallmark of Japanese naval operations. The force was composed of thirty-six Nakajima Kate horizontal bombers, led by the overall strike commander, Lieutenant Joichi Tomonaga, thirty-six Aichi Val dive bombers, led by Lieutenant Schoichi Ogawa, and thirty-six Zero-Sen fighters, under the command of Lieutenant Masaharu Suganamai. After circling to gain height the large formation flew away eastwards, while on the four Japanese carriers men worked to get a second attack wave brought up on the flight decks and made ready for action.

Meanwhile, reconnaissance aircraft from the *Yorktown* and also from Midway Island were in the air, and at 5.30 a.m. the pilot of a PBY Catalina flying-boat sent back the message to his base, "Many bombers approaching Midway at 150 miles." Within a few moments other Catalinas were reporting the Japanese air activity, including the signal so urgently awaited by Admiral Fletcher, "Enemy carriers in sight." Ninety minutes later, the first machines of a large force of 116 Devastator torpedo bombers, Dauntless dive bombers and Wildcat fighters were roaring away from the *Enterprise* and *Hornet* to attack the enemy ships. At about the same time, four B-26 Marauders and six Grumman Avengers took off from Midway to undertake a torpedo strike against Nagumo's carriers.

Led by Lieutenant Tomonaga in a Nakajima Kate, the formation of Japanese bombers and fighters directed against Midway neared the island, to be met by the air defence of about twenty obsolescent Brewster F2A Buffaloes and six Grumman Wildcats, under the command of Major Floyd B. Parks. Hopelessly outclassed by Suganamai's new clipped-wing Zero-Sen variants, the American fighters were completely fought out of the sky, seventeen of their number being shot down; and the seventy-two Kates and Vals were able to pass virtually unhindered over Midway to drop their many bombs. The base suffered extensive damage, fuel tanks being set on fire and some hangars destroyed, but Tomonaga considered that another raid was necessary, and accordingly radioed back to *Akagi,* advising that the second wave be launched.

The first American attack of the day on Admiral Nagumo's carrier fleet, made by the unescorted Midway-based B-26 Marauders and Grumman Avengers, had no chance of success against such overwhelming fighter opposition; attacking with great courage at a very low height, all but three of the American aircraft were immediately shot down. Then a force of sixteen Marine Corps dive bombers, also from Midway, plunged down through the concentrated anti-aircraft fire with dozens of Zero-Sen fighters hammering savagely away at them, and released their bombs. Again, despite outstanding gallantry by the American pilots—their leader, Major Loftus R. Henderson, was seen to aim his machine at *Kaga* and crashed into the sea in flames almost alongside the carrier—nothing was achieved, for the loss of eight aircraft.

Before the Japanese guns had time to cool down, the alarm bells were clanging once more, warning of another enemy bombing attack, undertaken by fifteen B-17 Flying Fortresses from Midway. Flying in immaculate formation at a height of 20,000 ft., the big, four-engined monoplanes swung majestically over the scudding carriers; and at exactly the right moment the bombs fell, aimed with great accuracy by the Fortresses' remarkable and world-famous Norden gyro-stabilised bombsights. This was precision bombing at its best, and the *Hiryu* and *Soryu* disappeared momentarily from sight amid the huge fountains of water that erupted around the fleet, but they emerged unscathed, and Admiral Nagumo could breathe freely again. Finally his ships repulsed a determined but inexperienced attack by eleven Midway-based Marine Corps Vought-Sikorsky SB2U Vindicator dive bombers, slow and obsolete machines that were no match for the Japanese fighters. Heavily engaged, they dropped their bombs but failed to score any hits, two of their number being destroyed.

While these ineffective American attacks were taking place Admiral Nagumo received Lieutenant Tomonaga's message recommending that the second wave of Nakajima Kate and Aichi Val strike aircraft be sent off against Midway, but while his carriers were defending themselves, there was nothing he could do to implement it. As the last Vindicators fled back to their base, however, the Japanese commander gave orders for the second wave to be launched, also deciding that the Kate torpedo bombers should first re-equip with heavy bombs. Then, just as the re-arming was almost completed, a floatplane out on reconnaissance from the heavy cruiser *Tone* signalled, "Ten ships, apparently enemy, in sight." Admiral Fletcher's carrier force had been spotted at last.

An unpleasant and potentially very dangerous situation was now developing to worry Admiral Nagumo. The first attack wave, under Lieutenant Tomonaga, was due back from Midway and, indeed, the large formation of returning aircraft could already be seen on the horizon, short of fuel and expecting to be landed on without delay. Nagumo had not yet definitely been informed that the American fleet included carriers; but if it did, then his bomb-loaded second wave would have to change back to torpedoes and take off immediately to strike at the enemy ships. Urgently he signalled back to the floatplane from *Tone*, "Ascertain ship types and maintain contact."

The reply from the little catapulted seaplane, received on

board *Akagi* at 8.30 a.m., did nothing to ease Admiral Nagumo's peace of mind. "Enemy force accompanied by what appears to be an aircraft-carrier in the rear," stated the message, followed shortly afterwards by a more definite but no less alarming signal that two additional American heavy cruisers had been sighted, and the aircraft-carrier was almost certainly *Yorktown*. Now Admiral Nagumo was left in no doubt that a sizeable enemy fleet was within striking distance; and he decided to postpone the second assault on Midway in favour of an attack on the American carriers.

It was a difficult decision, and one destined to have fateful consequences for the Japanese Imperial Navy, but at the time all the extra work and further inevitable delay obviously seemed well worthwhile to Nagumo. At his orders, the aircraft of the second attack wave were lowered down to the hangar decks of the Japanese carriers to be re-armed with torpedoes, while Lieutenant Tomonaga's tired pilots began quickly and efficiently landing back on the vacated flight decks. Below, the sweating maintenance crews haphazardly piled the unwanted bombs out of the way in their haste to get the Nakajima Kates re-equipped in the shortest possible time. At last all the machines of the first attack wave were down, and the torpedo bombers and fighters of the second wave ready for return to the flight decks once more. From the *Akagi,* Admiral Nagumo signalled his ships: "Proceed to contact and destroy enemy task force."

Then, just as the carriers began to gather speed, there came a cry from the lookouts of "Enemy aircraft approaching!" and Admiral Nagumo found his fleet again under attack from American bombers. These were the Devastators and Dauntlesses from *Enterprise* and *Hornet*; but by the worst possible misfortune, the fifteen torpedo-carrying aircraft from the latter ship had lost touch with their escorting Wildcat fighters. Led by Lieutenant-Commander John C. Waldron, the gallant, ill-fated Torpedo Squadron Eight nevertheless headed directly for the Japanese ships, immediately being set upon by over fifty Zeros from Nagumo's routine air umbrella. Skimming the waves, the Devastators flew steadily on towards *Akagi* and *Hiryu,* attacking in two sections from both port and starboard sides. Every few moments, one of the bombers would burst into flames, lurch out of line and hit the sea in a shower of spray, while all four carriers twisted violently to avoid the white wakes of the torpedoes.

Then, abruptly, the American attack was over. Sad to relate, every machine of Torpedo Squadron Eight had been shot down; only one man, Ensign George H. Gay, was left alive, to be picked up by a roving Catalina flying-boat the following afternoon. There was a storm of triumphant cheering on board the Japanese ships, but Admiral Nagumo still had no time to fly off his own laden torpedo bombers, for the Devastators from *Enterprise* were already in sight, and bent on vengeance. As they attacked the enemy carriers from the starboard side, a striking force of twelve Devastators from the *Yorktown*—launched, with great foresight, by Admiral Fletcher an hour after his main groups in order to deliver a 'final blow'—roared in from the port side. The Japanese anti-aircraft fire was thus caught unawares and divided; but the American machines were again far outnumbered by the fast, expertly handled Zero-Sen fighters. Within minutes, the handful of escorting Wildcats, eleven of the fourteen Devastators from *Enterprise* and all but two of *Yorktown*'s aircraft had been destroyed. The cheering on the carriers broke out with renewed vigour—who could doubt now that this mightiest of all Japanese Imperial fleets, protected by the battleships and fighters from all sea and air attackers, was indeed invincible?

At last it seemed as if Admiral Nagumo could launch his torpedo striking force against the American carrier fleet, destroy it and win the day. But unfortunately for him, and ultimately Japan, there still remained a decisive factor that he had either forgotten or failed to appreciate existed—the dive bomber squadrons sent out by Admiral Fletcher. Of these Dauntless aircraft, the machines from *Hornet* had strayed far off course and eventually were forced to return to their parent carrier, so can be discounted. However, the two squadrons from *Enterprise,* under the command of Lieutenant-Commander Clarence Wade McClusky, although at first failing to sight the enemy ships, had turned northwards and were now circling unseen high above them. Also, seventeen more dive bombers, flown off by *Yorktown,* and led by Lieutenant-Commander Maxwell F. Leslie, had arrived just in time to join McCluskey's formation.

At 10.20 a.m. the four big Japanese carriers were turning into

the wind, their flight decks thronged with Kate torpedo bombers, Val dive bombers and Zero-Sen fighters. The air throbbed
with the roar of many warming engines; last-minute orders were
issued; pilots plugged in helmet leads; cockpit canopies were
slammed into place. Then, above the shouted warnings of startled look-out men, came the unforgettable, heart-stopping whine
of falling dive bombers, drowning the voices and rumble of
turning motors. Too late, Nagumo's airborne fighters, still
scattered after shooting down so many of the American torpedo
bombers, turned back to reform their vital air umbrella; the
grey-green Dauntlesses were already zooming to regain height,
their bombs released and falling inexorably towards the targets.

A moment later, the first 1,000-lb. bomb struck the *Akagi*'s
flight deck and exploded with tremendous force, blowing aircraft
and men high into the air and turning the after part of the ship
into a raging furnace. A second heavy bomb penetrated to the
hangar deck before exploding among the machines there to cause
frightful destruction. Flames spread through the ship, detonating
the piled bombs that there had been no time to return to the
magazines, setting alight petrol and fuel oil stores, until the
whole superstructure was ablaze. With reluctance, Admiral
Nagumo realised that the time had come to transfer his command, and agreed to leave the carrier; but the bridge was already
cut off from the rest of the ship, a blistering island in a vast,
heaving sea of fire. Persuaded to climb out of a side window, he
swung down a smouldering rope and was taken safely aboard the
Nagara, an escorting light cruiser.

While *Akagi* was burning, other dive bombers had scored
direct hits on the *Kaga*'s long, exposed flight deck, and also destroyed the bridge, killing everyone on it, including the commander. The effect of the explosions among the aircraft crowding the
carrier was appalling, and her many fires were soon beyond control. Without a captain or helmsman, she drifted aimlessly away
from the fleet, belching great clouds of black smoke; damage
repair parties, frequently overcome by the intense heat, would
spend the next seven hours desperately trying to save her.

Meanwhile, Lieutenant-Commander Leslie's squadron from
Yorktown had hurled a deluge of 1,000-lb. bombs into the *Soryu,*
which was steaming on *Akagi*'s starboard beam. Three direct hits

Above, the Fairey Swordfish three-seater, torpedo-spotter-reconnaissance biplane, one of the Fleet Air Arm's most outstanding aircraft during World War Two; *below,* the Mitsubishi A6M-3 Zero-Sen single-seater, one of Japan's most effective fighters

Above, the Arado Ar 196A floatplane, used throughout the Second World War by the German Air Force; *below,* the Fairey Barracuda torpedo-bomber, used by the Fleet Air Arm in 1943–45 and particularly for attacks on the *Tirpitz*

were taken by the carrier in rapid succession, opening up the flight deck, wrenching the lift back against the bridge and tangling the massed waiting aircraft into a jumble of bodies and wreckage. Fires broke out in the gutted hangar deck and surged through the crippled ship until she was blazing from end to end; twenty minutes later, the order "Abandon Ship" had been given, and men were jumping overboard.

For Admiral Nagumo a mere five minutes—the turning point in the Battle of Midway—had brought unparalleled disaster, coming with tragic irony just when it must have seemed that his fleet was indestructible. Now, only the *Hiryu,* which chanced to be far ahead of the other three carriers, remained; and it is to the credit of Nagumo's tactical commander, Rear-Admiral Hiroak Abe, that before 11.0 a.m. he had ordered a striking force of eighteen Aichi Val dive bombers and six Zero-Sen fighters to be launched against the Americans in spite of the great shock that the Japanese side had just sustained. Two hours later, on Admiral Nagumo's instructions, *Hiryu* flew off a torpedo striking force composed of ten Kates and six Zero-Sens—virtually the only Japanese aircraft that remained out of the vast number originally committed by Yamamoto in the assault on Midway.

The successful American dive bombers receded into the distance, bound for their parent carriers, leaving *Akagi, Kaga* and *Soryu* shaken by intermittent explosions and burning beyond control. The late flagship, her steering gear gone, drifted in circles for most of the day, being finally abandoned at 7.15 p.m. and sunk by torpedoes from the escorting destroyers during the night. *Kaga,* the proud sister of *Akagi,* fared no better; still blazing but afloat many hours after the American air attack, she was hit by torpedoes fired by the submarine U.S.S. *Nautilus.* Her fuel tanks exploded, and now completely consumed by fire, the carrier capsized, taking with her to the bottom some eight hundred officers and men. At about the same time *Soryu* also settled and sank with a great hissing of steam from her white-hot decks, leaving only fragments of debris and many floating bodies.

In spite of the catastrophe that had so swiftly overtaken his carrier fleet, Admiral Nagumo was determined to continue the battle—hence the two striking forces *Hiryu* had already sent on their way. Shortly before noon, while *Yorktown* was landing on her returning aircraft, the first wave of Japanese machines was detected by radar, and Wildcat fighters—including flights launched by *Enterprise* and *Hornet*—hurriedly formed a defensive air umbrella over the carrier. The eighteen Val dive bombers, led by Lieutenant Michio Kobayashi, made their attack from a height of 10,000 ft., while the six Zeroes strove vainly to hold back the swarms of Wildcats. Somewhere in the twisting, whirling dogfight that followed, two of the Japanese fighters were shot down. In perfect formation, the Vals still dived, one after the other falling in flames, until only eight remained.

The anti-aircraft guns on *Yorktown* and her escorting cruisers destroyed two more of the dive bombers. Another Val, hit and vomiting fragments, dropped its bomb only to disintegrate a moment later; but the five survivors struck hard at their target, from a minimum height. A bomb exploded on the flight deck, blowing a great hole in it, causing many casualties and exposing the hangar deck below. Simultaneously, a second bomb dropped neatly down the carrier's funnel and burst in the engine-room; and a third bomb exploded dangerously near the magazine. Crippled and on fire, the *Yorktown* lost speed and finally came to a standstill, although she was still able to land on many of her returned aircraft.

The Japanese pilots flew back to *Hiryu* to report a victory, but in fact their victim was under way again within two hours, thanks to the skill and endurance of her damage repair parties. Then the *Yorktown*'s radar again picked up enemy aircraft— actually the torpedo striking force from *Hiryu,* under the command of Lieutenant Joichi Tomonaga. With the Nakajima Kates only forty miles away and closing fast, there was only time to get a dozen Wildcat fighters into the air before *Yorktown* was once more battling for her very existence. Skimming the water, and split into two sections in a classic torpedo attack, the Japanese bombers weaved through the anti-aircraft barrage, almost hidden by the huge water splashes from bursting shells.

When the range had closed to 500 yd. Lieutenant Tomonaga released his torpedo but made no attempt to turn away; in a great eruption of flame the leading Kate struck *Yorktown* abaft the bridge, scattering wreckage over the flight deck. Four more of the attackers were shot down by the defending Wildcats and anti-aircraft fire. Then the torpedoes were crashing home, two exploding together on the port side with such force that the huge, 20,000-ton carrier seemed to leap out of the water. She settled with a list of 26 degrees, and her captain gave the order to abandon ship before she suddenly capsized. Oddly enough, the *Yorktown* failed to go down as anticipated, but drifted with dead engines on the calm Pacific sea for the next twenty-four hours, being finally reboarded by a salvage party of 160 members of her crew. Towed by the little minesweeper *Viereo,* she started the long, slow journey back to Hawaii; but her plight had already been spotted by a Japanese flying-boat, and she was irrevocably doomed.

At about the same time that Lieutenant Tomonaga hurtled to his death against *Yorktown*'s superstructure, reconnaissance aircraft sent out by Admiral Fletcher to try to find *Hiryu*'s new course and position reported back that they had located the enemy carrier. Immediately, twenty-four Dauntless dive bombers, again led by the tired but redoubtable McClusky, were launched by *Enterprise,* to arrive over *Hiryu* in the later afternoon. With all her aircraft gone, the Japanese ship could only put up a hasty anti-aircraft barrage and take evasive action as the bombers dived out of the sun, surprising her exhausted crew at a snatched meal. Four bombs struck the *Hiryu*'s flight deck, blasting the forward aircraft lift out of its guides and back against the bridge, and starting numerous fires. Within five minutes the carrier was stopped and well ablaze, her vast hull riven by explosions, and over four hundred of her crew killed or wounded.

When a striking force of sixteen dive bombers from the *Hornet* arrived to support McClusky's attack on *Hiryu,* it was obvious that the carrier's fate was already sealed, and their bombs were dropped on the battleship *Haruna* and the cruisers that formed the remnants of Admiral Nagumo's fleet. Somehow the hulk that had been *Hiryu* remained afloat during the night, lighting the sky for many miles around with the intense red glow of her fires. At 2.30 a.m. she was at last abandoned, and then sunk by torpedoes from her attendant destroyers, probably within a short time of *Akagi* going down.

Meanwhile, Admiral Yamamoto, on board the giant battleship *Yamato,* had been informed that *Yorktown* was being pulled at only three knots towards Pearl Harbour, with many of her compartments still flooded but the list to port slightly reduced. He issued orders for the carrier to be sunk by the nearest Japanese submarine, the long-range I-168, under the command of Lieutenant-Commander Yahachi Tanabe, then cruising under water not far from Midway Island. Around midday on 6th June the submarine sighted *Yorktown,* surrounded by seven destroyers and still making slow but sure headway; from periscope depth, four torpedoes were fired at close range by Tanabe, then he crash-dived in expectation of the depth charges that within minutes came tumbling down all around his boat.

The surprise attack was a complete success. One torpedo hit the destroyer *Hamman* squarely amidships, blowing her into two parts which sank almost at once, with heavy loss of life. The second torpedo missed, but the third and fourth slammed into *Yorktown,* and the big carrier groaned to a standstill. Now there could be no hope of saving her; she was taking in water fast and obviously would only stay afloat a matter of a few hours. Reluctantly, her commander, Captain Elliott Buckmaster, ordered the salvage party to abandon ship, and she was left to drift throughout the night, her hangar deck awash. At 6.0 a.m. the following morning *Yorktown* turned quietly over and went down, her battle flags flying to the end.

With the destruction of Admiral Nagumo's Carrier Striking Force, the Battle of Midway was over, although neither side realised it for some days and indecisive cruiser actions were fought that did nothing to affect an outcome already decided. The Japanese fleet, without large carriers, no longer had any hope of invading Midway; and moreover Yamamoto's battleship squadron was now terribly exposed to air attacks from the *Hornet* and *Enterprise*. At midnight on 5th June, therefore, the man who had brought about one of the greatest carrier battles in naval history acknowledged defeat, and the following morning issued the order from *Yamato*: "The Midway operation is cancelled."

The Japanese ships retreated westwards, harried by American surface units and U.S. Army B-17 Flying Fortresses from Midway; but Marine Corps dive bombers, also based on Midway, and striking forces from the *Hornet* and *Enterprise* were finally responsible for sinking the damaged heavy cruiser *Mikuma* and crippling her sister ship *Mogami*. Probably the last enemy warship to be attacked by carrier-borne aircraft in the whole battle was the destroyer *Tanikaze,* which escaped unscathed after a massive dive bomber strike flown off the two American carriers had failed to score a single hit on her.

For Admiral Yamamoto it was a long way back to the Inland Sea and the security of home waters; but eventually, shortage of fuel compelled his American pursuers to break off the action and harass him no longer. Also, Rear-Admiral Raymond A. Spruance, flying his flag in *Enterprise,* was naturally a little wary of taking his carriers within too easy reach of the enemy battleship squadron's mighty guns, and his aircrews were exhausted to the limit of their endurance. For both sides, it was 'game, set and match' at Midway, the end of a dream for Yamamoto and the beginning of a new era for Admiral Nimitz.

When all the opposing warships that had survived the battle were back in port there remained only the inevitable balance sheet of war. For both Japan and the United States, after Midway it proved to be a tragic account that had been settled. Yamamoto had lost the fleet carriers *Akagi, Kaga, Soryu* and *Hiryu,* the heavy cruiser *Mikuma* and about five thousand officers and men. Various other ships, including the cruiser *Mogami,* had been seriously damaged, and 322 aircraft of all types destroyed, including those that went down with the carriers.

As for the Americans, there could be no doubt in Washington or Tokyo that they had achieved an overwhelming victory, but a surprisingly heavy price had been paid. The fleet carrier *Yorktown* and the destroyer *Hamman* had been sunk, 150 aircraft destroyed and three hundred officers and men killed in action. But the bitter blow to American pride of December 1941, was at last assuaged—"Pearl Harbour has been partially avenged," said Admiral Nimitz—whereas Japanese morale, already shaken by the Battle of the Coral Sea and Doolittle's raid, had plunged to the lowest depths.

Yamamoto and his admirals knew only too well that Midway was no ordinary setback; it was the first major Japanese defeat at sea for over three hundred years.

15

END OF AN AIR POWER: 1944

~~~~~~

Midway has been called "the battle that doomed Japan", and there can be no doubt that within a matter of months after the shattered Imperial fleet had limped back into the Inland Sea the tide of conquest had begun to ebb for Admiral Yamamoto. Even so, the war lords in Tokyo were unwilling to admit the possibility of any defeat—the full story of the Midway catastrophe did not become fully revealed to the Japanese people until long after 1945—and every naval engagement in the Pacific continued to be fought with a savage, fanatical determination that brought little reward and invariably ended in terrible, prohibitive numbers of casualties. As a typical example, the struggle for Guadalcanal in the Solomons archipelago, vital to both sides as an air base, began in August 1942, when eleven thousand American Marines landed to recapture the tiny, humid, malaria-infested island from the Japanese, and it did not end until February 1943, after every member of the garrison had been killed or wounded, and six major naval battles fought to decide who would retain it.

And tragic, often pointless actions they were. The first took place off Savo Island on 9th August 1942, when one Australian and three American heavy cruisers were sunk; then there was the Eastern Solomons on 24th August, a carrier-versus-carrier engagement in which Admiral Nagumo attempted to reverse the fortunes of Midway and lost the 20,000-ton *Ryujo* to American dive bombers, followed by the inconclusive Cape of Hope battle on the night of 11th–12th September. Five weeks later, from 26th–28th October, came Santa Cruz, scene of heavy attacks on Yamamoto's fleet by aircraft from *Enterprise* and *Hornet,* resulting in heavy damage to his battleships and cruisers; the culminating, desperate fight to retain Guadalcanal in "one of the most furious sea battles ever fought" on 12th–14th November, resulting in heavy losses on both sides; and finally Tassafaronga on 30th November, the bloody, vicious end of the Solomons affair.

The land fighting in the steaming, putrefying jungles of Guadalcanal preceded many other similar American amphibious operations against the fanatically defended groups of islands scattered across the Pacific that had become stepping-stones to the Japanese mainland. But after Guadalcanal the enemy battle fleet never again played such an important part in opposing those assaults, for Admiral Isoroku Yamamoto, the architect of Pearl Harbour and the tactical genius of the Imperial Japanese Navy, was dead. And with him died Japanese sea power in the Second World War. "If in spite of everything I have to fight, then all must be over in six months or a year," he had written in 1940. "I cannot take responsibility for a two-year war against the United States." By 1943 the longer conflict that Yamamoto had feared was haunting Japan, as American naval and air strength literally increased by the hour; and there was no other strategist in Tokyo with anything like the same ability to halt the gradual downhill slide to disaster.

All these facts were acknowledged in Washington as well as Tokyo, and it was Yamamoto's importance to Japan that finally brought about his execution. On 17th April 1943 a coded signal from the flagship *Yamato* off Truk was intercepted by the U.S. Navy reception post at Dutch Harbour in the Aleutians and relayed to Washington, where it arrived within minutes on the desk of the American Secretary of the Navy, Frank Knox. At first sight the message was of little consequence; nothing more than the itinerary for a tour of inspection by Admiral Yamamoto of Japanese bases in the South-west Pacific area. The visits were scheduled to last for about forty-eight hours, beginning the following morning at 6.0 a.m., when the admiral would take off from Rabaul in a twin-engined Mitsubishi Ki. 21 (code named 'Sally' under the Allied system) accompanied by a second bomber of the same type containing his chief of staff and the remainder of his party. There was to be an escort of six Mitsubishi Zeke fighters. It seemed like dull and uninteresting routine work, familiar to any high-ranking officer, but the detailed information was all there, including times of arrival, and Navy Secretary

Knox realised that here was a heaven-sent opportunity to destroy Yamamoto.

A discussion between Knox and General 'Hap' Arnold, commander-in-chief of the U.S. Army Air Force, led to their asking the advice of Colonel Charles Lindbergh, the lone transatlantic pilot of the 'twenties and now an expert on long-distance flights, and Frank Meyer of the Lockheed aviation company. Thus was finalised Operation *Vengeance,* the definite plan to kill Yamamoto. It was decided to intercept the Japanese aircraft just before they came in to land at Kahili airstrip on Bougainville at 9.30 a.m., using twin-engined Lockheed P-38 Lightning fighters from Henderson Field, Guadalcanal. Unfortunately, there was a serious snag—the distance involved was nearly 500 miles, far beyond the normal range of a P-38. And on the afternoon of 17th April there were no auxiliary fuel tanks available at Henderson Field.

The operation against Admiral Yamamoto now became possible only because such a remarkable system of logistics and flight planning existed on the American side in the Pacific zone. Two messages were despatched from Washington bearing Secretary Knox's signature: one to General Kenney, commander of the South-west Pacific Air Forces, requesting immediate supply of long-range tanks to Guadalcanal; the other to Major John W. Mitchell, commander of No. 339 Squadron, equipped with Lockheed P-38s, at Henderson Field, calling him and his two flight leaders to headquarters. In the makeshift hut at Tassafaronga, with the inevitable tropical rainstorm beating through the palm trees outside, Mitchell was handed Admiral Yamamoto's death warrant. It read:

"Washington, 17.4.43, 15.35. Top Secret. Secretary Navy to Fighter Control Henderson. Admiral Yamamoto accompanied chief of staff and seven general officers imperial navy including surgeon admiral grand fleet left Truk this morning eight hours for air trip inspection Bougainville bases stop Admiral and party travelling in two Sallys escorted six Zekes stop escort of honour from Kahili probable stop admiral's itinerary colon arrived Rabaul Bucka 1630 hours where spend night stop leave dawn for Kahili where time of arrival 0945 hours stop admiral then to board submarine chaser for inspection naval units under Admiral Tanaka stop.

"Squadron 339 P-38 must at all costs reach and destroy Yamamoto and staff morning April eighteen stop auxiliary tanks and consumption data will arrive from Port Moresby evening seventeenth stop intelligence stresses admirals extreme punctuality stop president attaches extreme importance this operation stop communicate result at once Washington stop Frank Knox Secretary of State for Navy stop.

"Ultra-secret document not to be copied or filed stop to be destroyed when carried out stop."

Over a frugal dinner the three American fighter pilots formed their plan of attack on the enemy formation. Twelve P-38s, led by Mitchell, would provide the high-level cover at 20,000 ft., it was decided, ready to tackle Yamamoto's escort fighters; the remaining six Lightnings, flying at 11,000 ft., were to have the task of actually intercepting and destroying the two Mitsubishi Sally bombers. While Mitchell and his flight commanders were still in conference, four B-24 Liberators from Port Moresby rumbled overhead to land at Henderson Field with the special auxiliary fuel tanks. In pouring rain and pitch darkness the race against time to get the drop tanks unloaded from the Liberators and fitted to No. 339 Squadron's P-38s began for the American maintenance crews—arduous, exhausting work carried out in a sea of mud and water.

Soon after dawn the last Lightning fighter had been fitted with long-range tanks, and at 7.20 a.m. the squadron began to take off into the now surprisingly bright and cloudless sky. One machine burst a tyre, skidded at 100 m.p.h. off the steel netting of the airstrip and crashed in flames; another had fuel trouble and turned back to Guadalcanal with failing engines. The remaining sixteen P-38s circled the island once as they gained height, then set course for Bougainville. Skimming the thick jungle many miles away, and heading for the same fateful destination, flew two grey-green camouflaged Mitsubishi Sally bombers, in tight formation with their escort of six fighters.

At exactly 9.35 a.m., Mitchell and his squadron reached the coastline of Bougainville and immediately sighted the little group of enemy aircraft; it was a perfect, textbook interception, and a brilliant achievement. With the twin 1,425-h.p. Allison engines of his P-38 roaring at full power, Mitchell took his top cover section up to 20,000 ft., giving the four attack group Lightnings, piloted by Lieutenants Thomas G. Lanphier, Rex T. Barber, Raymond K. Hine and Besby T. Holmes, the opportunity to close in on the Japanese bombers. The escorting A6M Zekes broke formation to engage the big twin-boomed American fighters so suddenly upon them, and long-range tanks were dropped by both sides as they whirled into battle. The two Sallys, very close together and taking skilful evasive action, dived until the trees were flashing past just beneath their wings.

Lanphier, in company with Barber, headed directly for the second Sally—actually Yamamoto's aircraft—and was immediately attacked by three Zekes. Tracer flashed past the two P-38s, Lanphier hammered a short burst of cannon fire into a streaking radial-engined monoplane and saw it flick over on to its back, then he was through the escort cover and within range of the enemy bomber. The big, lumbering Sally swung into his sights and he opened up a continuous fire, seeing the cannon strikes jumping along the tree-tops before moving relentlessly on across the starboard wing of Yamamoto's aircraft. Smoke and flame streamed from the Sally's engine cowling, parts of the wing flew back into the slipstream and there was an immediate loss of speed. A moment later the bomber's undamaged port wing touched the trees, and instantly the aircraft was down, tearing a path of destruction through the dense jungle, vomiting great fragments of burning debris as it exploded. Lanphier turned away, leaving a pall of thick black smoke rising high into the air, the symbol of his victory.

Meanwhile, Barber had attacked the other Sally, which contained, among others, Admiral Matomi Ugaki, the chief of staff to Yamamoto. A series of short bursts caught the twisting, turning bomber at close range as it flew very low along the coastline. Part of the tailplane broke away and it crashed in shallow water. The two admirals in the machine, Ugaki and Kitamura, were both seriously injured, but eventually recovered after being rescued from the wreckage in quick time by Japanese patrol boats.

The task of his squadron having efficiently been carried out, Major Mitchell ordered his pilots to disengage from the angry

Zekes and return to base before enemy fighters arrived in great numbers from Kahili airfield. Three of Yamamoto's escort had been shot down, for the loss of one P-38 piloted by Lieutenant Hine, who had fought a courageous, impossible battle against a superior number of the very fast Zeke monoplanes. Long after the tired but jubilant American airmen had landed back at Henderson Field, a Japanese army patrol hacked a path through the jungle finally to reach the burnt-out debris of the Sally bomber destroyed by Lieutenant Lanphier. Including the crew, eleven men had boarded the aircraft at Rabaul; all now lay violently dead in or around the wreckage. The body of Admiral Yamamoto, charred but recognisable, was found some distance away from the others, his *samurai* sword still at his side.

A state funeral was ordered by the Emperor of Japan for Isoroku Yamamoto, an honour previously bestowed on only twelve other Japanese and just one admiral, the national hero and victor at Tsushima in 1905, Heihachiro Togo. Far away from grief-stricken Tokyo, where 65,000 people filed past the urn containing Yamamoto's ashes, the Allies continued to fight bitterly for every foot of ground in recapturing the vast Japanese empire that was so much a personal achievement of the small, energetic admiral considered by some authorities comparable to Nelson. In May 1943 came the powerful American assault on Attu, in the Aleutians; and the following November the Gilbert Islands were under attack by massive Allied combined land, sea and air forces. The Imperial Sun was setting in the east; but its faded light threatened to be the prelude to an evening of bloody carnage.

Never before had such a vast armada of landing craft—over eighty thousand ships of various types—been assembled, or amphibious operations visualised on the scale now being carried out by the United States in the Pacific zone. By 1944 American naval strength, completely recovered from the Pearl Harbour disaster, was overwhelming; but there still seemed no way to bring the campaign to a swift conclusion. Every one of the hundreds of Pacific atolls in Japanese hands had to be taken in the same slow, costly manner: first, a saturation bombardment from the sea and air; then wave after wave of infantry poured ashore from landing craft; and finally, occupation by the construction battalions with their mechanical shovels and bulldozers, building roads, bridges and airstrips at lightning speed. Almost without exception the attacking marines landed into a murderous cross-fire from light cannon and machine-guns in massive bunkers constructed of coconut logs and steel rails, staggered to form defence in depth, and manned by fanatical Japanese who believed that death in battle should be their greatest achievement.

The slogging match went on. The assault on Kwajalein, the largest atoll in the Gilbert Islands, was preceded by a tremendous bombardment that rained down 15,000 tons of high explosive in the area over a period of two months, and yet the infantry still met with fierce enemy resistance; when the cratered rubble of the island was finally captured, over eight thousand Japanese had been killed. In February 1944 the tragic pattern of attacking against massed machine-gun fire and then digging in to face waves of howling, suicidal defenders was repeated at Engebi in the Eniwetok Atoll, where over 3,400 Japanese were killed. "We cut them down like overripe wheat," wrote one American officer afterwards, "and they lay like tired children with their faces in the sand."

On 27th March Admiral Mineichi Koga, who had succeeded Yamamoto as Commander-in-Chief of the Japanese Fleet, was killed when the flying-boat taking him from Palau to Davao crashed in bad weather conditions. He left behind as a legacy for Admiral Soemu Toyoda, who took his place, the desperate plan that was to bring about the Battle of the Philippine Sea and, incidentally, the final and complete destruction of Japanese sea and air power. It was a fairly simple scheme in outline, reviving the old dream that had lingered for so long in Tokyo Bay—to draw the American fleet into a decisive surface action against the mighty 18-in. guns of such battleships as *Yamato* and *Musashi* and see it wiped out in another Tsushima. But in order to succeed, such a plan presupposed that the enemy fleet was inferior in numbers and lacked air superiority, whereas by 1944 the reverse of that situation existed. Large new American fleet carriers—the *Essex*, the new *Yorktown* and *Lexington* and many others—were by then in commission, backed by dozens of light carriers, operating in powerful task forces; and one of these, comprising four task groups, was moving in support of the next United States attack, directed against Saipan and Guam, in the Marianas.

On 11th June heavy bombing raids by American carrier-based aircraft against the Japanese bases on Saipan and Guam opened the massive Marianas operation, code-named *Forager,* and four days later the first waves of marines were fighting their way ashore. Some 400 miles from Vice-Admiral Marc A. Mitscher's Task Force 58 of seven fleet carriers and eight light carriers, heavily escorted by battleships, cruisers and destroyers, steamed the Japanese First Mobile Fleet of nine carriers, six battleships, eleven heavy cruisers, two light cruisers and thirty destroyers, all under the central command of Vice-Admiral Jisaburo Ozawa. The stage was set for the greatest carrier battle since Midway, where the outcome of all similar succeeding engagements had, in fact, been decided. It remained only for Admiral Ozawa's reconnaissance aircraft to sight the enemy battle squadrons.

The 19th June was a bright, perfect day in the Pacific, conjuring up vivid images of waving palm-trees and blue waters lapping warm coral sand—if an island could be found that had not been ploughed up by shellfire and piled high with dead. At 8.30 a.m. the first large-scale Japanese air strike, composed of forty-five bomb-carrying Mitsubishi Zero-Sen fighters, eight Nakajima B6N2 (code-named Jill) torpedo bombers, with an escort of sixteen Zeke fighters, took off from the light carriers *Chitose, Chiyoda* and *Zuiho*; to be followed half an hour later by twenty-seven Nakajima Jill torpedo bombers and fifty-three Yokosuka D4Y (or Judy under the Allied coding system) dive bombers, with an escort of forty-eight Zero-Sen fighters, from the fleet carriers *Taiho, Shokaku* and *Zuikaku.*

No sooner had the two air striking forces been launched on their way than the Japanese fleet suffered a heavy and unexpected blow. Admiral Ozawa's flagship, the new 32,000-ton carrier *Taiho,* was just flying off her last batch of fighters when she was shaken by a tremendous explosion and eventually brought to a standstill, on fire and listing to starboard. Hit by just one of a fan of torpedoes fired from the United States submarine *Albacore,* captained by Commander J. W. Blanchard, the *Taiho* was destined to meet with the same fiery end as her predecessors at Midway; despite every precaution, leaking fuel oil ignited in the hangar deck, turning her into a blazing inferno from stem to stern. In the late afternoon the giant carrier rolled over and sank some 500 miles west of Saipan, taking 1,500 of her crew down with her. Admiral Ozawa, having transferred his command to the cruiser *Haguro,* was now compelled to resume control of his fleet as best he could with the inadequate facilities that remained.

Meanwhile, American radar had detected the imminent arrival of the first enemy air strike, and Task Force 58 turned into the wind to fly off a vast number of Grumman Hellcat fighters. The ensuing air battle amounted to nothing less than a great massacre; the beginning of a long day of endless slaughter. Lacking in experience if not in courage, the doomed Japanese pilots corkscrewed and dived frantically in all directions, their formations broken up and dispersed, cut to pieces by the fast, heavily armed Hellcats. Aircraft exploded, spun down the sky out of control or fell burning into the sea; out of the first strike, only twenty-five machines returned to their parent carriers.

Shortly after 11.00 a.m. the second Japanese air striking force was picked up on the American radar screens, and again the enemy formations were intercepted by swarms of Hellcats. Once more the blue Pacific sky became filled with stricken crimson-circled torpedo bombers and fighters, until out of the 128 aircraft that had made the attack only thirty survived. A few of the more determined Nakajima Jills battled their way through to the gun-bristling carriers of Admiral Mitscher's fleet, and one or two even managed to drop their torpedoes, but they never had the remotest chance of success. In a matter of moments, all had been shot down, including one determined pilot who crashed his machine into the battleship *Indiana,* but without causing any serious damage.

A third Japanese air strike, this time launched from the carriers *Junyo, Hiyo* and *Ryuho,* was pitchforked into the furnace later the same morning. It consisted of seven Nakajima Jill torpedo bombers, twenty-five Zero-Sen fighter-bombers and fifteen Zeke fighters; of these forty-seven aircraft, only about twenty sighted the American ships, to be repulsed with heavy losses. The fourth and last air strike of the battle, flown off the *Shokaku* and *Zuikaku* at about 11.30 a.m., was composed of thirty-six Yokosuka Judy dive bombers, six Jill torpedo bombers, ten Zero-Sen fighter bombers and an escort of thirty Zeke fighters. These aircraft, too, strayed sadly off course, only a few actually succeeding in attacking Task Force 58; and all but one or two were immediately destroyed.

While the third and fourth Japanese strikes were still away, and the *Shokaku* and *Zuikaku* busily occupied in recovering the battered survivors of the two earlier assaults, Lieutenant-Commander H. J. Kossler, captain of the United States submarine *Cavalla*, was gazing at the enemy fleet through his periscope. Avoiding the screen of cruisers and destroyers, Kossler fired a close-range salvo of six torpedoes at the nearest carrier, *Shokaku*, hitting her on the starboard side. The sequence of disasters that had already overtaken the *Taiho* was at once tragically and inevitably repeated; petrol-fed flames surged through the *Shokaku*'s decks to erupt in violent explosions during the afternoon, and at last she gave up the ghost and slid beneath the waves. It was turning out to be a disastrous day for Admiral Ozawa, but he was as yet still unaware of the terrifying losses he had also sustained in aircraft.

Some fifty or sixty miles from the Task Force they were protecting, Admiral Mitscher's Hellcats continued to wreak fearful execution among the scattered, confused groups of enemy aircraft that remained. Some of the machines from the fourth Japanese air strike, heading for the doubtful security of Guam airfield, were intercepted over the island and many destroyed; others crashed when attempting to land on the bomb-cratered strip in the gathering darkness. At last, not a single enemy aircraft remained in the sky, after more than eight hours of running battles—the period between mid-morning and sunset on 19th June 1944, ever afterwards remembered by the U.S. Navy pilots as the Great Marianas Turkey Shoot. Unable to recover from the loss of over three hundred machines in a single operation, against a mere twenty-three Hellcats shot down, on that day Japanese air power in the Pacific finally died.

Admiral Ozawa's First Mobile Fleet retreated rapidly north-westwards, the flight and hangar decks of his carriers sadly emptied of aircraft. But it was now the turn of Admiral Mitscher to go over to the offensive, and in the early afternoon of 20th June a Grumman Avenger out on reconnaissance from the *Enterprise* sighted the Japanese ships. From his flagship, the *Lexington*, Mitscher ordered a full-scale attack by the whole Task Force, and at about 4.30 p.m. over two hundred bombers and fighters were launched from eleven of the twelve American carriers. The sun was already setting when the great armada of Avengers and Hellcats plunged down on the speeding enemy fleet, and less than thirty minutes later it was too dark for the action to be continued; but in that short time the aircraft of Task Force 58 sealed the victory already achieved by the United States in the Battle of the Philippine Sea. A torpedo attack by four Grumman Avengers led by Lieutenant George B. Brown stopped and set ablaze the big carrier *Hiyo* which sank two hours later; the *Zuikaku* was hit a number of times by dive bombers from the *Enterprise* and *San Jacinto* and two more carriers, the *Chiyoda* and *Junyo,* were also badly damaged. Of Admiral Ozawa's other ships, the battleship *Haruna,* at least two cruisers and a number of destroyers all sustained damage in varying degrees.

With great difficulty, the tired American pilots landed back on board their parent carriers in the darkness. Due to inexperience in night operations, many misjudged their landings and crashed on touching down or skidded wildly down the flight decks into the sea, while others were forced to ditch in the water owing to lack of fuel. Some eighty aircraft were lost in these hazardous night recoveries—only twenty had been shot down in the preceding action—but most of the pilots were rescued. Thus was brought to a conclusion the most decisive carrier battle to be fought in the Pacific zone since Midway; for by the 21st June Admiral Ozawa's shattered fleet was virtually within sight of home waters, and beyond the reach of his opponent's larger, more slow-moving Task Force.

The grim struggle for Saipan lasted for almost another month, ending on the night of 6th–7th July with mass suicide attacks by thousands of Japanese, who inflicted heavy casualties among the men of the U.S. 27th Division before being repulsed. When the fighting died down, leaving Saipan in American hands, 23,811 of the defenders had been killed in action or were dead by suicide, including Lieutenant-General Saito, the military commander, and Vice-Admiral Chuichi Nagumo, the veteran of Pearl Harbour and Midway, long since relegated to a minor shore position. On 20th July the first American troops streamed ashore on smoking, bomb-scarred Guam; and three days later Tinian was captured.

By the middle of August, Operation *Forager* was almost completed.

It remained only for the Japanese to play a last, desperate trump card in attempting to stave off their inevitable defeat—an offensive launched against the American fleet by élite *Kamikaze* suicide pilots, dedicated to die for the Emperor. Like a ghostly breeze from Japan's medieval past, 'the sign of the Divine Wind' was at hand.

16

VICTORY IN EUROPE: 1945

In July 1941 the first British single-seater monoplane fighters to be taken into service aboard aircraft-carriers of the Royal Navy were embarked in *Furious* and, later, *Indomitable,* as a partial solution to the ever-present Fleet Air Arm problem of having to operate with slow or obsolescent machines. Following upon the unexpected success of R.A.F. pilots in flying off and landing Hawker Hurricanes carried in the ill-fated *Glorious* during the 1940 Norwegian campaign, a number of special variants of the type had been projected for naval use, known as Sea Hurricanes. This was the time when Germany's most notorious maritime reconnaissance bomber, the four-engined Focke-Wulf Fw 200 Condor—acknowledged by the Prime Minister Winston Churchill to be the "scourge of the Atlantic"—had virtually gained air supremacy over the northern sea lanes; and yet the Condor posed a serious threat only to Allied shipping because no light escort carriers or long-range fighters initially existed as a defence against it.

Designed by Focke-Wulf's Technical Director, Kurt Tank, the Fw 200 was originally intended as a commercial transport aeroplane for Lufthansa, the third prototype, named *Immelmann III,* being completed for the personal use of Adolf Hitler. When adapted for the maritime bombing role it displayed various shortcomings, and proved especially vulnerable to light anti-aircraft fire. Also the maintenance crews of *Kampfgeschwader* 40, which operated Condors from bases in Norway and later in Northern France, found their machines plagued with many servicing problems, together with some disastrous structural failures that occurred after taking violent evasive action. Nevertheless, the type remained in service pending production of the Heinkel He

177, and in the six months between August 1940 and February 1941 Focke-Wulf Condors, working in close liaison with U-boats, sank some 363,000 tons of Allied shipping. Soon afterwards the following directive was issued by Winston Churchill, "Extreme priority will be given to fitting out ships to catapult, or otherwise launch, fighter aircraft against bombers attacking our shipping."

Thus, as so often in time of war, necessity proved to be the mother of invention. A strengthened version of the sturdy Hawker Hurricane IA, commonly known as the Hurricat, emerged for use on board catapult-equipped merchant ships, to join the Mediterranean and Russian convoys. The first of these so-called CAM-ships was the s.s. *Michael E,* which was sunk by a U-boat before its aircraft could be launched; but more than thirty merchantmen were fitted out to carry and launch Hurricanes, and mixed into convoys with considerable success. The disadvantages were obvious, and not easily to be overcome: once launched, the fighter had been expended, for of course it could not be recovered; and the pilot had to bale out in the hope of being picked up from the water, often almost an impossibility in bitter Arctic seas.

The extremely useful, but still inadequate, CAM-ships inevitably led the way for small escort carriers known as MAC-ships, or merchant aircraft carrier ships—basically nothing more complicated than merchantmen fitted with short flight decks having room for six parked fighters. The first of these 'pocket' carriers was the motor ship *Empire Audacity* of 5,600 tons, formerly the captured German vessel *Hanover,* which in her new and unfamiliar guise joined the Mediterranean convoys in the summer of 1941, flying Grumman Martlets and, later, Sea Hurricanes. So much good work was done by this first MAC-ship in flying anti-submarine patrols and making Focke-Wulfs keep their distance that she was taken into Royal Navy service as H.M.S. *Audacity.* The following November her Martlets again proved their worth by shooting down four Fw 200s during just one voyage to Gibraltar.

On 21st December 1941 the little *Audacity* was sunk by torpedoes from a U-boat, with heavy loss of life, but about forty other MAC-ships provided invaluable air cover for Atlantic,

Mediterranean and Russian convoys during the next three years. In due course they would be supplemented by larger escort carriers, again utilising merchant ship hulls, but including a hangar and workshop layout reminiscent of the seaplane carriers of the First World War. The fighters normally operated were again Sea Hurricanes, complemented by one or two Fairey Swordfish for anti-submarine attack duties.

In support of the Murmansk and Archangel convoys, Sea Hurricanes and other fighters flown off escort carriers provided inestimable service, and played a vital part in breaking the back of Admiral Doenitz's U-boat campaign. Air cover for the North Russia ships became particularly important after April 1942, when twin-engined Heinkel He 111 and Junkers Ju 88 torpedo bombers were moved into new airfields in Norway specifically to attack Allied convoys taking the arduous Arctic route. A number of the PQ-coded convoys, without escort carriers, had suffered heavily at the hands of these aircraft from *Kampfgeschwader* 26 (flying He 111s) and *Kampfgeschwader* 30 (Ju 88s), terminating in the fearful slaughter imposed on PQ-17, which lost twenty-three ships out of a total of thirty-six in convoy. The brighter side of the coin was revealed when PQ-18 departed from Loch Ewe for Russia, to be joined by the merchant carrier *Avenger,* which had embarked twelve Sea Hurricanes and three Swordfish. For three successive days the convoy was under continuous attack by waves of Norwegian-based enemy torpedo bombers, and although a number of ships were sunk, over forty German aircraft were destroyed or badly damaged by the defending fighters and anti-aircraft fire. Four Sea Hurricanes from the *Avenger* were shot down, but three pilots saved.

The problem of providing air cover for every stage of the long journey to North Russia had thus been solved; for after PQ-18 had shown its aerial teeth, the He 111s and Ju 88s from Banak and Bardufoss never again repeated their earlier successes. For the remainder of the war, convoys on the Arctic route continued to enjoy the protection of escort cruisers, until merchant ship losses from enemy air attack became negligible and the torpedo bomber strikes eventually faded away. In fighting the equally worrying U-boat menace, Fairey Swordfish flown from escort carriers in the anti-submarine role valiantly and gloriously brought their long career to a close, on at least one occasion—in September 1944—destroying four of the heavily armed underwater craft during a single voyage.

Meanwhile, Sea Hurricanes operated by the large fleet carriers of the Royal Navy were slowly but surely gaining air supremacy in the Battle of the Mediterranean, which had been raging almost without respite since 1940. Typical of the convoy operations being undertaken by 1942 in the desperate struggle to keep Malta supplied—and at the same time a striking example of British fleet carriers in action—was the decisive engagement fought in August of that year. It involved an important convoy that left the Clyde early in the month to rendezvous with the largest force of escorting warships so far committed: the aircraft carriers *Victorious, Indomitable, Argus* and *Eagle*; the battleships *Rodney* and *Nelson*; seven cruisers; thirty-two destroyers; and four corvettes. The Fleet Air Arm fighters embarked for the voyage were many and varied, including Sea Hurricanes, Martlets and Fulmars, while aboard the veteran carrier *Furious,* which also joined the convoy, was a squadron of Royal Air Force Spitfires to assist in the air defence of Malta. On paper, such a powerful defence against U-boats and enemy bombers seemed invulnerable, but for three days the Allied ships would be within easy range of the massed German and Italian squadrons based on Sicily and Sardinia.

In brilliant summer weather the convoy sailed quietly to Gibraltar, where *Argus* was left behind. On 9th August the great armada was again at sea, and an Italian reconnaissance aircraft, the first of many watchful shadowing machines, was seen in the distance, circling just out of range. The same afternoon an enemy submarine fired a torpedo that struck the *Eagle,* and the carrier shuddered to a standstill. Riven by a tremendous explosion and on fire, she rolled over and sank ten minutes later, after most of her crew had been rescued. The outcome of the battle about to break in a great storm of destruction over the convoy now depended almost entirely on the fighters aboard *Victorious* and her sister-ship *Indomitable,* for during the evening *Furious* launched her Spitfires on their way to Malta and then turned back to Gibraltar, as previously arranged.

On 11th August the first wave of Junkers Ju 88s struck at the

Allied ships, only to be repulsed by Sea Hurricanes from *Indomit-able* and Fulmars from *Victorious* before they could inflict any serious damage. The following day brought the convoy within reach of even single-engined fighters operating from the Italian mainland, and until nightfall huge formations of Ju 87 Stukas, Ju 88s, Cant Z.1007s and Savoia-Marchetti Sm 79s, heavily protected by Messerschmitt Bf 109s and Macchi C.200s, attacked through the anti-aircraft barrage at varying heights and speeds. During a whole series of savage air battles, hitherto unequalled in Mediterranean convoy operations, the carrier-borne fighters—particularly the Sea Hurricanes of Nos. 800 and 880 Squadrons from *Indomitable*—fought back the masses of enemy raiders, destroying forty of them and damaging many more. It was like trying to stem an endless tide; but in the end they succeeded, and the great roaring of bomber engines faded away.

In the warm darkness the ships steamed on at top speed, while the exhausted fighter pilots and maintenance crews rested in preparation for the expected violence of another day. It could not possibly be worse than the one that had just ended, just as it would be unlikely for greater courage and determination to be displayed; one pilot alone, the Battle of Britain ace Sub-Lieutenant R. J. ('Dickie') Cork, had shot down no less than six enemy aircraft. As for those who sped the airmen on their way, it is sufficient to record that they worked without a break of any kind throughout that embattled August day, despite bombs, bullets, petrol fumes from idling engines and the intense heat of summer, often below decks and unaware even of which duels were being won or lost in the bright sunshine overhead.

Shortly after dawn on 13th August the convoy came within range of Royal Air Force fighters based on Malta, and full daylight brought a squadron of powerful twin-engined Bristol Beaufighters to play their part in defending the ships so long awaited by the besieged island. Again the enemy torpedo and dive bombers came thundering down; but all the heart had already been beaten out of their attacks, and they were lacking in determination. At last the fleet carriers could safely leave their merchantmen under the protection of Malta's Beaufighters and Spitfires and return to Gibraltar. It was a sadly depleted convoy that continued on its way, having endured many submarine and

E-boat onslaughts, apart from the continuous bombing raids; of the fourteen merchant ships that had left the Clyde only a few days before, less than half that number now remained. The escort losses were scarcely comparable but heavy in tonnage, for although the *Eagle* was the largest warship sunk during the voyage, two cruisers had also gone down and two more were badly damaged.

Finally three scarred but heavily laden cargo ships limped triumphantly into Valetta, and the oil tanker *Ohio,* perhaps the most essential vessel in the whole convoy, was later towed into harbour. The vital lifeline to Malta remained open, as it continued to do until the end of the war, by which time all the German forward air bases in Sicily and Italy had long been captured by our forces and the Mediterranean was at peace once more. Indeed, after 23rd October 1942, when General Montgomery launched his great offensive at El Alamein, heralded by a mighty barrage from a thousand guns, the Germans began to fall back in the Western Desert, and the amphibious Anglo-American invasion of Morocco and Algeria code-named Operation *Torch* finally sealed the fate of Rommel and his *Afrika Korps* divisions. "This is not the end," announced Winston Churchill. "It is not even the beginning of the end. But it is, perhaps, the end of the beginning!"

The sands of time were beginning to trickle out for Adolf Hitler, not only in the Mediterranean theatre of operations, but also in Russia, where the German Sixth Army was held, and finally destroyed, at Stalingrad in the winter of 1942–43. There was only misfortune, too, for the Fuehrer's battleship raiders, as they became more and more restricted in their activities. In December 1943 a large Allied convoy bound for Russia lured the 30,000-ton battle-cruiser *Scharnhorst* out of her Norwegian lair into the North Atlantic. But the Royal Navy close escort of three cruisers and a destroyer screen was backed at a discreet distance by the powerful battleship *Duke of York,* the cruiser *Jamaica* and four more destroyers. The steel jaws of Admiral Sir Bruce Fraser's trap opened to receive *Scharnhorst,* which began pounding away at the convoy about 150 miles north of North Cape and was engaged by the escorting cruisers *Belfast, Norfolk* and *Sheffield* while the British heavy units raced to join the battle. It was the late afternoon of a bitterly cold Christmas Day when the

Duke of York opened fire at 12,000 yd. with her huge 14-in. guns, and began the duel that came to an end soon after 7.0 p.m., when *Scharnhorst,* shattered and burning, went down. Out of a complement of 1,970 officers and men, only thirty-six were saved from the icy seas.

There now remained only a few warships in the German fleet, but undoubtedly one of these constituted a most serious threat to Allied shipping for no other reason than her immense power, which was contained, latent but not sleeping, in the remote fastness of Kaafiord, at the northern tip of Norway. The 42,000-ton battleship *Tirpitz,* sister ship to the *Bismarck* that had gone so valiantly to her doom in 1941, had not been completed long enough to see more than the briefest of actions, but her presence brooded over the Anglo-American convoys on the Arctic route like a watchful giant who might at any moment run amuck and wreak unimaginable destruction. The simple answer, of course, to the problem of *Tirpitz* was to immobilise her at anchor; and in September 1943 this had actually been achieved by British midget submarines which succeeded in penetrating the anti-torpedo nets around the battleship to attach limpet mines against her hull. The resulting heavy explosions shook *Tirpitz*'s engines loose in their mountings and caused other extensive damage, which Allied experts considered would need attention by a large, well-equipped dockyard.

Nevertheless, within six months repairs to the *Tirpitz* had almost been completed, without her once having been moved from the security of Kaafiord, and it became obvious to the Allies that another attack would have to be made before she was again ready for sea. A heavily escorted air strike by Fleet Air Arm dive bombers gave the most promise of success since the enemy battleship's anti-torpedo defences had been heavily reinforced; and towards the end of March 1944 six aircraft carriers, the *Victorious, Furious, Emperor, Fencer, Pursuer* and *Searcher,* were assembled under the overall command of Admiral Sir Michael Denny. The aircraft embarked for the action were Fairey Barracuda three-seater bombers and Vickers Supermarine Seafire, Grumman Wildcat and Hellcat and Chance Vought Corsair single-seater fighters—perhaps the most reliable Fleet Air Arm machines ever gathered together in a single operation.

Intended as a replacement for the Fairey Albacore, the far from beautiful Barracuda shoulder-wing monoplane was initially designed as a torpedo bomber, although it became much more of an all-purpose Fleet Air Arm machine before the war ended. The prototype had, in fact, made its maiden flight as far back as December 1940, but for various reasons production was delayed for over two years and the type did not go into operational service until January 1943. Even then, Barracudas saw very little action until the following September, when they were carried in *Illustrious* to support the Allied landings at Salerno. Despite their somewhat unfortunate appearance—that wide shoulder wing with curious Fairey-Youngman flaps, together with the long-legged undercarriage and high-set tailplane, took some time to win over those who preferred more conventional aircraft—Barracudas proved to be more than welcome in the Fleet Air Arm and were extensively used for anti-shipping operations until the arrival of VJ Day.

The carrier-borne version of the Supermarine Spitfire fighter, named the Seafire, inevitably followed the Sea Hurricane into Fleet Air Arm service after the Hawker aircraft had demonstrated that very fast, modern fighters could be operated from carriers; and a number of Merlin-engined Seafire variants were produced up to 1945. The Seafire was, of course, superior in general performance to the American-built Wildcat and Hellcat single-engined fighters also used by the Fleet Air Arm during the later years of the war; but they were sturdier, more rough-and-ready machines, and rendered excellent service, particularly from escort carriers.

It was a fine, warm day on 3rd April 1944, and the sun was shining brightly over the Norwegian mountains as forty-two Fairey Barracudas in two groups of twenty-one, from Nos. 827, 829 and 830 Squadrons (*Victorious*) and No. 831 Squadron (*Furious*) approached their unsuspecting target. High above the two formations roamed the fighter cover of eighty Seafires, Wildcats, Hellcats and Corsairs, watching for the first glint of enemy wings in the morning light; the days of hastily planned, unprotected Fleet Air Arm attacks by gallant but obsolete aircraft were gone for ever. Far below and ahead, the dive bomber pilots suddenly saw the fiord they were seeking, almost hidden by the high mountains that surrounded it, and prepared to strike at the great warship anchored there.

For the German seamen languishing at Kaafiord this was also a very important day. By a curious coincidence, their long winter of discontent in the *Tirpitz* had just ended, for the battleship was scheduled to run her steaming trials in Altenfiord that very afternoon. Her decks were a hive of industry as preparations went ahead to make the departure; in such a lonely place anything out of the ordinary was an event, and besides, a *Tirpitz* ready for trials promised more intensive action in the near future. Then the first group of ungainly Barracudas swooped between the towering sides of the fiord, the full-throated roaring of their Rolls Royce Merlin engines lost in the mountains until the deep, shattering sound broke suddenly over *Tirpitz*, overwhelming her with noise. The battleship's astonished anti-aircraft gun crews leapt desperately to man their weapons, but the heavy armour-piercing bombs were already crashing home on decks and superstructure. A fierce blaze broke out amidships, and within minutes the whole fiord was wreathed in thick black smoke.

The first wave of Barracudas had scarcely departed, clawing frantically for height to get away from those menacing mountains, when the second group plunged down, to bomb blindly through the smoke and now intense anti-aircraft fire. Then the last dive bombers had gone, leaving behind them death and destruction in the solitude of Kaafiord. Throughout the whole action, the fighters had most courageously kept very close escort, despite the danger of twisting and turning at their high speeds in such mountainous surroundings; and now they closed in to protect the Barracudas on the flight back to their carriers. Three of the dive bombers and one fighter had been lost.

The attack, over within a few violent moments like an abrupt blow from a mailed fist, was an unqualified success. Fifteen armour-piercing 1,000-lb. and 500-lb. bombs had squarely alighted on the *Tirpitz*, and she had been shaken by a large number of near misses. The upper deck had been badly holed, some bulkheads blasted out of place, at least three hundred men killed and many others wounded, and the great fire started amidships would still be burning some hours later.

The long, wearisome business of repairing the *Tirpitz* began all over again. Her defences were heavily strengthened, and within a short time included a smoke screen and artillery observation posts scattered in the surrounding hills. Grand Admiral Doenitz was determined that his last big battleship would have at least one more chance of putting to sea. Nevertheless the Fleet Air Arm remained equally undaunted, and on 17th July the fleet carriers *Formidable, Indefatigable* and *Furious* flew off forty-five Barracudas, escorted by fifty Corsair fighters, to strike at *Tirpitz* after a smaller attack on 15th May had brought no success. Hidden by her smoke screen, from which was hurled up a fearful barrage of high-velocity cannon fire, the battleship again made a most difficult target, but some minor damage was inflicted by near misses alongside the hull. During the following weeks further attacks were made by aircraft from the same three fleet carriers, but supported by the escort carriers *Nabob* and *Trumpeter,* which flew off some of the single-seater fighters.

On 22nd August the *Tirpitz* surprised her attackers by firing her main armament of 15-in. guns at them in pairs in twin turrets from a range of fifteen miles. All succeeding strikes were therefore carried out from the south to avoid unnecessary casualties; but the artificial smoke generators remained the battleship's best defence. However, on 24th August an armour-piercing, 1,000-lb. bomb grazed the bridge, tore through the upper deck and finally came to rest, unexploded, far below in the central control-room. The resulting damage was of little consequence, but a number of men were killed or wounded.

Other attacks by Barracudas were made on the *Tirpitz* up to the end of August, and some notable anti-shipping and photographic reconnaissance operations were carried out against the battleship by Fairey Fireflies from *Indefatigable*—the first actions in which these new Fleet Air Arm two-seater monoplanes participated. Having a general resemblance to its immediate predecessor, the Fairey Fulmar, the Firefly was much faster, had a more powerful armament, and could be used in a wide variety of roles; it later saw extensive action in the Far East theatre of operations, and remained in service (as the modified Mark 4) until 1956.

The repairs to the *Tirpitz* continued, but not for long without interruption. On 15th September 1944 a strong force of Royal Air Force four-engined Avro Lancasters, each carrying one of the special deep-penetration 12,000-lb. 'Tallboy' bombs invented by Dr Barnes Wallis, and operating from Archangel in North Russia, attacked the battleship. Yet again *Tirpitz* was saved from destruction by her smoke screen, although she came dangerously near to being capsized at anchor by some of the giant bombs, and one that exploded on contact with the water just alongside ripped open the armoured foredeck and split a number of forward bulkheads.

Because of the deteriorating situation in northern Norway— the German garrisons were soon to be withdrawn for service in more embattled zones—it was decided to move *Tirpitz* in order to make use of her as a floating battery, and on a dark October night she was quietly towed into the Sandesund in Tromsö fiord. Despite so much secrecy, the new anchorage was spotted by Fleet Air Arm reconnaissance Fireflies almost at once, and on 22nd October an unsuccessful high-level attack was made on the battleship by thirty-six Lancasters of Bomber Command. The anti-aircraft defence, now reinforced by the batteries around Tromsö and two flak ships, accounted for four of the R.A.F. machines.

Then, on 12th November, the end came for Germany's tortured 'Lonely Queen of the North', as *Tirpitz* was known to her crew. Once again the air-raid warning klaxons blared out in the solitude of Tromsö fiord, the smoke-screen began to spread across the still waters and the barrels of many guns swung anxiously skyward. As the repeating thunder of anti-aircraft cannon reverberated around the cliffs that surrounded *Tirpitz*, the big, four-engined bombers came into sight; eighteen R.A.F. Lancasters from the famous No. 617 ('Dambusters') Squadron, and thirteen from No. 9 Squadron, each carrying a 12,000-lb. 'Tallboy' bomb. This time there was no escape for the German battleship, for the smoke-screen dissipated in the light morning breeze to expose completely her great hull. There followed a terrible, inevitable accuracy about the bombing that told of long practice and vast experience.

The Wallis-designed bombs, looking like giant dustbins, plunged into the water on both sides of *Tirpitz*, lifting enormous water spouts higher than her masthead. One missile struck the battleship amidships, almost on the catapult, throwing pieces of one of her Arado Ar 196 floatplanes into the air; another exploded between two of her twin-gun main turrets, blowing them up to the sky to fall back into the water. Shrouded in black smoke, she began to list to port, steadily rolling over until the port-side guns had to cease firing and the inclinometer needle was flickering past 70 degrees. At 100 degrees the *Tirpitz* capsized.

The roar of gunfire died away and the booming thunder of detonating 'Tallboy' bombs was heard no more. Having rolled to 135 degrees, *Tirpitz* lay bottom up with her rudder and propeller shafts visible above the shallow waters of Tromsö fiord, a vast steel tomb for over 1,200 brave men. The last of Hitler's big capital ships had been destroyed, her fate inexorably set in motion by carrier-borne aircraft of the Fleet Air Arm and sealed by the heavy bombers of the Royal Air Force. With the *Tirpitz* died the German dream of whole oceans haunted by surface raiders, snapping like aggressive dogs at Allied convoys, roaming at will to sink where and when they wished. From the very beginning there had been too few of them; and towards the end they had been taught the hard lessons already learned by *Prince of Wales* and *Repulse* in the South China Sea—that without adequate air cover the battleship was doomed.

The U-boat menace remained, slowly but surely to be vanquished by destroyers, often working in co-operation with anti-submarine aircraft flown off the invaluable little escort carriers that did so much to win the Atlantic and Mediterranean battles. Long before Hitler committed suicide in devastated Berlin and Admiral Doenitz found himself Fuehrer of a crumbling and defeated Third Reich, the Allies had achieved complete command of the seas—but only because air supremacy had also been accomplished over those same waters. Sea Hurricanes, Seafires, Martlets, Corsairs, Wildcats and Hellcats; Swordfish, Albacores, Barracudas, Fulmars, Fireflies and Avengers; all had played their part in the sea war and not been found wanting, from the sunlit walls of Malta to the icy Polar wastes.

On 8th May 1945—VE Day—the war in Europe finally ended, and the guns thundered for the last time. "This is your victory," Winston Churchill told the wildly cheering London crowds. "In all our long history we have not seen a greater day than this!"

The crews of the aircraft carriers, in common with so many other servicemen, would dearly have loved to call it a day and return home. But the grim war in the Far East still went on, despite relentless, unceasing bombing raids by the United States Air Force that were steadily reducing every major Japanese city to ashes, and signs of collapsing morale among some of the enemy leaders. Ahead lay the forbidding prospect of recapturing all the myriad islands of the Pacific in Japanese hands, almost certainly at the cost of heavy casualties; over four thousand American dead on Iwo Jima alone indicated a grey future for those who were far away from the rejoicing in London and New York. Well might they crouch in foxholes, load shells into huge guns, sweat over aircraft engines between hot steel decks, and wonder "How long, O Lord? How long?"

17

THE WIND OF FATE: 1945

~~~~~~

Major Katashige Takata, a fighter pilot of the Imperial Army Air Force, was almost certainly the first Japanese airman to sacrifice his life deliberately under the complex, symbolic *Bushido* code of honour that called for blind obedience to the Emperor and the active desire to seek everlasting life through a glorious death. On 17th May 1944 Takata, flying a Mitsubishi A6M Zero-Sen fighter, dived his machine at full speed on to the superstructure of an American destroyer off Biak, New Guinea; there was a tremendous explosion, the ship caught fire and it eventually went down with the loss of many crew members. Nevertheless, this was an isolated, individual act of self-destruction—or "falling like a cherry blossom in the spring" as it became known—and merely preceded a highly organised Japanese plan to wipe out the American carrier forces in the Pacific with a series of hammer blows that would take friend and enemy alike to death in battle.

The adoption of *Kamikaze Tokubetsu Kogekitai—Kamikaze* Special Attack Squads—to deal with the critical situation facing Japan by 1944 was originally suggested by Captain Iyo, commanding the aircraft-carrier *Chiyoda,* but his proposal was at first rejected. However, the idea was brought up again by the fighter ace Captain Okamura, and received favourable consideration in high circles, particularly from Vice-Admiral Takijiro Onishi, commander of the Japanese air forces in the Philippines. There was great enthusiasm in Tokyo, and by July 1944 seventeen *Kamikaze* groups had been formed, each equipped with the latest Zeke 52 single-seater fighters, armed with 500-lb. bombs. Volunteer pilots for the suicide squadrons were not difficult to find; mostly young and inexperienced, already disciplined to believe that their life belonged to the Emperor, they were easily persuaded into an elaborate way of death for the beloved home-land. Wearing the ceremonial belted tunic with black buttons, on his chest the special emblem of the corps—a cherry blossom with three leaves—and around his throat a silk muffler inscribed with traditional poems, each pilot was carefully taught to accept, in cold blood and without hatred, the idea of his own contrived, violent end.

On 13th October the American Pacific Fleet under the command of Admiral William 'Bull' Halsey entered Leyte Gulf in the northern Philippines, and the now familiar pattern of landing against heavy opposition under cover of a naval bombardment began according to schedule; but the remnants of the Imperial Japanese Navy, supported by *Kamikaze* units, were also at sea, about to make a last-ditch attempt to save face with even a small victory. Led by the mighty 64,000-ton battleship *Musashi,* the enemy fleet included four other battleships, a task force of four aircraft-carriers, and many cruisers and destroyers—almost everything afloat that remained. Halsey, who had waited and hoped for just such a final engagement, gladly accepted the Japanese challenge; and so the opening shots were fired in the Battle of Leyte, perhaps the greatest struggle at sea ever to take place in the long history of naval warfare.

Between 14th October, when Vice-Admiral Masabumi Arima led three squadrons of bomb-carrying Zero-Sen fighters in to attack the American fleet with the sole intention of taking his pilots to glorious, certain death, and 26th October, when a dozen Japanese aircraft similarly bent on suicide plunged down on Admiral Halsey's warships in the Gulf of Leyte, a number of *Kamikaze* actions were undertaken. They met with surprising success; one American carrier was sunk, four more seriously damaged, and numerous casualties inflicted. Admiral Arima hurled his machine on to the flight deck of the carrier *Hornet,* wreaking such havoc that she had to be temporarily withdrawn from service, and other Japanese aircraft that exploded into the carriers *Swanee, Franklin* and *Hancock* also more than justified their purpose. Even so, few American commanders realised at the time that the *Kamikaze* attacks were carried out according to a definite plan, and were not merely individual acts of sacrifice.

Both the Short Sunderland flying-boat, *top,* and the Consolidated Catalina, *middle,* were used in many theatres during the Second World War on ocean reconnaissance; *bottom,* the Saunders-Roe Princess, one of the largest flying-boats in the world.

Above, the Howard Hughes Hercules, the largest and most expensive flying-boat ever built, made only one short flight in a decade before being scrapped in 1953; *below,* the Blackburn Buccaneer, a torpedo-spotter-reconnaissance aircraft adopted by the Royal Navy as one of their main strike planes

Apart from the operations by Admiral Onishi's suicide squadrons, the Battle of Leyte Gulf, which lasted for four days of hard slogging between the two fleets, and straggled over thousands of miles of ocean, ended in a resounding Japanese defeat. Admiral Halsey, in command of the greatest armada of warships—including more than twenty aircraft-carriers—ever to put to sea, hounded the enemy down and destroyed him, sinking three battleships, including the flagship *Musashi,* the entire force of Japanese carriers, including the often-wounded *Zuikaku,* that last survivor of Midway, ten cruisers and at least twelve destroyers. In order to inflict such frightful losses risks had to be taken, and the United States forfeited a light aircraft-carrier, two small escort carriers and several destroyers—not a high price to pay for such a victory.

In November 1944 the last and biggest of the Japanese fleet carriers entered service. Originally laid down as a sister ship to the battleships *Yamato* and *Musashi,* the huge *Shinano* displaced some 72,000 tons, and after conversion was the largest aircraft-carrier in the world, with a heavily armoured flight deck and a hangar deck capable of holding more than eighty machines. At anchor in Tokyo Bay she was the pride of the tattered Japanese Navy but a sadly inadequate reply to Admiral Nimitz's massive Pacific Fleet, and her fate revealed beyond doubt that the Battle of Leyte had sealed the doom of Japanese sea and air power. On 28th November the *Shinano* left Yokusuka naval base to put to sea for the first time; and she was at the bottom only seventeen hours later. Heading for Osaka Bay, she was sighted by the United States submarine *Archerfish,* which fired a salvo of torpedoes into her, and although the supposedly unsinkable ship did indeed stay afloat for the next seven hours, she finally went down with all her aircraft and five hundred men, taking beneath the warm Pacific waters Japan's last hopes of striking back at her enemies in any force.

Everything now depended on the *Kamikaze* units, and they were publicised out of all proportion to their strength and real value. Some special attacks were deliberately highlighted to impress the Japanese people, as on the occasion when Tokyo radio announced that the American cruiser *Nashville,* which carried General MacArthur's staff, would soon be destroyed by

Kamikaze aircraft. Sure enough, on 13th December 1944, a Mitsubishi Zero-Sen fighter carrying two 500-lb. bombs headed directly for the *Nashville* despite a heavy and concentrated barrage of anti-aircraft fire, and struck the cruiser's bridge at full speed. Although most of the high-ranking officers on board escaped without serious injury, severe damage was inflicted on the forward superstructure and over three hundred men killed or wounded, proving that even the most heavily defended warships were extremely vulnerable to attack by suicide pilots.

Meanwhile, a new type of expendable aircraft had been evolved to equip the *Kamikaze* groups based on the airfields of Kyushu, the most southerly of the islands forming the Japanese mainland. This was a small single-seater monoplane flying bomb, only 15 ft. in length, carrying a 2,000-lb. charge of high explosive in the nose and having a maximum speed of over 600 m.p.h. Designed by Captain Niki, the little Oka 4, or *Baka* (meaning 'madman') as it became known to the Americans, was propelled by four rockets which gave five or ten minutes flight duration, and had a very simple enclosed cockpit containing only the most elementary controls. It was intended to be carried into action slung beneath the fuselage of a Mitsubishi G4M (code-named Betty) twin-engined bomber, then released within comparatively easy reach of a number of targets, so that the *Kamikaze* pilot could quickly select one and dive upon it. Some eight hundred of these manned flying-bombs, which had a general resemblance to the German V-1 'doodlebugs' of the same period, were constructed, but only about fifty launched before hostilities ended.

1944 dragged wearily into 1945 and the United States forces in the Pacific zone began their next assault, against the strategically important little island of Iwo Jima. Never before had they encountered such fanatical opposition; more than two months of unceasing preliminary bombardment from air and sea seemed to have silenced only a few of the hundreds of enemy machine-gun nests hewed out of the volcanic rock and then reinforced with concrete. Iwo Jima was an island fortress, networked with hidden blockhouses and pillboxes that took a terrible toll of the attacking American marines. They struggled ashore and were mown down in their hundreds, established a beachhead and held it, against repeated *Banzai* charges, then slowly but surely battled their way up the barren hillsides to the highest point on the island, Mount Suribachi. At last, after twenty-six days of bitter fighting, the sheer weight of men and material landed on the eight square miles of Iwo Jima overcame Japanese resistance, and the island was captured. The Americans suffered twenty thousand casualties, including over four thousand killed; but with flame-throwers and mortars, bazookas and grenades, knives and axes, anything that came to hand, they had slain twenty-one thousand of the defenders.

The last stepping-stone to the Japanese mainland was the large island of Okinawa, some 360 miles south-west of Kyushu, and even more heavily fortified than Iwo Jima, with a garrison of 70,000 troops, many concrete emplacements and numerous batteries of large-calibre guns. It had to be invaded and seized to act as a springboard for the final blow at Japan; but the crippling losses already suffered by the Allied forces gave them cause for sombre thought and some hesitation. However, on 22nd March 1945 the American Fifth Fleet, under the command of Admiral Raymond A. Spruance, commenced the tremendous bombardment of Okinawa that was to last for the next ten days, while the greatest armada of warships and troop transports yet assembled for invasion purposes in the Pacific moved into position off shore and waited, ironically enough, for April Fools' Day.

From 26th March, the British Pacific Fleet, commanded by Admiral Sir Bruce Fraser, commenced diversionary attacks in support of the American forces arrayed against Okinawa, and aircraft flown off the carriers *Indomitable, Indefatigable, Illustrious* and *Victorious* successfully put out of action a number of Japanese airfields. Meanwhile, American Boeing B-29 Superfortress bombers, hurriedly landed on Iwo Jima, struck at the large enemy bases on Kyushu. The bombardment from sea and air thus gradually mounted to a crescendo; but during all these Allied preliminary actions, only isolated instances of *Kamikaze* attacks occurred, although two enemy fighters deliberately crashed on to the flight decks of *Indefatigable* and *Victorious* respectively, causing some damage.

On 1st April—Easter morning—the 1,300 ships of all shapes and sizes massed off Okinawa landed some 100,000 troops at three points around the island's coastline, yet the Japanese still chose to bide their time, and at first the invasion forces met with little resistance. Nevertheless, the warlords in Tokyo, shrunken now in stature, were only too well aware of the danger to their homeland. "It is a matter of just a short time before the rise or fall of our people will be decided," stated the Japanese radio when announcing that Okinawa was under assault, and Premier Kuniaki Koiso had already warned that: "The enemy now stands at our front gate. It is the gravest moment in our country's history."

The time had come for the Divine Wind of Imperial Japan to blow with hurricane force through the American fleet gathered off Okinawa. At dawn on 6th April a large formation of aircraft from Kyushu—mostly Zero-Sen fighters but including a few twin-engined bombers and obsolete floatplanes—appeared over the great multitude of invading warships, and was immediately engaged by swarms of American fighters; but the pilots who wore the white scarf of their dedication wrapped around their black helmets refused to be deviated from their deadly purpose. Dozens were shot down into the sea, but the remainder dived through the streaking, interlaced tracer of the Allied fighter umbrella, made no attempt to avoid the terrifying barrage of anti-aircraft fire thrown up by the warships, and exploded into their targets. The curious last screams of defiance that were shouted, such as "Babe Ruth, now go to hell!" or "Die, reckless Yankee Doodles!" seemed as fantastic in modern war as the *samurai* swords often clutched between the *Kamikaze* pilot's knees; the grand suicide gesture itself no more hopeless than the future of doomed Japan. How many *Kamikaze* aircraft left their bases for the last time on that day will probably never be accurately assessed, but at least three hundred were shot down or deliberately destroyed themselves, whereas only two American fighters were lost.

By a miracle the suicide pilots failed to sink any of the larger Allied ships, but a number of carriers were damaged, including H.M.S. *Illustrious,* which narrowly escaped disaster when her accurate gunfire deflected an enemy aircraft just before the moment of impact. In truth, the great Japanese *Kamikaze* offensive had opened as little more than a second Marianas Turkey Shoot for the American fighter forces, but Vice-Admiral Ugaki, who commanded the squadrons based on Kyushu, could still muster some seven hundred machines, and decided that more large-scale suicide attacks should be carried out the following day. Not that he had any real choice. All the airfields on Kyushu were daily being more heavily bombed by Allied carrier-based aircraft; and since early March the giant four-engined B-29 Superfortresses from the Marianas, bearing such exotic feminine names as *Samantha, Dolores, Janie Girl!, Miss Judy,* or more hopefully *Dina Might!,* had ranged far and wide over the Japanese homeland, turning city after city into ashes. To such an appalling situation there was only one solution—a glorious death for the Emperor.

Again the United States Hellcats and Corsairs rose in strength to cut the enemy *Kamikaze* formations to pieces, but despite their many successes a number of suicide aircraft penetrated the fighter screen and damaged many of the American ships, including the carrier *Hancock,* which was put out of action. Meanwhile, the only task force the beaten Japanese navy could now muster, composed of Admiral Yamamoto's old flagship, the 73,000-ton battleship *Yamato,* the heavy cruiser *Yahagi* and eight destroyers, had left the Inland Sea and was heading proudly for Okinawa also to seek an honourable and contrived destruction at the hands of the United States fleet. Some fifty miles south-west of Kyushu, 380 American carrier-based dive bombers and torpedo aircraft fell like eagles on the enemy battle squadron, which lay naked and helpless without a single fighter for protection. The *Yahagi* was first to go down, firing her guns to the end; then the *Yamato* abruptly vomited a great fountain of orange flame and disintegrated, leaving no survivors. Out of the whole task force, only four badly damaged destroyers chose to escape from the deluge of bombs and torpedoes so reminiscent of the rain of death that had overwhelmed *Prince of Wales* and *Repulse* in December 1941, all those many weary months ago.

The Japanese navy had committed suicide in vain. But the *Kamikaze* aircraft—Zero Sen fighters, *Baka* flying bombs and, later, almost anything that would fly—continued to strike at the Allied invasion fleet, day after day, until the strain began to tell on the warships' crews. On 11th April the battleship *Missouri* and the carrier *Enterprise* were repeatedly hit and badly damaged; and

in a massed attack the following day the battleships *New Mexico,*
Idaho and *Tennessee* were damaged, one destroyer sunk and six
others temporarily put out of action. The Japanese losses were
staggering—something like a hundred aircraft a day. Nevertheless, machines were raked together from all possible sources
in order to step up the *Kamikaze* offensive, and at the same time
Japanese resistance on Okinawa stiffened, bringing the invading
forces to a standstill.

During May the large fleet carriers of the British and American
forces were selected as the principal objectives for *Kamikaze*
attacks. A suicide aircraft hit the flight deck of the *Formidable,*
setting her island ablaze; another struck the *Indomitable,* but failed
to explode; and two more crashed into *Victorious,* causing some
casualties. On the American side the carriers *Bunker Hill* and
Enterprise were knocked out of action, the latter ship—Admiral
Mitscher's giant 'Big E'—barely escaping complete destruction.
Similarly, Admiral Spruance's flagship, the huge battleship *New*
Mexico, had to be withdrawn from service. Overwhelmed by
such a succession of disasters, the Allies were forced to contem-
plate raising the siege of Okinawa; meanwhile, they called for
increased supplies of anti-aircraft ammunition and many more
fighters.

The *Kamikaze* offensive could not stand the pace, of course.
After a last, mad fling on 24th May, when two American ships
were sunk and about twenty others damaged for a loss of three
hundred aircraft, the attacks petered out; there were too few
pilots left on Kyushu, now that so many had "fallen like cherry
blossoms in the spring" to be shattered against the steel hulls of
the American fleet. On 21st June, after a campaign lasting eighty-
two days. Okinawa was finally overcome by the American infantry,
who were astounded actually to witness hundreds of symbolic
Japanese suicides by the sword. The usual frenzied *Banzai*
charges to meet certain death continued right up the the bitter
end, until, amazingly, over 109,000 defending troops had been
killed. The Allied casualties, too, were high: 12,500 dead and
missing in action, 36,000 wounded.

At last it was possible for the invading forces to assess the cost
of the *Kamikaze* offensive, which had proved by no means as
ineffective as the Japanese considered. Thirty-four American

warships had been sunk off Okinawa; 288 ships of all classes damaged, including carriers, battleships and cruisers; 12,000 men killed and 33,700 wounded. Soon the United States navy yards were filled with vessels under repair, many requiring months of work before they could put to sea. Such heavy losses could not have been sustained indefinitely, and a United States Strategic Bombing Survey compiled on the suicide attacks came to the conclusion that if they had been carried out "in greater power and concentration they might have been able to cause us to withdraw or revise our strategic plans."

But the total loss in pilots of the *Kamikaze Tokubetsu Kogekitai* was equally prohibitive to the Japanese; and in the single fact that not one of the attacking aircraft was ever intended to return lay the weakness of the whole offensive, for it could only last as long as men and machines still remained. By the time that Okinawa fell into Allied hands, at least two thousand—and possibly as many as four thousand—suicide aircraft of various types had been destroyed, taking about the same number of dedicated young men on the wings of the Divine Wind to meet their personal Sons of Heaven. "Whatever you may think about the *Kamikazes*," the director of suicide operations in Tokyo, General Kawabe, told an American court of enquiry after the war, "you can be certain that the pilots died happily in the firm conviction that their sacrifice was one more step towards the Emperor's victory."

Perhaps not all the white-suited *Kamikaze* airmen died quite as happily as General Kawabe so steadfastly believed; but in any event there had not been enough of them to serve any real purpose in the life-or-death struggle for Japan. Also, the inevitable end was not to be prolonged for very much longer, as the weeks of July slid past and Tokyo radio persisted that there would be no capitulation. At 1.45 a.m. on 6th August a Boeing B-29 Superfortress named *Enola Gay,* piloted by Lieutenant-Colonel Paul W. Tibbets, took off from Tinian airfield in the Marianas and rose ponderously but smoothly into the early-morning sky. Six hours later the same big four-engined bomber was over Hiroshima, a pleasant city of some 343,000 people; and from the modified bomb bay fell a large black object, descending lazily by parachute until it vanished into the maze of streets and buildings far below. The B-29 *Enola Gay* banked around, just as a terrible blinding light, "brighter than a thousand suns", lit up Hiroshima, to be followed by that ghastly mushroom cloud soon to become familiar to the whole world. In that infinitesimal moment of time, sixty per cent of the city disappeared as if it had never existed, and some 78,000 civilians died. The Atomic Age had come to a world sadly unprepared to cope with the monstrous genie its scientists had created.

Three days later, at 11.02 a.m., another ugly black atomic bomb dropped from the opened belly of a B-29, this time on Nagasaki, the large supply port on Kyushu Island. Again a giant pillar of flame erupted towards the sky, proving that the destruction of Hiroshima had been no mere half-hearted warning, but the precursor of "a rain of ruin from the air, the like of which has never been seen on this earth," in the words of President Harry S. Truman of the United States. The appalling devastation and horrifying death roll at Nagasaki staggered even the most hardened and fanatical of the Tokyo warlords, and on 15th August 1945 the Japanese government surrendered.

Of the *Kamikaze* units that had attacked in such a blaze of glory at Okinawa, only a handful of volunteers remained, but they had one last gesture to make before the end. On 16th August, just two weeks before the first United States troops arrived in Tokyo, two small formations of Japanese fighters took off from their bomb-cratered airfield for the last time and headed out over the open sea. Some thirty machines deliberately crashed at full speed on to the American base established on Okinawa; the second suicide squadron simply flew on over the vastness of the Pacific, to plunge at last, out of fuel, into the water. There were, of course, no survivors. For those men, to whom the strange, harsh code of *Bushido* was more dear than life, there could be no question of defeat, and they had chosen to die rather than witness the final disgrace.

On 2nd September 1945 the formal Japanese instrument of surrender was signed by representatives of both sides on board the United States Pacific Fleet flagship *Missouri,* anchored in Tokyo Bay. All around the 45,000-ton battleship lay the might of the Allied navies, including the carrier task forces, their always dangerous and often wearisome duties at last completed; it had been largely a war between carrier-borne aircraft, and without these ships there might well have been a different end to the Japanese dream of Pacific conquest. Yet, curiously enough, there was little jubilation on this occasion, only gratitude for a difficult job well done. To many people, the scratching of silver-plated fountain pens in the shadow of Mount Fujiyama conveyed nothing except that it was all over in the East; the generals and admirals could sit back to write their memoirs and the soldier-civilians return home.

18

FUTURE INDEFINITE

∿∿∿

During the age of austerity that followed the Second World War, the flying-boat as a type slid into obscurity and finally died out, forty years of steady development having been brought to an end by the remarkable advances that had taken place in extending the range of land-based aircraft. It did not fade quietly away, but rather seemed to consume itself, growing apace in size to hasten the speed of its own unwilling departure, from the big Blohm und Voss Bv 238 and Kawanishi H8K (Emily) boats of 1945 to the huge Saunders-Roe Princesses of 1952. The amphibian class remained in existence only a little longer, although there was a brief post-war boom in small civil seaplanes featuring wheeled undercarriages, particularly in the United States. The last notable amphibians to appear on the British aviation scene were the twin-engined Short Sealand and Vickers-Supermarine Seagull of 1948, both of which were successful for a while but soon became obsolete owing to the increasing versatility of helicopters.

The giant Blohm und Voss Bv 238, with a wing span of 197 ft., was evolved by Dr Ing. Richard Vogt and his design team from Germany's contemporary of the Short Sunderland, the six-engined Bv 222 *Wiking,* which had been produced in small numbers as a long-range maritime reconnaissance flying-boat for the Luftwaffe. Only one prototype Bv 238 had been completed by 1944, and this was destroyed at its moorings on Lake Schaal by low-flying American P-51 Mustang fighters shortly before the collapse of the Third Reich, bringing to a halt an interesting new phase in large flying-boat development. However, the sweeping lines of the Sunderland were more closely followed—though not deliberately—by the biggest of the Japanese flying-boats, the Kawanishi H8K, code-named Emily under the Allied system.

With a maximum speed of 290 m.p.h. and having a range of some 4,000 miles, the four-engined Type 2, as it was also known, brought flying-boat design in the Far East to a successful, but ultimate conclusion; the close of hostilities had doomed the class to an early extinction in those waters.

In the United States the conventional wartime Consolidated PB2Y Coronado and Martin PBM Mariner flying-boat types were succeeded by the much larger Martin XPB2M Mars, with a wing span of 200 ft. Powered by four 2,200-h.p. Wright R-3350-18 Duplex Cyclone radial air-cooled engines, the Mars had a payload of 30,000 lb., and for a decade gave outstanding service in the cargo transport role. The four freight-carrying (JRM) craft used by the U.S. Naval Air Transport Service for round trips between California and Hawaii were, at that time, the largest flying boats in military service anywhere in the world; and on 27th August 1948 one JRM machine, the *Caroline Mars,* established a non stop flight record for seaplanes over a total distance of 4,748 miles. Nevertheless, the introduction of high-speed jet transport aircraft brought about the demise of all the Mars boats by 1956, and, apart from one or two experimental machines such as the Martin P6M Seamaster, the class had vanished from American service before 1960.

Flying-boat development in Great Britain terminated on a grand scale with the Saunders-Roe SR.45 Princess, originally designed for operation by B.O.A.C. on the post-war Atlantic routes. Work on the three boats ordered for civil use commenced at Cowes in 1946, and it soon became obvious that they would be true giants of the airlines, larger and heavier even than the American Martin Mars, which had hitherto seemed the ultimate conception in size and weight. The wing-spans of the Princess machines measured over 219 ft., and the hulls were 148 ft. in length. The range was some 5,500 miles and a maximum cruising speed of 380 m.p.h. could be attained. Each boat was powered by ten, 3,200-s.h.p./800 lb. thrust Bristol Proteus 600 propeller-turbine engines—an indication of the remarkable advances that had been made in power plant development—almost completely buried in the wide monoplane wing, which also featured retractable floats at the tips. The deep, amazingly roomy hull of the Princess was of figure-eight, or 'double-bubble' cross-section, for easier pressurisation, and passenger layouts were envisaged that included luxury accommodation for over a hundred people, with galleys, powder-rooms, sleeping-berths, a cocktail-bar and spiral stairways between the two decks. The spacious flight compartment, streamlined into the sweeping, rounded nose, featured the most modern achievements in aircraft engineering and instrument planning, with well-sited positions for captain and first officer, two flight engineers, navigator and radio officer. Everything about these Isle of Wight behemoths was grandiose in concept, attempting to recapture the pre-war splendour of the big Empire boats. But 1939 had been the end of an era in transoceanic flight, and the Princesses were emerging too late to save themselves.

The first Saunders-Roe Princess (G-ALUN) was quietly launched on 20th August 1952, and two days later could be seen in graceful flight over Cowes; but in due course considerable mechanical trouble developed in the complicated gearbox system of the double (paired) engines. Much valuable time was lost while modifications were carried out, and other aspects, political and economical, had meanwhile also arisen, eventually resulting in the cancellation by B.O.A.C. of all Princess requirements. To the bitter disappointment of their designer, Sir Arthur Gouge, the largest Saro boats ever built were soon afterwards retired completely from service, being cocooned and then beached at Calshot, where they remained until 1967, finally ending their sad days of enforced rest at the scrapyard.

Shortly before Saunders-Roe commenced construction of their ill-fated Princess boats, they had embarked upon the design of a revolutionary single-seater fighter flying-boat, powered by two side-by-side Metropolitan-Vickers F2/4 Beryl axial flow turbo-jet engines. This unique machine—the first of its type anywhere in the world—was designated the S.R.A./1. In general appearance it had the neat and streamlined layout of a miniature Sunderland or Mars, but the tailplane was much higher placed and the wing-tip floats were fully retractable. Armed with four 20-mm. fixed forward-firing cannon, and having a maximum speed of over 500 m.p.h., the S.R.A./1 was a most unusual and revolutionary aircraft, attempting to revive in the jet age a flying-boat type that had declined in popularity after the First World War, and during

1947 and 1948 it received a certain amount of favourable publicity. Nevertheless, like the giant Princess boats, the three S.R.A./1 prototypes arrived on the aviation scene at just that moment when marine aircraft were being ousted by jet-propelled, land-based machines, and consequently from the beginning they were doomed. Regretfully, two of these remarkable waterborne fighters had to go to the scrapyard; the other is retained for posterity in the collection of historical aircraft at the College of Aeronautics, Cranfield.

The Saunders-Roe S.R.A./1 is perhaps the most striking example of a flying-boat type that was faultless in design and apparently had many possibilities, yet failed simply because no advantageous service use could be envisaged for it at the time. But only in the United States, where the familiar 'bigger and better' theme in flying-boat construction was always sure of careful attention, can the story of that singularly beautiful class of marine aeroplane be properly ended; for there it was, at Long Beach, California, that the largest and most expensive craft of them all was finally assembled. It was once referred to as "the biggest thing man ever dreamed of sending into the sky", yet made only one short flight in a decade and cost a total of $23,000,000 to construct and keep in seaworthy condition.

The design of the Hughes H-4 (originally designated the HK-1) emerged in 1942 from a suggestion by the shipbuilding magnate, Henry Kaiser, to the effect that he was prepared to build a fleet of giant flying-boats for the transport of war materials or troops—airborne Liberty ships capable of roving far and wide around the world. Kaiser's project was approved by the United States government, but without any real enthusiasm, and the undertaking went ahead more or less as a private venture, meeting with innumerable delays and difficulties. Eventually, Kaiser persuaded Howard Hughes, the multi-millionaire racing pilot and aircraft factory owner, to join him in the construction of what was finally turning out to be an enormous monoplane flying-boat with a wing span of 320 ft. and a length of 219 ft. It was to be powered by no fewer than eight 3,000-h.p. Pratt and Whitney Wasp Major radial engines and the overall weight would be estimated at 425,000 lb.

Slowly—much too slowly—the Hughes H-4 took shape at the

millionaire's Culver City factory, through 1943 and into 1944. At a time when all available steel and aluminium in the aircraft industry was being allocated to fighter and bomber production, Kaiser and Hughes found it impossible to obtain any priority for the vast amount of light metal required by their machine, and it was decided that the construction should be entirely of wood. Millions of cubic feet of timber and gallons of glue were consumed by the insatiable monster that was being created, but the work dragged on and on, until eventually Kaiser quietly bowed out of the wearisome affair and the government contract for three aircraft of the H-4 type was cancelled.

Howard Hughes, typically refusing to accept defeat, continued with the building of his prototype H-4 boat, now formally named the *Hercules*. In June 1946 the wing, hull, tailplanes and engines were moved from the Culver City works to Long Beach, California, for assembly there. Along the twenty-five miles of road, all electric cables and telegraph poles had to be temporarily removed, a number of bridges reinforced to take the great weight and many hundreds of trees cut down. Finally, after two days and nights, the giant components arrived safely at their destination, the transfer alone having cost $55,000.

Just over a year later the Hughes *Hercules* was completed. It had an estimated cruising speed of 175 m.p.h., a normal range of nearly 3,000 miles, and there was room in the hull for seven hundred fully equipped troops, or even a 60-ton tank. Resting at its moorings the mammoth H-4 had to be seen to be believed, with a tail 100 ft. in height and a flight deck 20 ft. above the waterline. Most of those who came to see the great machine went away suitably impressed by its size but convinced that it would never take to the air. Nevertheless, on 2nd November 1947, while the H-4 was undergoing taxiing tests in Los Angeles harbour with Howard Hughes at the controls and some thirty of his technical advisers aboard, it was seen to lift smoothly off the water and climb steadily, levelling off at an altitude of about 80 ft. It remained in the air for over a mile, then Hughes gently settled the enormous hull back on to the choppy sea. "It felt so buoyant and good," he told reporters afterwards, "that I just pulled it up."

The ill-fated H-4 was destined never to fly again. It obviously needed more powerful engines, but these somehow never became available, and the big boat literally remained high and dry, doing precisely nothing except cost Hughes a lot of money for the next six years. In September 1953 it was seriously damaged in a storm by water flooding through the hull, and the estimated time needed to effect repairs—twelve months at a cost of over $5,000,000—finally brought Henry Kaiser's fantastic wartime dream to an end. With reluctance, Howard Hughes decided to abandon the project and allowed his only completed H-4 flying-boat to be scrapped.

Who can say if there is any future for the modern long-range commercial flying-boat? It would not seem so, in this era of very fast, efficient jet-propelled air liners; but as take-offs and landing speeds increase, more and more land is being swallowed up by the expanding airports of the world. Untroubled by limited run-way lengths, even the largest passenger-carrying flying-boats could still span the great air routes, with any amount of sheltered harbours available to act as bases—and more than a few of those seaports within easy reach of city air terminals. It is true that such a boat would have to be of the latest swept-wing layout, with extremely powerful jet engines, and, as a natural conse-quence, the streamlined mounting of such units awakens the problem of keeping the orifices clear from spray. Yet it can be successfully achieved, as the Saunders-Roe S.R.A./1 proved nearly twenty years ago, long before the conception of the hovercraft, which emulates, without fully replacing, waterborne flight.

One day the need may arise for a jet-age flying-boat, as swift and comfortable as the best equivalent land-based air liner. Too many years have passed since those supremely beautiful Short Empire boats encircled the world; it is just possible that another golden era in marine aviation lies over the horizon. If that time comes, let us hope that the design will be given every opportun-ity to prove itself, and the sad, lingering death of the Princess project not allowed to be repeated all over again.

For most of devastated Europe in the years immediately fol-lowing 1945 the so-called Atomic Age was also to be remem-bered as a time of austerity, with continued rationing, trouble between the Western Allies and Russia over the occupation of

Berlin, and many more of those drab, grey problems that were bound to arise after four years of conflict. In the great navies of the world there were suddenly too many warships and no more sea battles to be fought; Great Britain alone was left with four-teen battleships in service, apart from some others not yet com-pleted. However, the events of the Pacific campaign during and after Midway, followed by the successful atomic tests against shipping at Bikini Atoll, had firmly established the immense value of naval air power in modern war. Capital ships or aircraft carriers? It seemed that very soon the choice would have to be made.

In fact, for some nations, no real choice existed at all—just a temporary withholding of the economy axe where common sense dictated. Before 1945 was out, ten of Britain's fourteen battle-ships had been earmarked for the scrapyard, and the others soon afterwards made the same last journey. They were followed in due course by H.M.S. *Vanguard*, the last capital ship to be built by any navy after 1944, and only completed in 1946. Cruisers were also similarly cast out, no new warships of that class being built for almost a decade. Only the fleet aircraft-carriers—*Implacable, Indomitable, Indefatigable, Glory, Ocean* and the rest—were allowed to survive, although some had to be laid up in reserve and construction plans for the immediate future were drastically cut to pieces. This cautious attitude towards any new programme for Naval Aviation, as the Fleet Air Arm had become known by 1946, was at first shared to some extent by the United States, which had ended the war with over a hundred carriers of all types in service.

The onset of the jet engine brought a number of problems to the naval air arms of the world, not least being the high landing speeds of jet-propelled aircraft. On 3rd December 1945 Lieuten-ant-Commander E. M. Brown, R.N.V.R., flying a De Havilland Vampire twin-boomed single-seater jet fighter, circled the 14,000-ton light carrier *Ocean* while she was at sea off the Isle of Wight, then came in to make a neat and completely successful landing, stopping within 100 ft. During the next few days some fifteen take-offs and landings were made using the same carrier, this converted Vampire prototype—which preceded the produc-tion F.20 Sea Vampire—thus becoming the first jet aircraft in history to be operated from the flight deck of a carrier. Meanwhile, experimental landings on carriers by a jet aircraft were being attempted in the United States, using a strengthened Bell Airacomet acquired from the Army Air Force; but not until 21st July 1946 did Lieutenant-Commander James Davidson, flying a McDonnell XFD-1 twin-jet fighter operating from the *Franklin D. Roosevelt,* successfully accomplish the first American carrier jet take-offs and landings.

Another solution to the difficulties of handling the increasingly faster modern aircraft entering service with the naval air arms of the world was the angled flight deck—that is, a flight deck offset slightly from the ship's centre line in order to leave a clear runway, free of parked machines and catapult equipment. This new method of operating naval aircraft, invented by Captain D. R. F. Cambell, D.S.O., R.N., was incorporated for the first time in the 18,000-ton H.M.S. *Centaur,* which entered service in 1953, and thenceforth the angled deck became an important feature of all the latest carriers. The first American carrier to be so completed was the *Antietam,* in January 1953, followed by the mighty 75,900-ton *Forrestal,* at one time the largest warship in the world, with four lifts and hangar space for a hundred aircraft.

As always, necessity continued to be the mother of many inventions. The steam catapult, piston-driven by high pressure steam from the ship's boilers, was conceived by Commander C. C. Mitchell, O.B.E., R.N.V.R., and developed by Brown Brothers and Co. Ltd. of Edinburgh, to be finally introduced during 1954 into both the British and United States navies. It superseded the outmoded hydro-pneumatic system that had first appeared in the early 'thirties, and provided greatly increased launching power for all naval aircraft. The coming into general use of the helicopter, which could take off and land in a very small area, proved to be an invaluable asset to naval air operations, Sikorsky and Westland machines being first taken into service for ship-to-shore communications and later designed as anti-submarine aircraft. A third innovation was the mirror landing sight, developed to cope with the high approach speeds of modern aircraft, soon beyond the handling capabilities of even the most efficient batsman. It became an age of speed—speed in attack and defence, speed in operation of machines and movement of carriers; but much of this renewed activity in the world of naval aviation had followed as a natural consequence of the Korean war.

When North Korean forces invaded the Republic of South Korea on the morning of 25th June 1950 America and Great Britain were quickly drawn into action under the United Nations flag, participating in the ground warfare and undertaking block-ade duties with their naval units. The British fleet carrier *Triumph,* equipped with Supermarine Seafires and Fairey Fire-flies, was placed at the disposal of the overall commander, Gen-eral MacArthur, and operated for some weeks in conjunction with the United States carriers *Valley Forge, Sicily* and *Badoeng Strait,* flying mostly Grumman Panthers and war-weary Vought-Sikorsky Corsairs. Later, *Triumph* was relieved by H.M.S. *Theseus,* with modern Hawker Sea Furies. Aircraft from these carriers and their successors in the campaign—the British *Glory* and *Ocean,* the Australian *Sydney,* the American *Philippine Sea, Boxer, Princeton* and *Essex*—flew many thousands of arduous operational sorties during the next three years, mainly against ground targets, achieving results out of all proportion to the small forces employed and meanwhile gaining valuable exper-ience. There was usually only slight enemy air opposition off the Korean coast, but the few enemy fighters that were encountered frequently turned out to be very fast MIG-15 single-seater jet monoplanes; although far superior in all-round performance to all the Allied machines in service, except the North American Furies and Sabres used towards the end of the war, they were nevertheless always engaged in combat and not infrequently shot down.

The proven value of carrier-borne naval aircraft in such loca-lised wars as the Korean campaign not only provided the impetus for increased development in various aspects of sea flying, but also encouraged designs for faster and better aircraft. By 1960 the first Royal Navy single-seater jet fighter to serve in first-line squadrons, the Supermarine Attacker, had been super-seded by the Hawker Sea Hawk; and that extremely efficient machine was in turn being replaced by the even more modern swept-wing supersonic Scimitar, produced in time to equip the new 23,000-ton fleet carrier *Hermes.* Similarly, the Fairey Firefly piston-engined two-seater and the Westland Wyvern turbo-prop single-seater strike aircraft had given way to the twin-jet De Havilland Sea Vixen, followed by the world's first naval high-speed bomber in the low-level class, the Blackburn Buccaneer. This somewhat heavy-set, bulging monoplane with square-cut, sweptback wings, powered by twin Rolls-Royce Spey engines, is undoubtedly one of the finest carrier-borne strike aircraft ever designed, and certainly the best machine for its purpose so far introduced into the often neglected Fleet Air Arm.

In the United States, where the second 'super-carrier' of the giant *Forrestal* class was commissioned in 1956 under the name *Saratoga*, and a third, the *Ranger*, launched, considerable research in supersonic aircraft brought forth a succession of remarkably advanced naval fighters, from the Grumman F9F-6 Cougar and the North American FJ-2 Fury to the McDonnell F4H-1 Phantom and the Chance-Vought F8C-1 Crusader, both with a maximum speed of over 1,000 m.p.h. In the attack role, the twin-jet Douglas A3D-2 Skywarrior in its many variants and the small Douglas A4D Skyhawk must also be mentioned; for they remain the equal of any nuclear bomber in the world. During the decade that followed the Korean war, the aircraft-carrier became, in effect, the capital ship of the United States Navy, and the *Forrestal*-class 'fighting flat-tops' named *Independence, Kitty Hawk* and *Constellation* in due course joined their three predecessors in service. In 1964 the slightly smaller 65,000-ton *America* was launched, and three years later a sister-ship, the *John F. Kennedy*, entered the water for the first time; both are capable of carrying at least ninety aircraft, and perhaps represent the ultimate achievement in carrier development, with the exception of U.S.S. *Enterprise*.

Ordered for the United States Navy in 1956, launched in September 1960, and completed in December 1961 at a cost of £158,570,000, the *Enterprise*, of 75,700 tons, is not only the world's first nuclear-powered aircraft carrier—it has also taken the place of *Forrestal* as the largest warship in the world. Not experimental in any sense, but a fully operational carrier of the Pacific Fleet, the *Enterprise*, with a complement of a hundred aircraft and some three thousand officers and men, has the astonishing ability to remain at sea and under power for five years, if necessary, without refuelling. She can be considered as virtually a one-ship task force, capable of rushing her fighters and bombers to almost any trouble spot and then operating them to provide indefinite air support; a self-contained, heavily defended floating island. A triumph of modern naval engineering, the *Enterprise* might well prove to be the last and greatest of that long, splendid line of aircraft-carriers dating back to the *Furious* of 1917 and the little seaplane tenders taken to war in 1914; for sheer power, size and efficient handling of aircraft she will probably now never be equalled.

Sad to relate, in Great Britain the momentum given to naval aviation by the Korean war and the 1956 Suez crisis is now, after another decade, showing ominous signs of grinding to a standstill. Although it was at first stated that the existing Royal Navy carriers would continue to remain in service for some years, and *Eagle* and *Victorious* were scheduled for extensive refit and modernisation, the 23,000-ton *Bulwark* and, later, *Albion,* were converted to so-called commando carriers, each being equipped with Westland Whirlwind helicopters for the transport of Royal Marines—a completely new role. Drastic Treasury economies, and the expenditure of millions of pounds on such cancelled projects as the ill-fated British Aircraft Corporation TSR-2, have since slowly but surely begun to squeeze Royal Navy aviation out of existence; and the inevitable end of the road looms in sight with the announcement that all our present fleet carriers may be phased out—to use the cold official jargon—by 1972. The apparent alternative for attack or defence is the Polaris submarine—but can it honestly be accepted, with complete peace of mind, that this one (admittedly very powerful) weapon is able to fulfil all the many and varied roles of the carrier-borne, nuclear-armed strike aircraft?

Yet the die has already, it would seem, been cast. There will soon be no less than forty-one United States nuclear-powered submarines in service, each carrying sixteen nuclear-warheaded Polaris missiles, many of the latest A3 type with a range of over 2,500 miles. Thirty-one of these boats will be of the *Lafayette* class, probably the largest undersea craft ever built; five of the *Ethan Nathan* class, already operational; and five of the *George Washington* class, also in service and now considered virtually

outdated. For Great Britain the Polaris missile is carried by submarines of the *Resolution* class, each of over 7,500 tons, *Resolution*
and *Renown* being in service but *Repulse* and *Revenge* not yet completed.

The mighty Poseidon C3 missile, larger and infinitely more
powerful than Polaris, with twice the payload and a longer range,
is scheduled by the Americans to become operational by 1971,
and there can be little doubt that in due course it will also replace
the A3 in British submarines. Rightly or otherwise, after more
than half a century of glorious history and remarkable progress
British naval aviation shows every sign of being allowed to fade
gracefully away, and perhaps eventually the sea-flying air arm of
the United States and France will also be terminated, overwhelmed by the hurrying, nuclear age which could yet need
them. But not a few of us will be sorry to know the day when the
last carriers are moved down-river to the scrapyard; and it may
well be that in years to come sadder and wiser governments will
equally regret having lost those proud, if not always beautiful,
warships of a class that played no small part in winning two
world wars.

BIBLIOGRAPHY

CHICHESTER, FRANCIS, *Alone Over the Tasman Sea* (George Allen & Unwin Ltd., 1945)

CHURCHILL, WINSTON S., *The World Crisis, 1911–1918* (Macmillan edition, 1943)

CLOUSTERMANN, PIERRE, *Flames in the Sky* (Chatto & Windus 1956)

DETMERS, THEODOR, *The Raider Kormoran* (Wm. Kimber, 1959)

DUVAL, G. R., *British Flying-Boats & Amphibians, 1909–1952* (Putnam, 1966)

GREEN, WM., *Warplanes of the Second World War, Vol. V—Flying Boats* (McDonald, 1962)

GREEN, WM., *Warplanes of the Second World War, Vol. VI—Float-planes* (McDonald, 1962)

GREY, C. G., *Sea Flyers* (Faber & Faber, 1942)

HAWKS, ELLISON, *British Seaplanes in the Schneider Trophy Contests, 1913–1931* (Real Photographs, 1945)

HEINKEL, ERNEST, *He 1000* (Hutchinson, 1956)

HORSLEY, TERENCE, *Find, Fix and Strike* (Eyre & Spottiswoode, 1944)

JOY, WILLIAM, *The Aviators* (Angus & Robertson, 1966)

KEATS, JOHN, *Howard Hughes* (MacGibbon & Kee, 1967)

KEMP, P. K., *Fleet Air Arm* (Herbert Jenkins, 1954)

LORD, WALTER, *Day of Infamy* (Longmans, Green, 1957)

MACINTYRE, DONALD, *Wings of Neptune* (Peter Davies, 1963)

MATT, PAUL R., *U.S. Navy & Marine Corps Fighters, 1918–1962* (Harleyford, 1962)

NICHOLL, G. W. R., *The Supermarine Walrus* (Foulis, 1966)

NOWARRA, H. J., *Marine Aircraft of the 1914–1918 War* (Harleyford, 1966)

PALMER, HENRY J. JR., *The Seaplanes* (Morgan, 1965)

POLLINGER, GERALD, *Famous Aircraft of the World* (Muller, 1962)

POOLMAN, KENNETH, *Ark Royal* (Wm. Kimber, 1956)

POOLMAN, KENNETH, *Flying Boat* (Wm. Kimber, 1962)

POTTER, JOHN DEANE, *Admiral of the Pacific* (Heinemann, 1965)

RALEIGH, SIR WALTER & JONES, H. A. *The War in the Air* (Oxford University Press, 1922–37)

ROBERTSON, TERENCE, *Channel Dash* (Evans, 1958)

SAUNDERS, HILARY ST. GEORGE, *Per Ardua* (Oxford University Press, 1944)

THETFORD, OWEN, *British Naval Aircraft Since 1912* (Putnam, 1962)

YOUNG, DESMOND, *Rutland of Jutland* (Cassell, 1963)